Top Federal Tax Issues
FOR 2016 | CPE COURSE

Wolters Kluwer Editorial Staff Publication

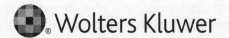

Contributors

Contributing Editors . . . . James A. Chapman, J.D., LL.M;

Donna Flanagan, J.D.;

Nitasha Kadam, J.D., LL.M;

Lawrence A. Perlman, CPA, J.D., LLM;

Robert Recchia, J.D., M.B.A., C.P.A.;

John W. Roth, J.D., LL.M.;.

James Solheim, J.D., LL.M;

Raymond G. Suelzer Jr., J.D., LL.M;

George L. Yaksick, Jr., J.D.

Technical Review . . . . George G. Jones, J.D., LL.M

Production Coordinator . . . . Gabriel E. Santana; Jennifer Schencker;

Vijayalakshmi Suresh; Muthuraman Lakshmanan

Production . . . . Lynn J. Brown

This publication is designed to provide accurate and authoritative information in regard to the subject matter covered. It is sold with the understanding that the publisher is not engaged in rendering legal, accounting, or other professional service. If legal advice or other expert assistance is required, the services of a competent professional person should be sought.

ISBN: 978-0-8080-4214-3

SUSTAINABLE FORESTRY INITIATIVE Certified Sourcing www.sfiprogram.org SFI-01042

Introduction

Each year, a handful of tax issues typically require special attention by tax practitioners. The reasons vary, from a particularly complicated new provision in the Internal Revenue Code, to a planning technique opened up by a new regulation or ruling, or the availability of a significant tax benefit with a short window of opportunity. Sometimes a developing business need creates a new set of tax problems, or pressure exerted by Congress or the Administration puts more heat on some taxpayers while giving others more slack. All these share in creating a unique mix that in turn creates special opportunities and pitfalls in the coming year and beyond. The past year has seen more than its share of these developing issues.

CCH's *Top Federal Tax Issues for 2016 CPE Course* identifies those recent events that have developed into the current "hot" issues of the day. These tax issues have been selected as particularly relevant to tax practice in 2016. They have been selected not only because of their impact on return preparation during the 2016 tax season but also because of the important role they play in developing effective tax strategies for 2016 and beyond. Some issues are outgrowths of several years of developments; others have burst onto the tax scene unexpectedly. Among the latter are issues directly related to the recent economic downturn and tax legislation designed to assist in a recovery. Some have been emphasized in IRS publications and notices; others are just being noticed by the IRS.

This course is designed to help reassure the tax practitioner that he or she is not missing out on advising clients about a hot, new tax opportunity; or that a brewing controversy does not blindside their practice. In addition to issue identification, this course provides the basic information needed for the tax practitioner to implement a plan that addresses the particular opportunities and pitfalls presented by any one of those issues. Among the topics examined in the *Top Federal Tax Issues for 2016 CPE Course* are:

- Employer Mandate of the Affordable Care Act
- Individual Mandate of the Affordable Care Act
- Tax Planning for Education
- Same-Sex Marriage
- International Tax Reporting
- Repair and Capitalization Guidance—What Now?
- Tax-Exempt Hospitals
- Reducing (Self-) Employment and NII Taxes in Passthrough Entities
- Tax Reform and Interim Measures

Study Questions. Throughout the course you will find Study Questions to help you test your knowledge, and comments that are vital to understanding a particular strategy or idea. Answers to the Study Questions with feedback on both correct and incorrect responses are provided in a special section beginning at ¶ 10,100.

Index. To assist you in your later reference and research, a detailed topical index has been included for this course.

Quizzer. This course is divided into five Modules. Take your time and review all course Modules. When you feel confident that you thoroughly understand the material, turn to the CPE Quizzer. Complete one, or all, Module Quizzers for continuing professional education credit.

Go to **CCHGroup.com/PrintCPE** to complete your Quizzer online. The CCH Testing Center website lets you complete your CPE Quizzers online for immediate results and no Express Grading Fee. Your Training History provides convenient storage for your CPE course Certificates. Further information is provided in the CPE Quizzer instructions at ¶ 10,200.

October 2015

CCH'S PLEDGE TO QUALITY

Thank you for choosing this CCH Continuing Education product. We will continue to produce high quality products that challenge your intellect and give you the best option for your Continuing Education requirements. Should you have a concern about this or any other CCH CPE product, please call our Customer Service Department at 1-800-248-3248.

COURSE OBJECTIVES

This course was prepared to provide the participant with an overview of specific tax issues that impact 2015 tax return preparation and tax planning in 2016. These are the issues that "everyone is talking about;" each impacts a significant number of taxpayers in significant ways.

Upon course completion, you will be able to:

- Recognize how the Affordable Care Act requires applicable large employers to offer or offset some of the costs of minimum essential coverage for health care insurance;
- Identify the individuals considered to be full-time or full-time equivalent employees of an applicable large employer;
- Identify the basic costs and coverage standards of the individual mandate;
- Identify the specific parts of Form 8965, *Health Coverage Exemptions*, that must be completed by taxpayers claiming exemptions from maintaining coverage;
- Recognize how savings plans, such as Section 529 plans, and U.S. savings bonds may be used to pay qualified educational expenses and how the investments can be coordinated;
- Identify the benefits and restrictions of the American opportunity tax credit and lifetime learning credit;
- Recognize the differences in the tax treatment of married and unmarried couples;
- Identify couples' contribution deductions for traditional IRAs and maximum contributions for traditional and Roth IRAs;
- Recognize the differences between the FBAR and FATCA reporting requirements;
- Recognize the civil and criminal penalties associated with noncompliance with the FATCA and FBAR requirements;
- Recognize how taxpayers that did not file changes in accounting method on Form 3115 for the 2014 tax year may file them in 2015;
- Identify how building lessors may deduct expenditures traditionally treated as capitalized leasehold improvements;
- Identify factors considered under the community benefit standard applied to tax-exempt hospitals;
- Identify the community health needs assessment requirements established for tax-exempt hospitals under the PPACA;

- Recognize some of the taxes that apply to the owners of passthrough entities;
- Identify circumstances when employment taxes, self-employment tax, additional Medicare tax, and net investment income tax apply in the context of trades or businesses conducted by passthrough entities;
- Identify the working group and committee initiatives that lawmakers have created to examine tax reform; and
- Recognize standalone tax bills that have passed the House, Senate, or both chambers.

One **complimentary copy** of this course is provided with certain copies of CCH publications. Additional copies of this course may be downloaded from **CCHGroup.com/PrintCPE** or ordered by calling 1-800-248-3248 (ask for product 10024491-0003).

Contents

4 Same-Sex Marriage

MODULE 3: RECENT REPORTING AND COMPLIANCE CHALLENGES

5 International Tax Reporting

6 Repair and Capitalization Guidance—What Now?

x

MODULE 1: HEALTH CARE—Chapter 1: Employer Mandate of the Affordable Care Act

¶ 101 WELCOME

The *Patient Protection and Affordable Care Act of 2010* (PPACA, or the Affordable Care Act) is a lengthy and complex law, with many requirements and features. The IRS has been issuing detailed guidance since the law's enactment in 2010. Some of the law's complexity reflects the law's jumble of effective dates, but by 2014, most of the major provisions of the law took effect, except for the employer shared responsibility payments *(employer mandate)* and the tax on "Cadillac" health plans. The first employer mandate provisions became effective on January 1, 2015, but transition relief from certain requirements is available for 2015. Cadillac plan limitations are scheduled to take effect in 2018.

Most employers are affected either directly or indirectly by the individual and employer mandate provisions. The *individual mandate* (individual shared responsibility payment) requires most individuals and their families to carry adequate health insurance or face a penalty; if that insurance is not provided by their employer, that employer may face a penalty. The employer mandate requires most employers to provide essential, affordable health insurance coverage or face a penalty. The premium tax credit, available to help low-and middle-income Americans pay for health insurance, is a critical component of the continued viability of both the individual and the employer mandates. As such, the Supreme Court's recent approval in *King v. Burwell* (SCt, June 25, 2015) of use of the premium tax credit on federal as well as state exchanges essentially turns back any viable challenge to the Affordable Care Act, along with its individual and employer mandates, for at least into the foreseeable future.

¶ 102 LEARNING OBJECTIVES

Upon completion of this chapter, you will be able to:

- Recognize how the Affordable Care Act requires applicable large employers to offer or offset some of the costs of minimum essential coverage for health care insurance;
- Identify the individuals considered to be full-time or full-time equivalent employees of an applicable large employer;
- Recognize when each of the two payment regimes applies to applicable large employer members;
- Identify the measurement methods used to determine whether an employee must be offered coverage; and
- Identify IRS requirements for annual information reporting using Forms 1094-C and 1095-C.

¶ 103 INTRODUCTION

"Employer mandate," "pay or play," and "employer shared responsibility (or ESR)" are all names for the same thing.

Before the Affordable Care Act (ACA), health coverage costs were born by employers, the government, and individuals. The ACA formalizes that arrangement through a system of coverage obligations and "shared responsibility payments."

Under the shared responsibility system, individuals must do their part either by obtaining and maintaining minimum essential coverage (MEC) throughout the calendar year or by paying into the system through the individual mandate. There are numerous exceptions to the mandate allowing an individual to escape liability, but the main one for financial purposes is lack of affordable coverage.

This is where the government comes in. With the premium tax credit, the federal government significantly subsidizes coverage for lower- and middle-income households so that affordability is no longer an issue. This credit is often paid in advance through lower premiums when an individual obtains coverage through a marketplace.

¶ 104 APPLICABLE LARGE EMPLOYER (ALE) STATUS

The employer mandate or "pay or play" is a key part of the shared responsibility system. The employer shared responsibility rules require applicable large employers (ALEs) to either offer a certain level of health coverage to their full-time employees (i.e., "play"), or make shared responsibility payments to the IRS to help the government defray the cost of providing the premium tax credit (i.e., "pay"). Either way, ALEs are shoulder a financial responsibility.

Only ALEs are subject to the employer mandate and associated reporting requirements. An employer qualifies as an ALE for a calendar year if the trade or business averages 50 or more full-time and full-time equivalent employees during the prior year. Transition rules for 2015 employer shared responsibility payments apply for employers that employ on average at least 50 full-time employees (including full-time equivalents) but fewer than 100 full-time employees (including full-time equivalents) on business days during 2014.

¶ 105 FULL-TIME EMPLOYEES AND PART-TIME WORKERS' HOURS COUNT TOWARD ALE STATUS

ALE status turns on both the actual number of full-time employees and the number of "full-time equivalent" (FTE) employees, a number that is based on a combination of part-time hours. This approach makes it difficult for an employer to escape ALE status by converting a full-time position to multiple part-time positions.

An employer's status as an ALE for a calendar year is determined by adding the following, and dividing the total by 12:

- The total number of full-time employees (including any seasonal workers) for each calendar month in the preceding calendar year; and
- The total number of FTEs, including any seasonal workers, for each calendar month in the preceding calendar year.

If the result is not a whole number, it is rounded to the next lowest whole number. If the result is 50 or more, the employer is an ALE for the current calendar year, unless the seasonal worker exception applies.

New Employers Use Reasonable Expectations

An employer not in existence throughout the preceding calendar year is an ALE for the current calendar year if the employer reasonably expects to employ an average of at least 50 full-time employees (taking into account FTEs) on business days during the current calendar year, and in fact it does so. An employer is treated as not having been in existence throughout the prior calendar year only if the employer was not in existence on any business day in the prior calendar year.

NOTE: A transition rule for 2015 applies to employers with between 50 and 100 employees applies. See the later discussion of how to determine ALEs in those circumstances.

COMMENT: An employer that expects to be an ALE but turns out to be wrong will not owe any shared responsibility payment under the mandate, so an employer has nothing to lose in terms of mandate liability by treating itself as an ALE.

EXAMPLE: Autodrive, an employer, is incorporated on January 1, 2016. On January 1, 2016, the company has three employees. However, prior to incorporation, Autodrive's owners purchased a car-sharing business intended to open within two months of incorporation and to employ approximately 100 employees. By March 15, 2016, the Autodrive has more than 75 full-time employees. Because Autodrive can be reasonably expected to employ on average at least 50 full-time employees on business days during 2015, and actually employs an average of at least 50 full-time employees on business days during 2016, Autodrive is an ALE.

Full-Time Employees

A *full-time employee* with respect to any month is an employee who is employed on average at least 30 hours of service per week. Regulations treat 130 hours of service in a calendar month as the monthly equivalent of 30 hours of service per week ((52×30) ÷ $12 = 130$). This monthly standard takes into account that the average month consists of more than four weeks. It means that an employee may be full-time for a month even though he or she worked less than 30 hours a week for one or more weeks during a that month.

Full-Time Equivalent Employees (FTEs)

A *full-time equivalent employee* (FTE) is a combination of employees, each of whom individually lacks the hours to count as full-time, but whose hours, added together, are counted as the equivalent of a full-time employee solely for the purpose of determining ALE status. The number of FTEs is determined by adding the number of hours of service of employees who are not full-time employees (but not working more than 120 hours per employee) for the month, and then dividing by 120. Fractions are taken into account. An employer may round the number of FTEs for each calendar month to the nearest one hundredth.

EXAMPLE: Manhattan Co. has 5 part-time employees for the month of January. Four of them worked 90 hours each and one worked 123 hours, for a total of 483 hours. The maximum taken into account for a single employee is 120, so the total for purposes of determining FTEs is 480. Based on the service hours of its part-time workers, the Manhattan must add four FTEs (480 aggregate hours of service ÷ 120) to the number of its full-time employees for January.

CAUTION: FTEs are used for adding together full-time employees for purposes of determining ALE status, but that is all. FTEs are not used in the full-time headcount when a trade or business calculates employer shared responsibility payments. The reason is that part-timers are not owed MEC, and a part-time employee who obtains subsidized coverage through a marketplace does not trigger employer mandate liability, even in combination with other part-time employees.

Individuals Not Counted as Employees

Individuals who do not count as employees include the following:

- Sole proprietors;
- Direct sellers;
- Partners in a partnership;
- 2 percent or more S corporation shareholders; and
- Real estate agents.

In addition, the hours of certain employees do not count towards their status as full-time, including volunteers for government or tax-exempt entities, and students under a government sponsored work-study program. However, educational employees are not considered part-time merely because they have limited summer hours.

Leased employees are the responsibility of the agency/employer rather than the entity for which they provide services. However, the IRS will not allow employers to convert their employees to leased employees just to avoid their ACA responsibilities.

STUDY QUESTION

1. A full-time equivalent employee:

    a. Works more than 30 hours per week but is not included as a full-time employee for hours exceeding the minimum

    b. Combines the hours of employees who in combination are considered equivalent of full-time employees for determining ALE status

    c. Is disregarded in determining an employer's applicable large employer (ALE) status

    d. Includes S corporation shareholders who hold 2 percent or more of S corporation shares

Seasonal Workers

An employer is exempt from the shared responsibility rules if the seasonal worker exception applies. The exception applies for an employer if:

- The sum of the employer's full-time employees and FTEs exceeds 50 full-time employees for no more than 120 days during the preceding calendar year; and
- The employees in excess of 50 employed during the 120-day period are seasonal workers.

Four months is treated as the equal of 120 days. The four months or 120 days need not be consecutive. For new employers, if the employer reasonably expects that the seasonal worker exception will keep it from being an ALE for the current calendar year, the employer will not be treated as an ALE for the current calendar year.

> **CAUTION:** Just because an employer relies on seasonal workers does not necessarily mean the employer can take advantage of the seasonal worker exception. The exception applies only for employers that exceed 50 full-time employees (including seasonal workers) for 120 or fewer days during the calendar year. So, for example, an agricultural employer that relies heavily on seasonal workers for longer periods (as many do) would not qualify for the exception if the employer's full-time employee head count (including seasonal workers) exceeds 50 for more than 120 days during the year.

COMMENT: The seasonal worker exception only applies for determining ALE status. There is no seasonal worker exception when administering the shared responsibility rules.

CAUTION: Even if the employer's full-time headcount remains over 50 due to seasonal workers for only 4 months per year, the exception does not apply if the headcount goes over 50 for an additional period for some other reason (such as a surge in part-time hours).

EXAMPLE: During 2015, the Shopping Season Co. has 40 full-time employees for the entire calendar year, none of whom is a seasonal worker. In addition, it has 80 seasonal full-time workers who work for the company from September through December 2015. The company has no FTEs during 2015. Before applying the seasonal worker exception, Shopping Season has 40 full-time employees during each of 8 calendar months of 2015 and 120 full-time employees during each of 4 calendar months of 2015, resulting in an average of 66.5 employees for the year (rounded down to 66 full-time employees). However, the workforce equaled or exceeded 50 full-time employees (counting seasonal workers) for no more than 4 calendar months (treated as the equivalent of 120 days) in calendar year 2015. The number of full-time employees would be less than 50 during those months if seasonal workers were disregarded. Therefore, the seasonal worker exception applies, and the company is not considered to employ more than 50 full-time employees. Shopping Season is therefore not an ALE for 2016.

Related Employers as Applicable Large Employer Members

In determining the number of full-time employees, all employers treated as a single employer under the IRS's controlled group aggregation rules are treated as one ALE. *Related employers* include controlled groups of corporations, partnerships and proprietorships under common control, and affiliated service groups. Each individual employer in an ALE is an *applicable large employer member* (ALEM).

CAUTION: The controlled group rules are complex, and their application should be left to attorneys.

COMMENT: According to the IRS, a single-member ALE has one ALEM. An ALEM does not include a person or entity that is not an employer, or only an employer of employees with no hours of service for the calendar year.

The determination of whether an employer is an ALE is made by adding together the full-time and full-time equivalent (FTE) employees of each ALEM making up the aggregated ALE group.

EXAMPLE: Clothing companies Mamon and Pere are related under the aggregation rules. Mamon averaged 40 full-time employers in the prior year, and Pere averaged 10 full-time employees in the prior year. Together they averaged 50 full-time employees, and therefore together they are a single ALE. Mamon and Pere will be considered separately by the IRS in assessing shared responsibility payments, and they will have to file separately with respect to information reporting.

CAUTION: Because related businesses are aggregated, a business owner cannot reduce its headcount by simply creating a different company and transferring employees to that company. The rules must be checked carefully because controlled groups can often include companies that appear to be separate (e.g., companies owned by different family members).

STUDY QUESTION

2. An agricultural employer will *not* qualify for the employee head-count exception if the employer's head count exceeds:

    a. 50 averaged for the tax year

    b. 25 seasonal workers employed for fewer than 120 days during the year

    c. 50 for more than 120 days during the year

    d. The minimum 120 days applied for both the ALE status and seasonal worker exception

¶ 106 EMPLOYER SHARED RESPONSIBILITY UNDER THE TWO PAYMENT REGIMES OF CODE SEC. 4980H(a) AND (b)

Employer shared responsibility payments are determined at the applicable large employer member (ALEM) level. Under the regulations, single-employer ALEs are considered to have one ALEM, as discussed above.

> **NOTE:** The discussion below uses ALEM to describe an employer subject to the shared responsibility payment rules. That would include both ALEMs in multimember ALEs and an ALEM in a single-member ALE. A later discussion covers transition relief under Code Sec. 4980H(a) for 2015 if the ALEM has 100 or more employees.

Employer shared responsibility payments are not triggered for a reporting month unless at least one of an ALEM's full-time employees is receiving government subsidized coverage (generally, a premium tax credit) through a marketplace. Full-time equivalent (FTE) employees do not count for these purposes: The employee must be an actual full-time employee to trigger employer liability.

> **COMMENT:** Marketplaces are supposed to provide certification to employers of such coverage (Section 1411 Certification), but sometimes they often fail to do so.

The Two Payment Regimes

If the employer is an ALEM, and at least one of its full-time employees qualifies for subsidized coverage through a marketplace, one of two mutually exclusive assessed payment regimes may apply:

- One applies to ALEMs that fail to offer MEC to substantially all of their full-time employees; and

- The other regime applies to ALEMs that do offer such coverage, but nevertheless have one or more full-time employees who obtain subsidized coverage through a marketplace because the employer coverage is not affordable or does not provide minimum value.

Code Sec. 4980H(a) regime for failure to offer coverage. The first regime is found in Code Sec. 4980H(a). It applies to an ALEM that does not offer substantially all of its full-time employees (and after 2015, their dependents) the chance to enroll in a company health plan for MEC. The amount of the shared responsibility payment is based on total number of the employer's full-time employees (with certain subtractions) whether some of them are offered coverage or not.

Code Sec. 4980H(b) regime for employee's subsidized coverage through marketplace. The second regime is found in Code Sec. 4980H(b). It applies if: (a) the first regime does not apply because the ALEM does offer a plan with MEC to substantially all of its full-time employees, but nevertheless (b) at least one full-time employee obtains subsidized coverage through a marketplace either because the employer did not offer coverage to that particular employee, or the offered coverage did not satisfy affordability or minimum value requirements. The resulting employer shared responsibility payment is based on the number of full-time employees qualifying for subsidized individual coverage (normally, a much lower figure than the total number of full-time employees).

> **PLANNING POINTER:** Generally, shared responsibility payments under the first regime are far more costly than shared responsibility payments under the second regime. An employer can satisfy requirements of the first regime by broadly offering relatively inexpensive coverage. The second regime requires that the offered coverage satisfy affordability and minimum value requirements for employees, which means a higher cost of coverage for the employer. Some employers choose to provide inexpensive coverage for all full-time employees and thus avoid big liability under the first regime, and take their chances with liability under the second regime.

An ALEM is never liable under both regimes for the same calendar month. If the ALEM is liable under the second regime, the payment is capped so that it cannot be more than the amount that would apply under the first regime. As a result, no ALEM that offers coverage to substantially all of its full-time employees is ever worse off for doing so.

Under transition relief, shared responsibility payments will generally not be assessed for 2015 against an ALEM that belongs to an ALE with fewer than 100 full-time employees, effectively pushing the start date for the employer mandate back a year to 2016 for ALEs with between 50 and 99 full-time employees (reporting duties still apply, however).

Limited Nonassessment Periods

A limited nonassessment period is essentially a grace period before an ALEM has to offer coverage to an otherwise eligible full-time employee. In general, an ALEM has three full calendar months before it has to offer coverage to an employee who is hired as or becomes full-time. This grace period is contingent on the ALEM offering ACA-compliant coverage at end of the period. There are a number of other limited nonassessment periods, including one for employers that become ALEMs for the first time.

¶ 107 SHARED RESPONSIBILITY PAYMENTS UNDER CODE SEC. 4980H(a) FOR FAILING TO OFFER COVERAGE TO SUBSTANTIALLY ALL FULL-TIME EMPLOYEES

Transition Relief in 2015 for ALEMs with Fewer Than 100 Employees

For employers that had fewer than 100 full-time employees (including full-time equivalents) in 2014 and that meet the conditions described below, no employer shared responsibility payment under Section 4980H(a) or (b) will apply for any calendar month during 2015. For employers with noncalendar-year health plans, this applies to any calendar month during the 2015 plan year, including months covered by the 2015 plan year that fall in 2016.

If an ALEM fails to offer its full-time employees and (after 2015) their dependents the opportunity to enroll in MEC under an eligible employer-sponsored plan for any calendar month, and at least one full-time employee qualifies for a premium tax credit, a shared responsibility payment may be imposed. The payment is calculated based on the total number of full-time employees, minus 30 (80 in 2015 only under transition relief).

An ALEM is treated as offering coverage to its full-time employees (and their dependents) for a calendar month if, for that month, it offers such coverage to all but 5 percent (or, if greater, five) of its full-time employees. Under transition relief for 2015-only, employers may offer coverage to all but 30 percent of their full-time employees.

As a result, an offer to 70 percent for 2015 (95 percent for 2016 and thereafter) of an ALEM's full-time employees suffices to avoid the shared responsibility payment for failure to offer coverage. An employee in a limited nonassessment period is not included in the calculation.

> **EXAMPLE:** In 2016 (a post-transition year applying to 5 percent or 5 employees), Largo Production Co. is an ALEM with 120 full-time employees. It offers eligible employer coverage to all but 5 of these employees. Because 5 percent of 120 is 6, and 5 is less than 6, the Largo qualifies as offering coverage to its full-time employees. Note that if instead Largo had 80 full-time employees, it would still be treated as offering coverage to its full-time employees because of the 5 full-time employee floor.

Calculating Payment for Failing to Offer Coverage

The shared responsibility payment for not offering coverage equals the product of the applicable payment amount, which is 1/12 of $2,000 for any month (i.e., $166.67 per month), times the number of full-time employees for the month. The $2,000 amount is adjusted for inflation after 2014 (remaining at $2,000 for 2015 due to rounding). In computing the shared responsibility payment, the number of the employer's full-time employees for any month is reduced by 30 (80 for 2015). Allocation rules apply for ALEMs. The payment is determined on a calendar month basis.

Under the transition relief for 2015, the liability calculation replaces 30 with 80. Shared responsibility payments will generally not be assessed for 2015 against ALEs with fewer than 100 full-time employees, effectively pushing the start date back a year to 2016 for ALEs with between 50 and 99 full-time employees (reporting duties still apply, however). The 95 percent rate under the first regime is 70 percent for 2015, and the number subtracted from the full-time employee count is 80 rather than 30. An employer is not subject to a shared responsibility payment for 2015 for failing to offer dependent coverage if the employer takes steps during its 2014 plan year toward offering dependent coverage.

Each ALEM Responsible for Its Own Employees

Liability for a shared responsibility payment for a calendar month with respect to a full-time employee applies solely to the ALEM that was the employer of that employee for that calendar month. For an employee who was employed by more than one ALEM of the same ALE during a calendar month, liability for the shared responsibility payments applies to the ALEM for which the employee has the greatest number of hours of service for that period.

If the employee has an equal number of hours of service for two or more ALEMs of the same ALE for the calendar month, those ALEMs can treat one of those members as the employer of that employee for that calendar month, and if the ALEMs do not select one member or select in an inconsistent manner, the IRS will select a member to be treated as the employer of that employee for these purposes.

Allocating 30 Headcount Reduction to Multiple ALEMs

The shared responsibility payment for failing to offer coverage is based on an ALE's full-time head count, minus 30 (80 for 2015 under transition relief). For ALEs with multiple ALEMs, this figure is allocated to each ALEM based on their ratable share of full-time employees.

The allocation is made on the basis of the number of full-time employees employed by each ALEM during the calendar month (after application of the rules addressing employees who work for more than one ALEM during a calendar month).

If an ALEM's total allocation is not a whole number, the allocation is rounded to the next highest whole number. This rounding rule may result in the aggregate reduction for the entire group of ALEMs exceeding 30.

> **EXAMPLE:** In 2016, McKnead Co. is an ALEM in a single-employer ALE and fails to offer MEC to at least 95 percent of its full-time employees. McKnead has 100 full-time employees, 10 of whom receive a premium tax credit for the year for enrolling in a marketplace-offered plan. The inflation-adjusted applicable amount for a calendar month remains at $2,000 divided by 12. For 70 of McKnead's full-time employees (100 full-time employees – 30), the company owes $2,000 per employee, for a total shared responsibility payment of $120,000 ($2,000 × 70 full-time employees) for 2016, which is assessed on a monthly basis.

> **EXAMPLE:** ALEMs Zeta and Yeta are ALEMs in a two-employer ALE. Zeta employs 40 full-time employees in each calendar month of 2017. Yeta employs 35 full-time employees in each calendar month of 2017. Assume that for 2017, the applicable payment amount for a calendar month is $2,000 divided by 12. Zeta does not sponsor an eligible employer-sponsored plan for any calendar month of 2017 and receives a certification from a marketplace for 2017 with respect to at least one of its full-time employees. Yeta sponsors an eligible employer-sponsored plan under which all 35 of its full-time employees are eligible for MEC. Zeta is subject to an annual shared responsibility payment for 2017 of $48,000, which is equal to 24 × $2,000 (40 full-time employees reduced by 16 (its allocable share of the 30-employee offset ((40/75) × 30 = 16)) and then multiplied by $2,000). Yeta is not subject to a shared responsibility payment for failing to offer coverage for 2017.

STUDY QUESTION

---

3. The Code Sec. 4980H(b) regime applies only if:

   a. No full-time employee was offered MEC under Code Sec. 4980H(a) rules

   b. The ALEM is liable under both regimes for the same calendar month

   c. The ALEM does offer MEC to substantially all of its full-time employees but at least one obtains marketplace coverage because of affordability or MV requirements

   d. No full-time employee obtained subsidized coverage through a marketplace

---

¶ 108 SHARED RESPONSIBILITY PAYMENTS UNDER CODE SEC. 4980H(b) FOR OFFERING COVERAGE THAT DOES NOT MEET MINIMUM VALUE OR AFFORDABILITY STANDARDS

A shared responsibility payment is imposed for a calendar month on an ALEM that:

- Offers its full-time employees (and after 2015 their dependents) the opportunity to enroll in MEC under an eligible employer-sponsored plan for any month; but

- Has at least one full-time employee for that month in a qualified health plan offered through a marketplace with respect to which the employee qualified for subsidized coverage.

The amount of a shared responsibility payment under Code Sec. 4980H(b) is the product of:

- The number of the full-time employees receiving a premium tax credit for the purchase of health insurance through a state or federal health marketplace for the month, times

- An amount equal to 1/12 of $3,000 for any month (i.e., $250 per month) (Code Sec. 4980H(b)). After 2014, the $3,000 amount is adjusted for inflation (remaining at $3,000 for 2015 due to rounding) (Code Sec. 4980H(c)(5)).

Employees Excluded from Calculation

Just because a full-time employee qualifies for subsidized government coverage for a calendar month does not necessarily mean the employee will count in the shared responsibility payment calculation for that month. Employees do not count toward the penalty if they obtained coverage during a limited nonassessment period, or if the employee was offered the opportunity to enroll in an MEC policy under an eligible employer-sponsored plan that satisfied minimum value and met one or more of the affordability safe harbors (discussed below).

Cap Based on Hypothetical Liability for Failing to Offer Coverage

The aggregate amount of shared responsibility payment under Code Sec. 4980H(b) may not exceed the amount that would apply if the employer were instead liable under Code Sec. 4980H(a) during that calendar month for failure to offer coverage (Reg. § 54.4980H-5(a)). As a result, an employer cannot be held liable for a larger penalty for offering coverage that does not meet affordability or minimum value (MV) standards than for not offering coverage at all.

> **EXAMPLE:** In 2016, Weldrite Co. offers health coverage and has 100 full-time employees, 10 of whom receive a premium tax credit for the year for enrolling in a marketplace-offered plan. For each employee receiving a tax credit, Weldrite owes $3,000 (assuming no inflation adjustment from 2014), for a total shared responsibility payment of $30,000 ($3,000 × 10 employees). The maximum amount of the shared responsibility payment for Weldrite Co. is capped at the amount of the shared responsibility payment that the company would have been assessed for a failure to provide coverage, or $140,000 ($2,000 × 70 full-time employees (100 full-time employees – 30)). Because the calculated shared responsibility payment ($30,000) is less than the overall limitation ($140,000), Weldrite owes a $30,000 for 2016.

Minimum Value (MV)

An eligible employer-sponsored plan generally provides MV if the plan's share of the total allowed costs of benefits provided under the plan is at least 60 percent of those cost (Code Sec. 36B(c)(2)(C)(ii)). There is an online MV calculator made available by the Department of Health and Human Services and the IRS. There are also safe harbors.

Affordability

Coverage under an employer-sponsored plan is affordable to a particular employee if the employee's required contribution to the plan does not exceed 9.5 percent of the employee's household income for the tax year (9.56 percent in 2015 and 9.66 percent in 2016). Household income for this purpose is the modified adjusted gross income (MAGI) of the employee and any members of the employee's family (which would include any spouse and dependents) who are required to file an income tax return. MAGI is adjusted gross income on individual's federal income tax return plus any excluded foreign income, nontaxable Social Security benefits (including tier 1 railroad retirement benefits), and tax-exempt interest received or accrued during the tax year. It does not include Supplemental Security Income (SSI).

Employer safe harbors for affordability. Because employer knowledge of its employee's income circumstances is limited, the IRS has provided safe harbors that protect the employer from employer mandate liability based on information the employer has available. For premium tax credit purposes, an employee who qualifies for the premium tax credit on affordability grounds is still qualified for the credit even if, for employer mandate purposes, the employee falls under a safe harbor. The safe harbor is determined at the ALEM level for aggregated employers.

An employer may use one or more of the safe harbors, but only if its full-time employees and their dependents have the opportunity to enroll in MEC under an eligible employer-sponsored plan that provides MV with respect to the self-only coverage offered to the employee.

Use of any of the safe harbors is optional, and an employer may choose to apply the safe harbors for any reasonable category of employees, provided the employer does so on a uniform and consistent basis for all employees in a category. Reasonable categories generally include specified job categories, nature of compensation (hourly or salary), geographic location, and similar bona fide business criteria. The safe harbors include the following:

- The *Form W-2 safe harbor* applies if an employee's required contribution during the entire calendar year (excluding COBRA or other continuation coverage except with respect to an active employee eligible for continuation coverage) does not exceed 9.5 percent of that employee's Form W-2 wages from the employer (and any other ALEM of the same ALE that also pays wages to that employee) for the calendar year;

- The *rate of pay safe harbor* applies with respect to an hourly employee for a calendar month if the employee's required contribution for the calendar month for the ALEM's lowest cost self-only coverage that provides minimum value does not exceed 9.5 percent of an amount equal to 130 hours multiplied by the lower of the employee's hourly rate of pay as of the first day of the coverage period (generally the first day of the plan year) or the employee's lowest hourly rate of pay during the calendar month; and

- The *federal poverty line safe harbor* applies with respect to an employee for a calendar month if the employee's required contribution for the calendar month for the ALEM's lowest cost self-only coverage that provides MV does not exceed

9.5 percent of a monthly amount determined as the federal poverty line for a single individual for the applicable calendar year, divided by 12.

¶ 109 OFFER OF COVERAGE

A key factor in applying the employer shared responsibility rules is determining whether an employer offered coverage to its full-time employees (and after 2015 their dependents). To qualify as an offer, the employee must have an effective opportunity to:

- Elect to enroll in the coverage at least once with respect to the plan year; and
- Decline to enroll if the coverage offered does not
    - Provide minimum value, or
    - Meet affordability standards.

For a new full-time employee, a limited nonassessment period applies. The ALEM must offer coverage effective no later than end of the first three full calendar months after the employee becomes otherwise eligible for coverage.

The offer of coverage must include "dependents." A dependent for employer mandate purposes is a child (including an adopted child) of an employee who has not attained age 26. A child attains age 26 on the 26th anniversary of the date the child was born.

Although employers are free to offer coverage to an employee's spouse, step-children, grandchildren, or foster care children, they are not required to do so under the employer mandate. An offer of coverage for a child who is a citizen or foreign national of another country is not required unless the child is a resident of the United States or a country contiguous with the United States.

Any employer that takes steps during its plan year that begins in 2014 or 2015 (or both) to expand its offer of coverage to dependents of full-time employees will not be liable for any shared responsibility payment solely because of a failure to offer coverage to the dependents for that plan year.

STUDY QUESTION

---

4. The employer shared responsibility payment under Code Sec. 4980H(b) for 2015 is $250 times:

- **a.** The full-time employees and the seasonal workers employed for more than three consecutive months
- **b.** The number of full-time employees receiving a premium tax credit for purchasing health insurance through a marketplace
- **c.** The number of employees enrolled in MEC times the number of dependents offered coverage in the employer's plan
- **d.** The full-time and part-time employees not covered by any employer plan times 1/12

¶ 110 COUNTING EMPLOYEE HOURS TO IDENTIFY FULL-TIME EMPLOYEES

Hours of Service

Hours are counted to determine both (1) whether an employer averages at least 50 full-time employees and qualifies as an applicable large employer, and (2) whether an applicable large employer member must offer a particular employee coverage that satisfies the employer shared responsibility requirements.

Hour of services include both work hours and time-off hours for which an employee is paid (or at least entitled to be paid). This time may include time off for vacations, holidays, illnesses, incapacity (including disability), layoffs, jury duty, military duty, or leaves of absence, provided the employee is entitled to be paid for this time. Hours of service do not include service performed as a bona fide volunteer. They also do not include hours of service performed in a federal work-study program, outside the United States, or for a different ALEM.

A *bona fide volunteer* is an employee of a government entity or a Code Sec. 501(c) organization that is exempt from taxation whose only compensation is in the form of:

- Reimbursement for (or reasonable allowance for) reasonable expenses incurred in the performance of services; or
- Reasonable benefits (including length of service awards), and nominal fees, customarily paid by similar entities in connection with the performance of services by volunteers.

Measurement Methods

The IRS has provided two methods of using hours of service to determine full-time status: the monthly measurement method and the lookback safe harbor measurement method. These methods provide minimum standards for the identification of full-time employees. Employers may always treat additional employees as eligible for coverage, subject to compliance with any nondiscrimination or other applicable requirements.

> **COMMENT:** ALEMs report their monthly full-time total (minus employees in a limited nonassessment period) on Form 1094-C. The also report their total employee count, including employees that are not full-time and employees in a limited nonassessment period, for each calendar month. The employer selects a day of the month to determine the total employee count.

Hourly and salaried employees. Under the both the monthly and the lookback measurement methods, for hourly employees an employer must calculate actual hours of service from records of hours worked and hours for which payment is made or due.

For employees paid on a nonhourly basis, an employer must calculate hours of service by using one of the following methods:

- *Actual hours of service* from records of hours worked and hours for which payment is made or due;
- *Days-worked equivalency,* whereby the employee is credited with 8 hours of service for each day for which the employee would be required to be credited with at least 1 hour of service in accordance with the rules for hourly employees; or
- *Weeks-worked equivalency,* whereby the employee is credited with 40 hours of service for each week for which the employee would be required to be credited with at least 1 hour of service in accordance with the rules for hourly employees.

Change in methods. An employer must use one of the three permitted methods for calculating the hours of service for nonhourly employees. An employer is not required to use the same method for all nonhourly employees, however. An employer may apply different methods for different categories of nonhourly employees, provided the categories are reasonable and consistently applied.

An ALEM is not required to apply the same methods as other ALEMs of the same ALE for the same or different categories of nonhourly employees, provided that in each case the categories are reasonable and consistently applied by the ALEM. An employer may change the method of calculating the hours of service of nonhourly employees (or of one or more categories of nonhourly employees) for each calendar year.

Monthly measurement method. Under the monthly measurement method, an ALEM determines each employee's status as a full-time employee by counting the employee's hours of service for each calendar month.

> **COMMENT:** The monthly method is simple, and an ALEM can act quickly if an employee is no longer eligible for coverage (there is a significant lag time with the lookback method). The downside is the employer's monthly duties to an employee in terms of offering coverage are determined at the end of the month. This is not a problem for full-time employees or for part-time employees that are rigorously kept below 130 hours a month. But for employees at the hourly margin or variable-hour employees, it could result in the employer discovering it needed to offer coverage for a month only after the month ends. This problem is mitigated by a three-month limited nonassessment period for offering coverage to employees who become eligible for coverage for the first time. But that can only be used once for each employee (unless employment is terminated, and then the employee is rehired).

Weekly rule option for measurement periods lasting four or five weeks. If the employer uses the monthly measurement method for a category of employees, the employer may determine full-time employee status over a period that lasts four or five weeks rather than length of a calendar month. Permissible periods include periods that either:

- Begin on the first day of the week that includes the first day of the calendar month, provided that the period over which hours of service are measured does not include the week in which falls the last day of the calendar month (unless that week ends with the last day of the calendar month, in which case it is included); or

- Begin on the first day of the week immediately subsequent to the week that includes the first day of the calendar month (unless the week begins on the first day of the calendar month, in which case it is included), provided the period over which hours of service are measured includes the week in which falls the last day of the calendar month.

> **EXAMPLE:** Special Solder Co. uses the monthly measurement method in combination with the weekly rule to determine full-time status. The company uses the period of Sunday through Saturday as a week, and includes the week that includes the first day of a calendar month and excludes the week that includes the last day of a calendar month (except in any case in which the last day of the calendar month occurs on a Saturday). Special Solder measures hours of service for the five weeks from Sunday, December 27, 2015, through Saturday, January 30, 2016, to determine an employee's full-time employee status for January 2016; for the four weeks from Sunday, January 31, through Saturday, February 27, 2016, to determine an employee's status for February 2016; and the four weeks from Sunday, February 28, through Saturday, March 26, 2016, to determine an em-

ployee's status for March 2016. For January 2016, the employer treats an employee as a full-time employee if the employee has at least 150 hours of service (30 hours per week × 5 weeks). For February and March 2016, the employer treats an employee as a full-time employee if the employee has at least 120 hours of service (30 hours per week × 4 weeks).

COMMENT: The weekly rule allows flexibility in administration of the employer shared responsibility rules. However, it cannot be used to determine ALE status.

Limited Nonassessment Period after Employee First Becomes Eligible for Coverage

If an employer is using the monthly method, and one of its employees becomes otherwise eligible for coverage for the first time in a calendar month, the employer has the benefit of a limited nonassessment period before the employer has to offer coverage. The period is three full calendar months. So, for example, if an employee first becomes otherwise eligible on May 15, the employer does not have to offer coverage in June, July, and August. Coverage must then be offered on September 1.

The forgiveness applies for Code Sec. 4980H(a) liability for failing to offer coverage only if the employee is offered coverage no later than the day after the end of that three-month period. It applies for Code Sec. 4980H(b) liability for failing to offer affordable coverage that provides minimum value only if the offered coverage provides minimum value.

This rule cannot apply more than once per period of employment of an employee. However, if an employee terminates employment and returns under circumstances that would constitute a rehire, this rule may be used again for the same employee.

Leave and rehire rules. Employees who take an extended leave and return to work face two possible rules. If they are continuing employees, their employer must be offer coverage upon resumption of service. In contrast, if rehired employees are treated as new employees, the employer may use the new employee limited nonassessment period before offering coverage. The length of leave determines whether an employee is treated as continuing or as terminated and rehired. Special rules apply for educational employers.

Employees treated as terminated and rehired after at least 13/26 consecutive weeks of leave. An employee who resumes providing services to an employer after a certain period during which the individual was not credited with any hours of service may be treated as having terminated employment and having been rehired. The period must be at least 13 consecutive weeks immediately preceding the resumption of services (26 weeks for an educational employer).

Employees treated as continuing if less than 13/26 consecutive weeks of leave. A continuing employee is treated the same way as an employee who has not experienced a period with no hours of service. A continuing employee who is full-time employee is treated as offered coverage upon resumption of services if the employee is offered coverage as of the first day that employee is credited with an hour of service, or, if later, as soon as administratively practicable. For this purpose, offering coverage by no later than the first day of the calendar month following resumption of services is deemed to be as soon as administratively practicable.

Optional rule of parity for short-term employees for determining length of leave. For purposes of determining the period after which an employee may be treated as having terminated employment, an ALEM may choose a shorter period for recent hires. The period is measured in weeks and must last at least four consecutive weeks. The period must exceed the number of weeks of that employee's period of employment with the ALEM immediately preceding the period.

> **EXAMPLE:** If an employee works for a noneducational employer for 2 weeks immediately preceding the leave, the employer can use a 4 week period under the rule of parity. If the employee works 8 weeks, the employee must use a period of at least 9 weeks.

Look-back measurement method. The lookback method uses standard measurement periods to determine employee status, and employees are treated according to that status in subsequent associated stability periods. Regulations provide separate rules for ongoing employees, new full-time employees who are not seasonal, and new employees who are variable-hour, seasonal or part-time employees. Special rules apply for new variable, seasonal or part-time employees as they transition to ongoing employees. Special rules are also provided for employees rehired after termination or resuming service after an absence.

The lookback method and the monthly method may be used concurrently for different categories of employees. Transition rules are provided for changes in employment status resulting from a change in the full-time employee determination method.

> **COMMENT:** The lookback method is relatively complex and inflexible compared to the monthly method, and it can result in the employer having to offer coverage to an employee for some time after the employee is no longer otherwise qualified for an offer of coverage under the plan. However, the lookback method provides stability and a degree of certainty. Employees will not simply be popping into and out of coverage. Also, employers may tailor their lookback rules for greater flexibility by using shorter periods or lean toward stability with longer periods.

> **CAUTION:** The lookback method applies only for determining an ALEM's obligations and liability under the employer mandate. It cannot be used for determining ALE status.

Standard Measurement Periods for Ongoing Employees

An ALEM uses a standard measurement period as a lookback period for ongoing employees to determine full-time status in a subsequent stability period. If the employee was full-time during that period, the employer treats the employee as full-time for a subsequent associated stability period even if the employee is not actually full-time during the stability period. Employers may insert an administrative period of up to 90 days between a standard measurement period and its associated stability period.

An *ongoing employee* is an employee who has been employed by an employer for at least one standard measurement period.

A standard measurement period is chosen by the ALEM. It cannot be less than 3 and not more than 12 consecutive months. If the employer determines that an employee was employed on average at least 30 hours of service per week during the standard measurement period, the employer must treat the employee as full-time during a subsequent stability period, regardless of the employee's number of hours of service during the stability period as long as the employee remains employed during the period.

The stability period must be at least the greater of six consecutive calendar months or the length of the associated standard measurement period. If the employee is determined not to have worked full-time during the standard measurement period, the employer may treat the employee as not a full-time employee during the immediately following stability period.

90-day administrative period may be inserted between measurement and stability periods. An employer may insert an administrative period between a measurement period and its associated stability period. The administrative period may last up to 90 days. It may neither reduce nor lengthen the measurement period for the stability period. It must overlap with the prior stability period so that during any such administrative period, ongoing employees who are enrolled in coverage because of their status as full-time employees based on a prior measurement period will continue to be covered.

New full-time, nonseasonal employees. For a new employee who is reasonably expected at the employee's start date to be a full-time employee (and is not a seasonal employee), an ALEM determines employment status based on the employee's hours of service for each calendar month. If these hours equal or exceed an average of 30 hours of service per week, the employee is a full-time employee for that calendar month. Once such an employee becomes an ongoing employee, the rules for ongoing employees apply for determining full-time employee status.

A limited nonassessment period applies when an employer hires a new full-time, nonseasonal employee. The employer will not be subject to an assessable payment under Code Sec. 4980H(a) for failing to offer coverage for a three-month period beginning with the first day of the first full calendar month of employment if, for the calendar month, the employee is otherwise eligible for an offer of coverage under a group health plan of the employer.

This rule applies only if the employee is offered coverage by the employer no later than the first day of the fourth full calendar month of employment if the employee is still employed on that day. If the offer of coverage provides minimum value, the employer also will not be subject to an assessable payment under Code Sec. 4980H(b) for offering unaffordable coverage that does not meet minimum value standards.

> **COMPLIANCE TIP:** The nonassessment period does not apply if the employer does not follow through with an offer of coverage, in which case the employer will be open to shared responsibility liability for those months.

The determination whether a new employee is full-time or not must be reasonable based on the facts and circumstances at the employee's start date. Factors to consider include, but are not limited to:

- Whether the employee is replacing an employee who was (or was not) a full-time employee;

- The extent to which hours of service of ongoing employees in the same or comparable positions have varied above and below an average of 30 hours of service per week during recent measurement periods; and

- Whether the job was advertised or otherwise communicated to the new hire or otherwise documented (for example, through a contract or job description), as requiring hours of service that would average 30 (or more) hours of service per week or less than 30 hours of service per week.

Initial measurement periods. For new variable-hour, seasonal, or part-time employees, an ALEM may determine full-time status using an initial measurement period of no less than 3 consecutive months and no more than 12 consecutive months (as selected by the employer).

The start of the initial period must begin on:

- The employee's start date (for example, April 27 if the employee started work on that date); or

¶110

- On any date up to and including the first day of the first calendar month following the employee's start date (for example, May 1 for an April 27 start date); or

- On the first day of the first payroll period starting on or after the employee's start date, if later (for example, May 4 if the next payroll period after April 27 starts on that date).

The employer measures the new employee's hours of service during the initial measurement period and determines whether the employee was employed on average at least 30 hours of service per week during this period. The stability period for such employees must be the same length as the stability period for ongoing employees.

As with ongoing employees, employers may use measurement periods and stability periods that differ either in length or in their starting and ending dates for the categories of employees.

Identifying variable-hour employees. A new employee can be treated as a variable-hour employee if, based on the facts and circumstances at the employee's start date, the employer cannot determine whether the employee is reasonably expected to be employed on average at least 30 hours of service per week during the initial measurement period. Factors to consider include:

- Whether the employee is replacing an employee who was a full-time employee or a variable-hour employee;

- The extent to which the hours of service of employees in the same or comparable positions have actually varied above and below an average of 30 hours of service per week during recent measurement periods; and

- Whether the job was advertised or otherwise communicated to the new employee (for example, through a contract) that weekly hours might vary above and below an average of 30 hours of service per week.

For temporary staffing firms, additional factors include whether other employees in the same position of employment as part of their continuing employment:

- Retain the right to reject temporary placements that the temporary staffing firm offers the employee;

- Typically have periods during which no offer of temporary placement is made;

- Typically are offered temporary placements for differing periods of time; and

- Typically are offered temporary placements that do not extend beyond 13 weeks.

Identifying part-time employees. A *part-time employee* is a new employee who the employer reasonably expects to be employed on average less than 30 hours of service per week during the initial measurement period, based on the facts and circumstances at the employee's start date.

STUDY QUESTION

5. All of the following are reasons that employers report employee hours for purposes of the employer shared responsibility payments *except:*

    a. Whether an ALEM must offer employee coverage that satisfies the employer shared responsibility requirements

    b. Whether volunteer service hours are counted toward the determination of full-time employees for the employer shared responsibility payments

    c. Whether an employer averages at least 50 full-time employees per month of coverage

    d. Whether an employer qualified as an ALE

¶ 111 APPLICABLE LARGE EMPLOYER REPORTING ON FORMS 1094-C AND 1095-C (CODE SEC. 6056)

Applicable large employers have to report the coverage they provide to their full time employees to help the IRS determine the coverage status of each of employee. This duty falls on each ALEM in an ALE or the sole employer in a single employer ALE.

For each of its full-time employees, the employer must file an annual return with the IRS and furnish a statement to the employee reporting whether an offer of health coverage was or was not made to the employee. If an offer was made, the employer must report the required information about the offer. Therefore, even if an employer does not offer coverage to any, or only some, of its full-time employees, that employer must file returns with the IRS and furnish statements to each of its full-time employees to report information specifying that coverage was or was not offered.

ALE reporting serves two purposes. First, it forms the basis for the process leading to any assessment of employer shared responsibility payments against the ALEM. Generally, a payment will be assessed if the employer either does not offer MEC to its full-time employees (and their dependents) or the coverage offered is not affordable or does not provide MV, and one or more of the full-time employees receive a premium tax credit for purchase of coverage on the marketplace. By requiring employers to report the coverage that was offered to each employee, the IRS hopes to be able to verify whether the employer has satisfied its shared responsibility obligations.

Second, ALE reporting allows the employees who receive the statements to determine whether they are actually eligible for the premium tax credit under Code Sec. 36B. The advance and refundable Code Sec. 36B premium tax credit helps individuals afford health insurance coverage purchased through a marketplace. An employee is not eligible for the premium tax credit if the employee is either offered affordable MEC under an employer-sponsored plan that provides MV or is enrolled in an employer-sponsored plan that provides MEC.

Form 1094-C, *Transmittal of Employer-Provided Health Insurance Offer and Coverage Information Returns,* acts as an annual transmittal form for one or more Forms 1095-C, *Employer-Provided Health Insurance Offer and Coverage,* and also summarizes month-by-month information about the employer so any applicable penalties can be assessed. An ALEM may choose to file multiple Forms 1094-C, accompanied by Forms 1095-C for some of its employees, provided that a Form 1095-C is filed for each employee for whom the ALEM is required to file. One "Authoritative Transmittal" Form

1094-C must be filed by each ALEM reporting aggregate employer-level data for all full-time employees of the ALEM.

If the ALEM self-insures plans, it will also have to report as a coverage provider, it does so using the same forms.

> **EXAMPLE:** If an ALEM files a separate Form 1094-C for each of its two divisions to transmit Forms 1095-C for each division's full-time employees, one of the Forms 1094-C filed must be designated as the Authoritative Transmittal and report aggregate employer-level data for both divisions.

In addition, ALEMs must file one Form 1095-C for each employee who was a full-time employee for any month of the calendar year. The ALEM is required to furnish a copy of the Form 1095-C to the employee. For purposes of reporting on Forms 1094-C and 1095-C, an employee in a limited nonassessment period is not considered a full-time employee.

Due Dates for Filing Form 1094-C and Form 1095-C

As of the time of this writing, for calendar year 2015, Forms 1094-C and 1095-C are required to be filed to the IRS by February 29, 2016 (March 31, 2016, if filed electronically). Filers of 250 or more information returns must file electronically. The first Form 1095-C is due to each full-time employee by February 1, 2016, by mail unless the recipient consents to receive the statement in electronic format.

STUDY QUESTION

6. Which of the following is **not** a reason that the IRS requires ALEs to report the coverage they provide to employees for the tax year?

    a. To verify whether the employer satisfied its shared responsibility requirements

    b. To follow the process under the ACA for assessing employer shared responsibility payments for the past year

    c. To offer employees who receive the statements to verify whether their employer-sponsored coverage will be applicable for the next reported term of coverage

    d. To report whether coverage the employer offers is affordable and provides minimum value coverage

¶ 112 CONCLUSION

The Affordable Care Act has imposed new and sweeping changes for employers, particularly employers that average 50 or more full-time employees and full-time equivalents during the prior calendar year. Between the employer mandate and employer information reporting, noncompliant employers will face hefty penalties and fines for noncompliance. Transition rules for 2015 further complicate compliance. Employers that have already taken steps to maintain compliance will require ongoing support, whereas those employers who have not taken action as of yet will need to immediately assess their position with regard to this law.

MODULE 1: HEALTH CARE—Chapter 2: Individual Mandate of the Affordable Care Act

¶ 201 WELCOME

The *Patient Protection and Affordable Care Act of 2010* (PPACA, or the Affordable Care Act) is a lengthy and complex law, with many requirements and features. The IRS has been issuing detailed guidance since the law's enactment in 2010. Some of the law's complexity reflects the law's jumble of effective dates, but by 2014, most of the major provisions of the law took effect, except for the employer mandate and the tax on "Cadillac" health plans. Most individuals and employers are affected by these provisions. They include the *individual mandate* (individual shared responsibility payment), which requires most individuals and their families to carry health insurance or face a penalty; the premium tax credit, which the IRS administers to help low- and middle-income Americans pay for health insurance; and the *employer mandate* (employer shared responsibility payment), which requires most employers to provide essential, affordable health insurance coverage or face a penalty. Beginning in 2014, an individual or family who purchases insurance through an exchange and whose income is below certain levels may apply and qualify for the premium tax credit under Code Sec. 36B. The credit is refundable to the taxpayer. Alternatively, the credit may be paid in advance directly to the insurer; the taxpayer then must pay any difference between the premium and the credit.

¶ 202 LEARNING OBJECTIVES

Upon completion of this chapter, **you will** be able to:

- Identify the basic costs and coverage standards of the individual mandate;
- Identify the specific parts of Form 8965, *Health Coverage Exemptions,* that must be completed by taxpayers claiming exemptions from maintaining coverage; and
- Recognize eligibility and filing requirements for the premium tax credit using Form 8962, *Premium Tax Credit.*

¶ 203 INTRODUCTION

Beginning in 2014, the Affordable Care Act (ACA) requires individuals to:

- Be covered by a health plan that provides basic health insurance coverage (known as *minimum essential coverage* or MEC);
- Qualify for an exemption from the coverage requirement; or
- Pay a shared responsibility payment.

This shared responsibility provision for individuals is also known as the *individual mandate.* Beginning on January 1, 2014, each individual is mandated to maintain qualifying health insurance coverage (known as "minimum essential coverage") for each month of the tax year. The provision applies to all U.S. citizens and resident aliens, including children and senior citizens, if not exempt.

If a taxpayer did not maintain qualifying health insurance coverage during the entire 2015 tax year and does not qualify for a statutory exemption from this requirement, then the taxpayer will have to make an individual shared responsibility payment when submitting their 2015 federal tax return in 2016.

Taxpayers are also responsible for making the payment for their "tax household," meaning their spouse (if filing jointly) and any person they claim as a dependent, if the dependent did not maintain coverage throughout the year and cannot claim an exemption from the mandate.

Generally, the payment is either a percentage of the taxpayer's household income or a flat dollar amount, whichever is greater. For 2015, the annual payment is the greater of: (1) 2 percent of the household income that is above the minimum tax return filing threshold for the taxpayer's filing status (i.e., single, married filing jointly, head of household), or (2) $325 per adult and $162.50 per child (capped at $975 for a family). However, the annual payment due for any individual in any case may not exceed the cost of the national average premium for a bronze level health plan available through the Health Insurance marketplace (also referred to as the "marketplace" or "exchange"). The term *marketplace* includes state marketplaces, regional marketplaces, subsidiary marketplaces, and the federally facilitated marketplace.

Unless otherwise stated, any reference to "taxpayer" in this chapter shall include all members of the tax household (i.e., the spouse, if filing jointly, and any dependents for whom the taxpayer can claim an exemption).

¶ 204 MINIMUM ESSENTIAL COVERAGE

Minimum essential coverage includes coverage provided under the following programs:

- Employer-sponsored coverage for employees and dependents, including coverage provided under self-insured plans, COBRA coverage, retiree coverage and certain expatriate coverage;
- Individual coverage purchased directly from an insurer, in the marketplace, or obtained through a student health plan;
- Medicare Part A coverage and Medicare Advantage plans;
- Comprehensive Medicaid coverage;
- Children's Health Insurance Program (CHIP) coverage;
- Comprehensive veterans' health coverage administered by the Veterans Administration;
- Most types of TRICARE coverage;
- Coverage provided to Peace Corps volunteers;
- Coverage under the Nonappropriated Fund Health Benefit Program;
- Refugee Medical Assistance supported by the Administration for Children and Families;
- Self-funded health coverage offered to students by universities (check with the university to see whether it qualifies);
- State high-risk pools (check with the state to see whether it qualifies); and
- Other coverage recognized by the Secretary of Health and Human Services (HHS) as MEC.

MEC does not include coverage providing only limited benefits, such as coverage consisting solely of excepted benefits (i.e., standalone vision care or dental care, workers' compensation, or accident or disability policies). Note that all members of the tax household need not be covered under the same policy or plan in order to satisfy the individual mandate.

CAUTION: Limited benefit government-sponsored programs that do not provide comprehensive coverage generally do not qualify as MEC.

Taxpayers who enrolled in one of these programs during the tax year and wish to avoid having to make an individual shared responsibility payment must claim an exemption by filing Form 8965, *Health Coverage Exemptions,* with their return.

If a taxpayer is enrolled in and entitled to receive benefits under a plan that is minimum essential coverage for any day during a month, the taxpayer is considered to maintain qualifying coverage for the entire month. For example, if the taxpayer started a new job on August 28, 2015, and was covered under the employer's health plan starting on that day, the taxpayer is considered to have had coverage for the entire month of August.

COMMENT: Employer-sponsored coverage is minimum essential coverage regardless of whether the employer is a governmental, nonprofit, or for-profit entity. Coverage provided to a business owner (such as a partner or sole proprietor) is minimum essential coverage if the plan is eligible employer-sponsored coverage with respect to at least one employee.

Evidence of Coverage

Documentary proof of coverage may include:

- Form 1095 series information statements from an employer, insurer, or marketplace (these are the best evidence and clients should bring them in with their other tax statements);
- Form W-2;
- Medical bill showing payment of amounts due by a health insurance company;
- Statement from an employer indicating health insurance coverage;
- Medicare card; or
- Record of advance payments of the premium tax credit.

In the absence of the documentation above, the IRS recommends tax practitioners exercise the same due diligence with regard to entering health insurance information as applies to entering nearly all other amounts on the tax return, such as charitable contributions. Specifically, after making appropriate inquiries, practitioners may rely in good faith and without verification upon information provided by the taxpayer, unless there is evidence that that information is incorrect, inconsistent, or incomplete.

Taxpayers are ultimately responsible for the accuracy of the information in the tax returns they sign.

Form 1040/Form 1040A/Form 1040EZ

If the taxpayer maintained minimum essential coverage for every month in 2015, then no additional forms need to be filed with the tax return. The taxpayer can simply check the box on Form 1040, 1040A or 1040EZ, indicating that he or she had MEC for all of 2015.

If the taxpayer did not maintain MEC for one or more months in 2015, then this box should not be checked. The taxpayer must either claim an exemption or make a shared responsibility payment.

STUDY QUESTION

1. The premium tax credit is:
   a. Not available to taxpayers who have not yet filed their federal income tax returns for the year
   b. Administered by the IRS
   c. Nonrefundable
   d. Targeted to individuals and families eligible for Medicaid

¶ 205 COVERAGE EXEMPTIONS

The ACA provides certain statutory exemptions from the individual mandate to obtain MEC. Some exemptions are available only from the marketplace, others are available only by claiming them on a tax return, and others are available from either the marketplace or by claiming them on a tax return. The most common types of exemptions are discussed here and all the exemption types for 2015 are summarized in Table 1.

Table 1. Obtaining Coverage Exemptions for 2015		
Coverage Exemption	Granted by Marketplace	Claimed on Tax Return
Income below the filing threshold		X
Coverage considered unaffordable		X
Short coverage gap		X
Citizens living abroad and certain noncitizens		X
Members of a health care sharing ministry	X	X
Members of Indian tribes	X	X
Incarceration	X	X
Aggregate self-only coverage considered unaffordable		X
Gap in CHIP coverage		X
Resident of a state that did not expand Medicaid		X
Limited benefit Medicaid and TRICARE programs that are not MEC		X
Members of certain religious sects	X	
Determined ineligible for Medicaid in a state that did not expand Medicaid	X	
General hardship	X	
Coverage considered unaffordable based on projected income	X	
Unable to renew existing coverage	X	
AmeriCorps coverage	X	

Indian Tribes

The Indian tribes exemption is available to a taxpayer who is either a member of a federally recognized Indian tribe or an individual eligible for services through an Indian care provider. The taxpayer may apply to the marketplace for this exemption by submitting the tribal exemption application form.

Low Income

The low-income exemption is available to a taxpayer whose income is below the minimum threshold for filing a federal tax return. The taxpayer is not required to file a federal income tax return solely to claim the coverage exemption. If the taxpayer files a return anyway (for example, to claim a refund), he or she can claim the coverage exemption with the return.

> **NOTE:** Low-income individuals may qualify for Medicaid, which generally qualifies as minimum essential coverage. Eligibility standards vary widely from state to state. Simply falling below the poverty line in some states does not guaranty coverage eligibility. In other states, Medicaid participants can have incomes up to 133 percent of the federal poverty line. It is important for tax professionals to know the eligibility standards in their states.

Short Coverage Gap

The short coverage gap exemption is available to a taxpayer who is without minimum essential coverage for fewer than three consecutive months during the year. If the taxpayer has more than one short coverage gap in a year, the exemption only applies to the first gap.

> **CAUTION:** If a taxpayer has a gap of three consecutive months or more, the individual is not exempt for any of those months. For example, if an individual has coverage for every month in the year except February and March, the individual is exempt for those two months, but if an individual has coverage for every month in the year except February, March, April, and May, he or she is not exempt for any of those months. The exception to this rule is if a gap spans two tax years, and the part of the gap in the first tax year is less than three months. In that case, no payment is due for the portion of the gap falling in the first tax year, regardless of how long the gap actually becomes. For example, if a gap lasted from November 2014 through June 2015, no payment is due for November and December 2014.

Hardship

The hardship exemption is available to a taxpayer who suffers a hardship with respect to obtaining coverage, as defined by the final regulations issued by HHS. The taxpayer must apply for the hardship application to the marketplace.

A special hardship exemption applies to individuals who purchased their insurance through the marketplace during the initial enrollment period for 2014, but due to glitches in the enrollment process, experienced a coverage gap at the beginning of 2014. Hardship exemptions will also be available on a case-by-case basis for individuals who face unexpected personal or financial crises that prevent them from obtaining minimum essential coverage. See the instructions to the hardship application (Form 8965, *Health Coverage Exemptions*) for possible situations in which the exemption may be granted and documentation required.

Affordability

The affordability exemption is available to a taxpayer who cannot afford coverage because the lowest cost coverage option through an employer sponsored plan or through a marketplace plan costs more than 8 percent of the taxpayer's household income. The taxpayer can apply for this exemption through the marketplace by submitting one of two application forms: the application form for individuals who are in a state with a federally facilitated marketplace or the application form for individuals in a state with a state-based marketplace.

The affordability exception is useful because some individuals slip through the cracks. For example, the premium tax credit is available only for individuals with income above the poverty line, and in any case, the amount of the credit is based on a benchmark non-smoker plan for which the taxpayer might not qualify. See the premium tax credit discussion below.

STUDY QUESTION

2. The short coverage gap exemption:
   a. Applies to a taxpayer who has no MEC for six or more months during the tax year
   b. Applies to only the first short coverage gap if the taxpayer has more than one gap in a tax year, each lasting fewer than three months
   c. Applies to the first three months of a coverage gap of any duration during the year
   d. Is not available if the gap spans December of the current year and the first two months of the following year

¶ 206 FORM 8965, *HEALTH COVERAGE EXEMPTIONS*

Taxpayers must report or claim coverage exemptions on Form 8965 and file it with their Form 1040, Form 1040A, or Form 1040EZ. Some exemptions are available only from the marketplace, others are available only by claiming them on a tax return, and others are available from either the marketplace or by claiming them on a tax return.

The three parts of Form 8965 are completed based on how the coverage exemption is obtained. Depending on the taxpayer's situation, one or more parts of Form 8965 may need to be completed.

Form 8965, Part I

If the taxpayer is granted a coverage exemption from the marketplace, Part I of Form 8965 must be completed. The religious conscience exemption and most hardship exemptions are available only by going to the marketplace and applying for an exemption certificate.

The exemptions for members of federally recognized Indian tribes, members of health care sharing ministries and individuals who are incarcerated are available either by going to the marketplace and applying for an exemption certificate or by claiming the exemption as part of filing a federal income tax return. If the taxpayer received one of the coverage exemptions from the marketplace, then Part I should be filled in. If the taxpayer wants to instead claim one of these exemptions on his or her return without applying to the marketplace, then the instructions for Part III below should be followed.

Part I requires the name and Social Security number of each person in the tax household who was granted a coverage exemption from the marketplace.

Taxpayers who are granted a coverage exemption from the marketplace are sent a notice with their unique exemption certificate number (or ECN), which ought to be entered in Part I. If the taxpayer has applied but has not yet received the ECN at the time of tax filing, then "pending" should be entered for each person listed.

Form 8965, Part II

Generally, if a taxpayer is not required to file a return, he or she is exempt from the shared responsibility payment and no further action is required. Part II of Form 8965 should be used to claim a coverage exemption if the taxpayer's household income or their gross income is below the filing threshold but the taxpayer is filing a return though he or she is not required to do so (to claim a tax refund, for example).

If the taxpayer qualifies for this exemption, everyone in the tax household is exempt from the individual mandate for the entire year.

Computing household income for Form 8965, Part II. Household income is calculated by combining the taxpayer's modified adjusted gross income (MAGI) plus the MAGI of each individual in the tax household who is claimed as a dependent and is required to file his or her own tax return. MAGI is calculated by taking the AGI and adding back any applicable deductions such as student loan interest, qualified tuition expenses, self-employment tax, tuition and fees, passive loss or passive income, IRA contributions, and rental losses.

Once the household income is calculated, it should be compared to the 2015 filing threshold for the taxpayer's age and filing status. If the 2015 household income is less than the filing threshold for the taxpayer's filing status, then "yes" should be checked on the appropriate line.

> **COMMENT:** Because household income is the sum of the MAGI of all members of the tax household with a filing requirement, the IRS has recommended that tax practitioners ought to, with appropriate consent, obtain copies of the tax return(s) for all members of the tax household in order to properly calculate the household income.

Calculating gross income for Form 8965, Part II. Gross income is calculated by combining all income the taxpayer has received in the form of money, goods, property, and services that are not exempt from tax, including any income from sources outside the United States, from the sale of the taxpayer's main home, the taxable part of Social Security benefits, and gains reported on Form 8949 or Schedule D. In determining gross income, income should not be reduced by any losses.

If the taxpayer's 2015 gross income is less than the filing threshold for the taxpayer's filing status, then "yes" should be checked on the appropriate line.

Form 8965, Part III

Part III of Form 8965 should be completed if the taxpayer wishes to claim a coverage exemption on his or her tax return. Taxpayers may claim an exemption on their return (instead of submitting an application for exemption to the marketplace) if they are a member of a federally recognized Indian tribe, eligible for services from an Indian health care facility, a member of a health care sharing ministry, or incarcerated. Taxpayers who lack access to affordable coverage, have a short coverage gap, experience certain hardships, or who are not lawfully present in the United States may only claim an exemption as part of filing a federal income tax return.

Under Part III, a line should be completed for each individual for whom the taxpayer is claiming a coverage exemption. If the taxpayer is claiming more than one coverage exemption for any individual, a separate line should be completed for each exemption.

> **COMMENT:** Coverage exemptions apply in the entire month if an individual is eligible for the exemption for at least one day in that month. For example, if an

¶206

individual was incarcerated following the disposition of charges from June 30 to July 30, the individual is eligible for the coverage exemption for June and July.

STUDY QUESTION

3. If the taxpayer's household income or gross income is less than the filing threshold for the filing status and he or she doesn't file a return, how can he or she still claim the coverage exemption?

   a. Using Form 8965, Part I

   b. Using Form 8965, Part II

   c. Using Form 8965, Part III

   d. No filing is required because the taxpayer is exempt due to low income and is not required to file a tax return

¶ 207 SHARED RESPONSIBILITY PAYMENT

For any month in a calendar year starting in 2015 that the taxpayer had neither health care coverage nor an exemption, the taxpayer will need to calculate his or her shared responsibility payment and submit it with the federal return for that year.

The instructions to Form 8965 provide a Shared Responsibility Payment Worksheet to calculate the payment. Any payment that is due on line 14 of this worksheet will be reported on the taxpayer's return under "Other Taxes". Taxpayers need not submit the worksheet with their return.

For each month that the taxpayer is without coverage or an exemption, the monthly payment due is 1/12 of the annual payment amount. The annual payment amount is the greater of:

- An applicable percentage (2 percent for 2015) of the taxpayer's household income that is above the tax return filing threshold for the taxpayer's filing status; or

- The taxpayer's flat dollar amount ($325 per adult, $162.50 per child, limited to a family maximum of $975 for 2015).

The applicable percentage is 2 percent for 2015 and 2.5 percent for 2016 and thereafter (capped at a national premium cost for bronze coverage). The flat dollar amount is the following:

- 2015, $325 per adult, $162.50 per child, and a family maximum of $975; and

- 2016 and thereafter, $695 per adult, $347.50 per child, and a family maximum of $2,085, adjusted for inflation in later years.

   COMMENT: The 2014 sums were close to nominal, and 2014 can be considered almost a practice year for taxpayers and tax return preparers. The sums quickly rise to serious amounts starting in 2015.

   COMMENT: Because household income is the sum of the MAGI of all members of the tax household with a filing requirement, the IRS has recommended that tax practitioners ought to, with appropriate consent, obtain copies of the tax return(s) for all members of the tax household in order to properly calculate the household income. As discussed above, MAGI is the taxpayer's adjusted gross income plus tax-exempt interest and excludable foreign earned income.

The individual shared responsibility payment is capped at the cost of the national average premium for a bronze level health plan available through the marketplace, which, for 2015, is $2,484 per individual ($207 per month per individual) and $12,420 for a family with five or more members ($1,035 per month for a family with five or more members).

> **COMMENT:** For 2015, therefore, the annual shared responsibility payment due for an individual with no dependents generally will be at least $325 ($27.08 per month) but not more than $2,484 ($207 per month).

The IRS may not use liens or levies to collect any individual shared responsibility payments, but may offset an unpaid liability against any tax refund that may be due. The absence of an enforcement mechanism is unusual for a tax provision, but a tax provision typically requires someone to act, and the individual share responsibility payment is levied on inaction by the taxpayer.

STUDY QUESTION

4. Eduardo and Julia Ruiz are married and have two children younger than age 18. They do not have minimum essential coverage for any family member for any month during 2014 and no one in the family qualifies for an exemption. For 2015, their household income is $70,000 and their filing threshold is $20,600. How much of a penalty will they owe?

    a. $487.50 ($162.50 × 3 dependents)

    b. $1,167.50 ($650 for the spouses + $487.50 for the dependents)

    c. $988 for the whole family

    d. $2,484

¶ 208 PREMIUM TAX CREDIT

The premium tax credit helps eligible taxpayers pay for health insurance obtained through the marketplace. The credit for eligible taxpayers is provided on a sliding scale, depending on the size of the family and household income.

An unusual (and complicating) feature is that all or a portion of the credit amount can be advanced at the taxpayer's election in the form of lower insurance premiums throughout the year. The advanced amount is based on a prediction of the taxpayer's income and circumstances. Differences between the advance and the actual credit amount are reconciled on the taxpayer's tax return.

The amount of the premium tax credit is determined on a sliding scale. A taxpayer with household income at 200 percent of the federal poverty line for the taxpayer's family size gets a larger credit to help cover the cost of insurance than a taxpayer with the same family size who has household income at 300 percent of the federal poverty line.

The premium tax credit is a refundable tax credit. That means that if the amount of the credit is more than the amount of the tax liability on the return, taxpayers will receive the difference as a refund. If no tax is owed, taxpayers can get the full amount of the credit as a refund. However, if a taxpayer receives advance premium tax credit benefits, he or she will need to reconcile the advanced amount against the actual credit amount calculated on the tax return.

Taxpayers Who Qualify for the Credit

A taxpayer is eligible for a premium tax credit if all of the following requirements are met:

- The taxpayer, spouse (if filing a joint return), or a dependent was enrolled at some time during the year in one or more qualified health plans offered through a marketplace;
- At least one of these individuals was not eligible for other MEC during the months they were enrolled in the qualified plan;
- The taxpayer's income is at least 100 percent but not more than 400 percent of the federal poverty line for the taxpayer's family size (unless the income is below 100 percent and the taxpayer, spouse, or dependent enrolled in a qualified plan is not a U.S. citizen, but is lawfully present in the United States and is not eligible for Medicaid because of immigration status);
- If married, the taxpayer and the taxpayer's spouse file jointly (unless the taxpayer's filing status is head of household, or the taxpayer is a victim of spousal abuse or abandonment); and
- The taxpayer cannot be claimed as a dependent by someone else.

Taxpayer's Tax Family and Tax Coverage Family

A taxpayer is allowed a premium tax credit only for months that a member of the taxpayer's tax family is: enrolled in a policy offered through the marketplace and not eligible for MEC (for example, from an employer or a government program). The *taxpayer's tax family* consists of the taxpayer, the taxpayer's spouse if filing jointly, and all other individuals for whom the taxpayer claims a personal exemption deduction. The family members who meet the above two requirements are the taxpayer's *tax coverage family*.

Effect of Employer Coverage

If an individual is eligible for MEC during the year from an employer, the individual cannot qualify for a premium tax credit for the months the individual is so eligible, unless the coverage is unaffordable or does not provide minimum value.

An individual who enrolls in an employer-sponsored plan (including retiree coverage) is not eligible for the premium tax credit for the months in which he or she is so enrolled. This holds true even if the plan is unaffordable or fails to provide minimum value. However, if only one spouse is enrolled in employer coverage that is not affordable and does not provide minimum value, the nonenrolled spouse may be eligible for a premium tax credit.

If the individual changed enrollment from marketplace coverage to employer-sponsored coverage during the year, the individual is a member of the coverage family only for the months the individual is enrolled in MEC through the marketplace and was not eligible for coverage under the employer-sponsored plan (or other MEC, such as Medicaid). An individual is eligible for employer-sponsored coverage for any month the individual is enrolled in the employer coverage or could have enrolled in employer coverage that is affordable and provides minimum value.

> **EXAMPLE:** Steve is single and has no dependents. When he enrolled through the marketplace in November 2014, his projected 2015 household income was $27,925. He enrolled in a qualified health plan, and the marketplace determined the advance credit payments for which he was eligible. However, Steve decided to wait and take all of the benefit of the credit on his 2015 return. In

August 2015, Steve began a new job and became eligible for employer-sponsored coverage on September 1st. Because Steve became eligible for employer-sponsored coverage on September 1st, he cannot claim a premium tax credit for any months in 2015 other than January through August.

Effect of Government Coverage

A premium tax credit is not allowed for an individual's coverage for the months that he or she is eligible for the government-sponsored coverage if the coverage qualifies as MEC. Therefore, an individual eligible for coverage through a government-sponsored program, such as Medicaid, Medicare, CHIP, or TRICARE, is not a member of the coverage family for the months in which he or she is eligible for government-sponsored coverage. This holds true even for taxpayers who live in states that chose not to participate in the Medicaid expansion.

Advance Premium Tax Credit (APTC)

At enrollment, the marketplace will project the taxpayer's income and family composition to estimate the amount of the premium tax credit the taxpayer would be able to claim. If eligible for advance credit payments, taxpayers may choose to:

- Have some or all of the estimated credit paid in advance to the insurance company to lower the insured's out-of-pocket cost for monthly premiums during the year; or
- Wait to get all the benefit of the credit when they file their tax return.

The amount of any advance credit payments will appear on Form 1095-A, *Health Insurance Marketplace Statement.*

CAUTION: The premium tax credit is a unique tax benefit in that is it made available well in advance of the date the taxpayer files the year's tax return. The advanced amount is a prediction based on past financial and family information that might not hold true for the tax year of the advance. The credit amount is ultimately determined on the taxpayer's tax return, and discrepancies must be reconciled at that time. If the prediction is sufficiently wrong, it might subject the taxpayer to underpayment of tax penalties. Form 8962, *Premium Tax Credit,* must be used to calculate the premium tax credit and to reconcile advance credit amounts with the actual credit amount.

Married Taxpayers

Married taxpayers can file separately and qualify for the credit only in one of two "situations" (as they are called in the instructions). In Situation 1, the taxpayer files as head of household for Form 1040 or Form 1040A, or as single for Form 1040NR due to living separately from the taxpayer's spouse.

In Situation 2, the taxpayer files as married filing separately because the spouses live apart at the time of filing and the taxpayer is a victim of domestic abuse or spousal abandonment. Taxpayers in this situation check the "Relief" box at the top of Form 8962.

If the taxpayer does not fall under either of these situations but nevertheless files as married filing separately, the taxpayer does not qualify for the credit and must repay any advances on the credit.

Form 8962, Premium Tax Credit

Part 1 of Form 8962 is used to calculate the amount the taxpayer is expected to contribute for coverage. All things being equal, the higher the taxpayer's income, the higher the expected contribution amount. The larger the family, the lower the expected contribution amount. Part 1 also filters out taxpayers who make too much to qualify for any credit.

In Part 2, that amount is compared to the cost of the second lowest cost silver plan (SLCSP). The premium tax credit amount makes up the difference. The credit amount is capped by what the taxpayer actually paid.

> **COMMENT:** The premium tax credit helps eligible taxpayers obtain relatively inexpensive middle-of-the-road coverage. If the taxpayer wants to go above and beyond that coverage, the taxpayer will have to pay for the enhanced portion of coverage entirely out of pocket. The cap ensures that if the taxpayer went for lower cost coverage, the taxpayer wouldn't receive more than his or her cost for the premiums. A downside for smokers is that the benchmark SLCSP plan is for nonsmokers, so the extra cost of coverage is born entirely by the insured with no help from the credit.

Part 3 is used to reconcile any advance against the actual credit amount as calculated in Part 2.

Part 4 is used if an individual for whom a Form 1095-A was issued was in more than one tax family during the year. This situation typically arises in marriage and divorce situations. Coverage amounts must be allocated in this case before Part 2 or Part 5 can be completed.

Part 5 provides an alternative calculation method if the taxpayer got married during the tax year. The alternative method allows the taxpayer to split the family in two based on his or her premarriage situation, for purposes of calculating the credit. The alternative method is limited to taxpayers filing joint returns who would otherwise have to pay back an advance premium tax credit.

Form 8962, Part 1, annual and monthly contribution amounts. In Part 1 of Form 8962, the taxpayer determines whether a premium tax credit is available based on:

- The number of members in the taxpayer's tax family;
- Household income; and
- The relationship between household income and the federal poverty level.

Part 1 also determines the amount the taxpayer is expected to contribute toward coverage, which is important when he or she determines the amount of the credit in Part 2.

Tax family. The tax family consists of the taxpayer, spouse (if a joint return), and dependents entitling the taxpayer to an exemption. The number of exemptions from Form 1040, 1040A, or Form 1040NR is used to determine the applicable federal poverty line.

Household income. To determine eligibility and the credit amount, the taxpayer's household income is compared to the applicable federal poverty line. Household income is the total of the taxpayer's MAGI, the spouse's MAGI if the couple is filing a joint return, and the MAGI of all dependents required to file a federal income tax return.

> **EXAMPLE:** Marguerite and Dean Carlton are married and file jointly. They have one child, Brian, who is 17. They claim him as a dependent. Brian works part time and has a filing requirement. Marguerite and Dean's household income calculation would include their MAGI, as well as Brian's MAGI.

MAGI is the adjusted gross income on the federal income tax return plus any excluded foreign income, nontaxable Social Security benefits (including Tier 1 Railroad

Retirement benefits), and tax-exempt interest. It does not include Supplemental Security Income (SSI).

> **COMMENT:** Worksheets are provided in the Form 8962 Instructions for both the taxpayer's, and the dependents' MAGI.

Federal poverty line. The federal poverty line is an income amount adjusted for family size that the government considers to be poverty level for the year. HHS publishes this information on its website for residents of the 48 contiguous states and Washington, D.C., and separately for the residents of Alaska and for Hawaii. Premium tax credit eligibility for a particular year is based on the most recently published set of poverty guidelines as of the first day of the annual open enrollment period. For example, the premium tax credit for 2015 is based on the 2014 guidelines.

For 2014 (which governs the premium tax credit for 2015), for residents of one of the 48 contiguous states or Washington, D.C., the following illustrates when household income would be between 100 percent and 400 percent of the federal poverty line:

- $11,670 (100 percent) up to $46,680 (400 percent) for an individual;
- $15,730 (100 percent) up to $62,920 (400 percent) for a family of two; and
- $23,850 (100 percent) up to $95,400 (400 percent) for a family of four.

The IRS provides federal poverty line tables in the Form 8962 instructions.

Household income as percentage of federal poverty line. The household income amount is divided by the federal poverty amount. To qualify for a credit, the result must be between 1.00 and 3.99. The instructions provide special rounding rules.

If the percentage is 400 or below, the "yes" box is checked. If the percentage is more than 400, there is no tax credit. If an advance was made, the taxpayer goes to Part 3 of Form 8962 for reconciliation.

Note that if the percentage is below 1.00, the credit is generally unavailable, except in two special circumstances. First, if the marketplace exchange estimated the taxpayer would qualify, advances were made, and the taxpayer otherwise qualifies, the taxpayer can qualify. Second, the credit is available for lawful aliens lawfully in the U.S. who do not qualify for Medicaid due to immigration status. In general, U.S. citizens whose income is at or below the poverty line qualify for Medicaid.

Contribution amounts. Go to Applicable Figure table in the instructions, and match income to poverty line percentage to the "applicable figure." This figure ranges between .0200 for percentages less than 133 percent and .0950 for percentages between 300 and 400 percent. There is a sliding scale for percentages in between. For example, if the percentage is twice the poverty line (200 percent), the applicable figure is .0630.

The taxpayer multiplies the applicable figure by the household income and enters the amount. That is the annual contribution for health care. That contribution is divided by 12 to determine the monthly contribution amount.

The contribution amount represents the amount the taxpayer is expected to provide for coverage out of pocket based on the taxpayer's circumstances. It will be subtracted from the cost of the benchmark SLCSP amount to arrive at the maximum possible (i.e., before capping) credit amount in Part 2.

Form 8962, Part 2, claiming premium tax credit and reconciling advance payment of credit. The taxpayer should have received a Form 1095-A information statement that covers each member of the tax household who obtained coverage through a marketplace. This form will contain the amount of the actual premiums, the amount of the SLCSP, and the amount of any advances on the credit, broken down by each month of the year. This information is used on Part 2 of Form 8962.

¶208

If there are multiple Forms 1095-A for the same taxpayer, he or she sums the amounts when filling out the columns in Part 2. If one Form 1095-A is shared between taxpayers (e.g., due to a marriage or divorce during the tax year), only the amounts allocated under Part 4 are entered. The "Instructions for Form 8962" provides a more detailed description of entering Form 1095-A information onto Part 2.

Final step in completing Part 2. If the taxpayer shares a policy with another taxpayer, a shared policy allocation will need to be done in Part 4 before continuing. In such a case, the taxpayer consults Form 8962, Part 4. Note that in these situations, Form 1095-A might have been sent to the other taxpayer, or the other taxpayer might need a copy of the form if it was received by the taxpayer.

If the taxpayer got married during the tax year, he or she may qualify for an alternative credit calculation that may reduce the amount of an advance that needs to be returned. A taxpayer and spouse may be eligible for the alternative method if they:

- Were unmarried on January 1 and were married by December 31 of the tax year;
- Are filing a joint return for the tax year;
- Have someone in the tax family enrolled in a qualified health plan before the first full month of marriage; and
- Have a premium tax credit advance for someone in the tax family during the tax year.

If the advance must be repaid because the taxpayer and spouse exceed the household income requirement for the credit, they can use the alternative method. If their household income qualifies them for the credit, they must fill out Worksheet 2 in the "Instructions for Form 8962" to determine whether they received an excess advance. If so, they may use the alternative method. This is described in Form 8962, Part 5.

Annual versus monthly reporting on Part 2. If Form 1095-A for the tax household includes coverage for January through December, with no changes in monthly amounts, the taxpayer should check "Yes" box, and report and calculate the credit on the basis of annual amounts. Otherwise, the taxpayer will have to fill out lines t for each month separately, January through December.

Taxpayers who have changes in monthly amounts not shown on Form 1095-A (for example, a taxpayer enrolled in a qualified health plan became eligible for employer coverage during the year, but did not notify the marketplace) must also do a monthly calculation to determine their premium tax credit.

Credit amount. The credit amount is the sum of the credit amount for each month. The credit amount for a month is the lesser of two amounts:

- The monthly premium for the plan or plans in which the taxpayer's family enrolled (enrollment premium); and
- The monthly premium for the taxpayer's applicable SLCSP minus the taxpayer's monthly contribution amount.

This calculation is done on Form 8962.

Form 1095-A will have the information needed for this part of the form, including the actual premium, the SLCSP premium, the advance (if any) for that month, and the contribution amount. If Form 1095-A does not include the SLCSP premium, or it is wrong due to changes in circumstances, these premiums can be obtained using the Second Lowest Cost Silver Plan (SLCSP) Lookup Tool on the healthcare.gov website.

On the form, the credit amount is determined in two steps. First, the maximum credit amount is determined by using the SLCSP premium in Column B as a benchmark. In Column D, the taxpayer's contribution is subtracted from that benchmark. What's left is the maximum premium tax credit amount. Next the credit is capped. That is done in Column E where the lesser of the maximum credit and the actual premium amount in Column A is entered. The cap might apply if the coverage was an inexpensive bronze plan, which is the most basic type of minimum essential coverage (catastrophic-only coverage does not count as MEC).

> **NOTE:** If the taxpayer is using the annual method because there was no change for any month, this work is done on the annual line. If the taxpayer is reporting on a monthly basis, these determinations are made on the separate monthly lines.

Net credit amount. The total tax credit amount and the total advance amount are netted. If the amount of the credit is greater than the advance, the advance is subtracted from the credit. If the amount is zero because the two amounts are the same, the form is complete. If the amount is positive, the amount is entered on Form 1040, Form 1040A, or Form 2040NR

If the amount is negative (i.e., the advance amount is greater than the actual amount), the taxpayer goes to Part 3 for reconciliation.

STUDY QUESTION

---

5. All of the following are qualifications for a married couple to use the alternative credit calculation for reconciling excess advance premium tax credit amounts to return *except*:

- **a.** Marriage between January 1 and December 31 of the tax year
- **b.** The filing status of married filing separately
- **c.** Enrollment of someone in their tax family in a qualified health plan before the first full month of their marriage
- **d.** Receipt of an advance premium tax credit for someone in the tax family during the tax year

---

Form 8962, Part 3, Repayment of Excess Advance Premium Tax Credit (Reconciliation). Reconciliation must be done if there was an advance, and any one of three circumstances applies:

- The advance amount is greater than the credit amount;
- The taxpayer checked the "no" box on Line 6 because the taxpayer's household income as a percentage of the federal poverty line was 400 or greater; or
- The taxpayer is filing married at the end of the tax year, but is filing as married filing separately and did not check the "relief" box because the taxpayer was not a victim of domestic abuse or spouse abandonment.

The excess of the advance amount over the credit amount is owed if the taxpayer's percentage is over 400. If the percentage is not over 400, a repayment limitation applies based on household income to federal poverty line percentage and filing status. This amount is determined using the Repayment Limitation Table in the instructions.

The smaller of the advance amount and the repayment limitation amount is entered on Form 1040, Form 1040A, or Form 1040NR

Form 8962, Part 4, Shared Policy Allocation. A shared policy allocation must be made if taxpayers' circumstances fall under one or more of the following situations:

- Taxpayers are divorced or legally separated during the tax year;
- Taxpayers are married at year end but filing separate returns;
- A policy is shared with an individual for whom another taxpayer claims the personal exemption; and
- A policy is shared by two or more tax families.

Taxpayers divorced or legally separated during the tax year. The allocation is 50/50 for taxpayers who were divorced or legally separated during the tax year, unless the taxpayers agree otherwise. This percentage is applied to premiums, SLCSP, and advances.

> **EXAMPLE:** Joe and Suzy Miller are married at the beginning of the year with three children. They enroll the children in qualified coverage with an effective date of February 1. They divorce in July. The children enroll in other MEC, and disenroll in the qualified plan effective August 1. Joe claims two of the children on his taxes, and Suzy claims one. They agree to allocate the amounts reported on Form 1095-A 67 percent to Joe, and 33 percent to Suzy. If they had not agreed, the split would have been 50/50.
>
> On Joe's Form 8962, he enters Suzy's Social Security number and 0.67. On Suzy's Form 8962, she enters Joe's Social Security number, and 0.33. They both enter 02 for the start month and 07 for the stop month.

Taxpayers married at year end but filing separate returns. Married taxpayers can file separately and qualify for the credit only if one of two "situations." In Situation 1, the taxpayer files as head of household for Form 1040 or Form 1040A, or as single for Form 1040NR due to living separately from the taxpayer's spouse. In Situation 2, the taxpayer files as married filing separately because the spouses live apart at the time of filing and the taxpayer is a victim of domestic abuse or spousal abandonment.

If the taxpayer files married filing separately and Situation 2 does not apply, the credit is not available, and the taxpayer must repay and advances.

Whether it is to claim the credit or repay advances, the taxpayer must take an allocation if:

- The spouses enrolled in the same qualified health plan; or
- The taxpayer or someone in the taxpayer's tax family was enrolled in the same policy as the taxpayer's spouse during the tax year.

In Situation 1 or 2, the taxpayer and spouse have separate tax families. The taxpayer enters .50 for the premium allocation, and .50 for the advance credit allocation. The SLCSP is not allocated. Instead, the taxpayer enters the applicable SLCSP for the taxpayer's tax family.

IRS Publication 974 provides information on the applicable SLCSP; information is also available on **www.healthcare.gov/taxes**.

If the taxpayer files married filing separately and is not in Situation 2, the premium cannot be claimed, so nothing is entered for premium allocation or for SLCSP. Allocation is needed to calculate the advance that needs to be repaid, and 0.50 is used.

> **EXAMPLE:** Jim and June Fittelo are married at the end of the year with one child. They have a qualified health plan for the year with an annual premium of $14,000 and an advance of $8,500. Jim moves out in May. They file individually, June as head of household with the child as dependent (Situation 1), and Jim as married filing separately. June enters Jim's Social Security number, 0.50 for premiums, and 0.50 for the advance amounts. She has to look up the correct SLCSP for her tax family. She takes into account $7,000 in premiums, and $4,250 in

advances. Jim does not qualify for the credit because he is filing married filing separately. He enters June's Social Security number and 0.50 for the advance. He leaves the premium column and SLCSP column blank because he does not qualify for the credit. He must repay the $4,250 (half of the total) in advances allocated to him (subject to any repayment limitation).

EXAMPLE: Larry and Elaine Shields are married at the end of the year with no dependents. They are enrolled in a qualified plan with a premium of $10,000 per year with an advance of $6,500. Elaine is a victim of domestic abuse, and files using the married filing separately status. She checks the "Relief" box at the top of Form 8962. Unless she notified the marketplace exchange, Elaine has to redetermine her family size, household income and SLCSP for the year. She takes into account $5,000 in premiums, and $3,250 in advances. She enters Larry's social number and 0.50 for allocation.

EXAMPLE: Adam and Cathy Dupchek are married with no dependents. They are both enrolled in a qualified health plan with advances of $8,700 for the tax year. They both file returns as married filing separately, so neither qualifies for the credit. They are each allocated 50 percent of the advances, which they must repay (subject to repayment limits). Note that if only Cathy had been enrolled, the entire $8,700 would be allocated to her alone.

STUDY QUESTION

---

6. Which of the following is **not** a situation in which married taxpayers filing separately may claim the premium tax credit?

    a. The taxpayers live apart at the time of filing, with one of the spouses being a victim of domestic abuse

    b. The taxpayers live apart at the time of filing due to one spouse abandoning the other

    c. The taxpayers share an abode but one of the spouses did not receive an advance credit

    d. The taxpayers live apart at the time of the filing, with one filing as head of household

---

Policy shared with individual for whom another taxpayer claims personal exemption. This situation may arise where a couple is divorced, and one former spouse enrolls a child in qualified plan, and the other former spouse claims the exemption. The allocation can be agreed upon, but if there is no agreement, the allocation is proportional to the number of covered in the plan. For example, if three individuals are covered and one is claimed as a dependent of the other spouse, the allocation would be 33 percent to the other spouse. The allocation formula applies to all three policy items, including premiums, advances, and SLCSP.

EXAMPLE: Joe and Alice McKinsey were divorced prior to the tax year, and have two children. Joe enrolled the two children in his qualified health plan. One child resides with Alice, and she claims the child as a dependent. Joe and Alice agree to allocate 20 percent of the credit to Alice, and 80 percent to Joe. If they had not agreed, the allocation would have been 67 percent to Joe, and 33 percent to Alice. Joe enters Alice's Social Security number, and enters 0.80 for the premium, the SLCPS, and the advance. Joe and Alice each determine the credit amount based on each of their tax family's household income and number of individuals in the family.

An allocation agreement may be changed month-to-month, but within the agreement period the same amount must be applied to all policy amounts.

Policy shared by two or more tax families. A policy may end up being shared by two or more families in a tax year in which a dependent decides to take his or her own exemption. If corrected and separate Forms 1095-A are not issued, the premium will need to be allocated. The allocation is done in proportion to the redetermined SLCSP.

> **EXAMPLE:** Gary Page and his three children are enrolled in a qualified plan for which the annual premium is $15,000. Two of the children are dependents. One of them, Tim, is not and may take his own premium tax credit if he qualifies. Unless separate and correct Forms 1095-A are issued, the premium will need to be allocated. The allocation percentages are based on the correct SLCSP. The SLCSP for Gary and his dependent children is $12,000, and the SLCSP for Tim is $6,000. Because 67 percent of the total SLCSP premium is Gary's, and 33 percent is Tim's, the actual premiums are allocated in the same percentages.

Additional shared policies. Information regarding allocations among additional policies may be made on the lines provided on the form. If there are additional shared policies, the additional information is to be attached in a statement. When done, the allocated and nonallocated amounts need to be totaled, and entered into the appropriate columns.

Form 8962, Part 5, Alternative Credit Calculation for Year of Marriage. An alternative credit calculation method may be available to taxpayers who got married during the tax year if they have an advance credit amount that needs reconciling. The alternative method uses separate "alternative size" families for both spouses, and splits the household income 50/50.

A taxpayer and spouse may be eligible for the alternative method if they:

- Were unmarried on January 1 and married on December 31 of the tax year;
- Are filing a joint return for the tax year;
- Have someone in the tax family enrolled in a qualified health plan before the first full month of marriage; and
- Have a premium tax credit advance for someone in the tax family during the tax year.

If the advance must be repaid because the taxpayer and spouse exceed the household income requirement for the credit, they can use the alternative method. If their household income qualifies them for the credit, they must fill out Worksheet 2 in the "Instructions for Form 8962" to determine whether there is an excess advance. If so, they may use the alternative method.

The alternative method is based on an "alternative family size," which includes the taxpayer and any individual in the tax family that qualifies as the taxpayer's dependent as defined for purposes of Form 1040 or 1040A

Individuals who are dependents of both spouses may be in either alternative family size, but cannot be in both.

> **EXAMPLE:** Catherine McHenry, Henry Wooster, and their son Ralph Wooster have lived together since July 2014. Catherine and Henry marry in August 2015. Each has coverage under a qualified health plan for the months before September. Ralph qualifies as Catherine's dependent and as Henry's dependent, and may be

included in either Catherine's or Henry's alternative family size but not in both of their alternative family sizes.

¶ 209 CONCLUSION

Of all of the changes under the Affordable Care Act, the requirement that individuals must either maintain minimum essential coverage for every month, qualify for a statutory exemption, or make a shared responsibility payment may be the most far-reaching. Because the individual mandate affects all U.S. citizens and resident aliens, it is extremely important for practitioners to be aware of its ramifications as well as possible methods (such as the premium tax credit) that would make the mandate more affordable.

If this chapter has done its work, two takeaways reflect major issues right now. First, the amount of individual shared responsibility payments ramps up this year. Clients need to be warned that 2014 was merely a practice run compared to 2015 and that they really need to get their coverage ducks in a row. Second, the premium tax credit can be a generous credit, but taking an advance payment can be a trap for the unwary taxpayer's whose circumstances change during the year. Practitioners should encourage clients to contact their marketplace if changes in income or family situation occur.

MODULE 2: MAXIMIZING INDIVIDUAL BENEFITS—Chapter 3: Tax Planning for Education

¶ 301 WELCOME

This chapter explores the variety of taxpayer incentives for funding secondary and higher education, including savings vehicles, tax credits, tax deductions, and student loans. Education tax incentives continue to evolve. A number of recent tax laws, starting with the *Taxpayer Relief Act of 1997* (P.L. 105-34), have added new tax breaks for financing higher education and have greatly liberalized the terms of those breaks that were already available. At the same time, however, enhanced reporting rules have been added, such as under the *Trade Preferences Extension Act of 2015* (P.L. 114-27, June 29, 2015), which requires a tuition statement to be attached to a return that claims a related credit or deduction. Although some of these added benefits have been made permanent, others continue to expire or are set to expire in the near future. "Permanent" means that the statute enabling the benefit has no fixed expiration date. Obviously, Congress can make changes at any time.

¶ 302 LEARNING OBJECTIVES

Upon completion of this chapter, you will be able to:

- Recognize how savings plans, such as Section 529 plans, and U.S. savings bonds may be used to pay qualified educational expenses and how the investments can be coordinated;
- Identify the benefits and restrictions of the American opportunity tax credit and lifetime learning credit; and
- Recognize what qualified student loan costs are deductible.

¶ 303 INTRODUCTION

Higher education is a forward-looking expenditure and planning is crucial. With myriad tax incentives and varying expiration dates, it was challenging for students and their parents to get an accurate picture of the after-tax cost of attending college.

Both the American opportunity tax credit and the above-the-line deduction for higher education expenses are closely interwoven with the lifetime learning credit (LLC). Determining which of these three benefits is the best to claim requires a complex financial analysis.

Some of the tax breaks encourage saving for college; others help to defray the cost of paying for it. Some breaks can be used in combination; others are mutually exclusive. Choosing the right credit, deduction, or other incentive is challenging, but can make a substantial difference. This course explains the 11 major tax incentives for higher education.

There are different types of federal tax incentives for higher education. Some are aimed at saving for college; others help to pay for college through tax savings. First, consider the tax incentives for saving for higher education, including the following:

- Qualified tuition programs;

- Coverdell education savings accounts (ESAs); and
- U.S. savings bond interest exclusion.

Next, note the breaks for paying for education expenses. These breaks include the following:

- If extended for 2015, an above-the-line deduction for higher education expenses (tuition and fees deduction);
- Education tax credits (American opportunity tax credit and lifetime learning credit);
- Scholarships and tuition reduction plans;
- Penalty-free Roth and traditional IRA withdrawals
- Exclusion from an employee's gross income of $5,250 of employer-provided education assistance; and
- Deduction for work-related education costs.

  NOTE: The last two tax breaks, used in connection with the taxpayer's status as an employee or self-employed worker, are beyond the scope of this course. The focus of this course is using tax provisions principally to assist in saving and paying for the higher education of a taxpayer's children, grandchildren, or other family members.

Finally, there is a break for those who borrowed funds for higher education expenses:

- Student loan interest deduction; and
- Exclusion for certain student loan forgiveness.

¶ 304 DIFFERENCES BETWEEN PREPAID TUITION PLANS AND STATE SAVINGS PLANS

Nearly every state has some type of qualified tuition program (QTP) in place. These plans are sometimes known as Section 529 plans, after the Internal Revenue Code section authorizing them. Generally, two types of plans exist: prepaid tuition plans and savings plans. Prepaid tuition plans are plans in which contributions are used to guarantee payment of state university tuition (or some comparable amount).

Prepaid Tuition Plans

Since 2002, private colleges and other institutions have been able to offer prepaid tuition plans, in addition to the state savings plans. Details of one such private plan, which has more than 270 participating colleges and universities, can be found at **www.privatecollege529.com.**

The savings plan is set up as a trust. The savings plan may or may not provide for guaranteed returns. Withdrawals from a private 529 plan for qualified higher education expenses have not been taxable to the beneficiary since 2004.

Qualified State Tuition Programs

To determine whether a state has a tuition savings plan and to compare various states tuition savings plans, interested individuals can go to **www.savingforcollege.com** or **www.collegesavings.org**.

Since 2002, withdrawals from a state 529 plan for qualified higher education expenses are not taxable to the beneficiary. This favorable treatment for qualified withdrawals, which had been temporary at first, has been made permanent.

EXAMPLE: Hilda Spear, mother of 8-year-old Jim Spear, prepays the state college's tuition. When Jimmy is 18 and if he attends a state university, the tuition will be fully covered. If Jim goes to an out-of-state school, his particular state college's plan allows for payment of those expenses. If Jim does not attend college or dies, the plan may refund contributions, less an administrative charge.

PLANNING POINTER: Funds in 529 savings accounts are treated as an asset of the parent in determining eligibility for a student's federal financial aid. Currently, a parent's expected contribution toward a child's college costs will include on average 5.6 percent of the value of the 529 account for each academic year; this is more favorable than the 20 percent applied to assets owned in a child's name or in a custodial account.

Code Sec. 529 (added by the *Small Business Job Protection Act of 1996,* P.L. 104-188) allows states to adopt tax-exempt, prepaid tuition savings programs. Code Sec. 529 is generally effective for tax years ending after August 20, 1996; however, a transitional rule (modified by the *Taxpayer Relief Act of 1997*) applies to preexisting programs if certain conditions are met.

Such state programs, allow a person either to:

- Purchase, in cash, tuition credits or certificates on behalf of a designated beneficiary which entitles the beneficiary to the waiver or payment of qualified higher education expenses, or

- Make cash contributions to an account established solely for the purpose of paying for qualified higher education expenses on behalf of the designated beneficiary.

The interest on the tuition account or the increase in value of the tuition credit is generally exempt from federal income tax while the funds remain in the plan.

Private institutions can establish qualified tuition programs provided they obtain a ruling or determination by the IRS stating that the program satisfies the requirements of Code Sec. 529 (Code Sec. 529(b)(1)). Such private qualified tuition programs must hold all contributions in a qualified trust (created or organized in the United States for the exclusive benefit of designated beneficiaries) and must meet the requirements for individual retirement account (IRA) trusts (i.e., a bank trustee or an individual trustee that meets applicable IRA requirements and trust assets cannot be commingled except in a common trust or investment fund). The *Pension Protection Act of 2006* (P.L. 109-280) repealed the "sunset" provisions of *the Economic Growth and Tax Relief Reconciliation Act of 2001* (EGTRRA) and allowed the IRS to prescribe regulations for administering qualified tuition plans, specifically to prevent abuse.

Distributions and rollovers. Distributions, in-kind or cash, are excluded from gross income to the extent the distribution is used for qualified higher education expenses. Further, distributions made by private-entity qualified tuition programs are also excludible from gross income (Code Sec. 529(c)(3)(B)).

Distributions that are not used for qualified higher education expenses are subject to the same penalty as Coverdell ESA withdrawals not used for education purposes under Code Sec. 530(d)(4). A 10 percent penalty will apply to qualified tuition program withdrawals not used for qualified higher education purposes, other than those made on account of the death or disability of the designated beneficiary.

Although Code Sec. 529(b)(4) prohibits the contributor and the designated beneficiary from directing the investment of the QTP's contributions and earnings, Prop. Reg. § 1.529-2(g) would permit the person establishing the account to select, at that time, an investment strategy from those designed by the program. Further, IRS Notice 2001-55,

¶304

2001-2 CB 299, permits a change in the investment strategy once every calendar year and upon a change in the designated beneficiary provided the selection is from broad-based strategies designed exclusively by the program and the program has established procedures and maintains records to prevent a change from occurring more frequently.

In order to provide increased benefits to a more broadly defined group of beneficiaries, over time the following definitions have been expanded and clarified:

- *Room and board expenses.* The definition of qualified higher education expenses includes room and board expenses in an amount up to the school's posted charges or $2,500 per year for students living off-campus and not at home Reg. § 1.529-1(c)(2). After 2001, the room and board expense limitation is equal to the amount allowed under U.S.C. § 108711 (for calculation of a student's costs of attendance for federal financial aid purposes), which, for students living off-campus and not at home, is equal to the amount of expenses reasonably incurred by the student for room and board (Code Sec. 529(c)(3)(B)). Room and board expenses constitute qualified higher education expenses only if the student is:

  - Enrolled in a degree, certificate or other program leading to a recognized educational credential at an eligible educational institution, and

  - Carrying at least half of the normal full-time work load for the course of study the student is pursuing;

- *Eligible educational institution.* An eligible educational institution is any college, university, vocational school, or other postsecondary institution that is eligible to participate in the Department of Education's student aid programs; and

- *Family member.* For purposes of account rollovers and beneficiary changes, the definition of a member of the beneficiary's family includes the beneficiary's spouse, anyone qualifying as a dependent under Code Sec. 152(a), or the spouse of anyone qualifying as a dependent. In addition to spouses, family members include parents, children, siblings, nephews and nieces, certain in-laws, first cousins, and the spouses of those relations.

Interaction with AOTC and LLC. To the extent that a distribution from a qualified state tuition program is used to pay for qualified tuition and fees, the distributee may claim the American opportunity tax credit (AOTC) or lifetime learning credit (LLC) under Code Sec. 25A as long as the same expenses are not used for both benefits. Similarly, the AOTC and lifetime learning credits may be taken for payments of qualified education expenses that are made in kind from a qualified state tuition program. Under coordination rules, qualified expenses are reduced by scholarships, fellowship grants, and education credits (including AOTC and LLC), after which the distributions from the qualified tuition program are applied. If the beneficiary receives distributions from a Coverdell ESA and a qualified tuition program that exceed the reduced expenses, the expenses must be allocated between the distributions (Code Sec. 529(c)(3)(B)). For purposes of this allocation, disregard any qualified elementary and secondary education expenses.

Coordination with education savings bonds. Taxpayers are entitled to redeem U.S. savings bonds and exclude the earnings under Code Sec. 135 (as if the proceeds were used to pay higher education expenses) if the redemption proceeds are contributed to a qualified tuition program on behalf of the taxpayer, the taxpayer's spouse or a dependent. In that case, the beneficiary's basis in the bond proceeds contributed on their behalf to the qualified state tuition program will be the contributor's basis in the bonds (i.e., the original purchase price). The amount of the exclusion is phased out in 2015 for taxpayers with MAGI's of $77,200 for single filers or heads of household and $115,750 for married filing jointly or qualifying widower and is fully phased out at $92,200 (for single filers and heads of household) and $145,750 (married filing jointly and qualifying widow(er) filers). The exclusion is not available to married taxpayers filing separately.

STUDY QUESTION

1. The savings programs for higher education costs are coordinated in that:

    a. Taxpayers may not claim an education tax credit for tuition expenses if payments of room and board or course materials are made from a qualified tuition plan

    b. Taxpayers may not redeem education savings bonds and contribute the proceeds to a qualified tuition program

    c. Qualified higher education expenses are reduced by education credits; then distributions from the qualified tuition program are applied to the remainder

    d. Taxpayers may not claim education credits in the same tax year as education savings bonds are redeemed

---

Gift and estate tax considerations. A contribution to a qualified state tuition program is treated as a completed gift of a present interest from the contributor to the beneficiary at the time of the contribution. Annual contributions are eligible for the gift tax exclusion under Code Sec. 2503(b) and are excludable for purposes of the generation-skipping transfer (GST) tax, provided that the annual gift tax exclusion limit ($14,000 for a single individual and $28,000 for a married couple electing gift splitting in 2013, 2014, or 2015) is not exceeded. Contributions are not eligible for the unlimited exclusion for direct payments of tuition under Code Sec. 2503(c). A contributor making a contribution in excess of the exclusion limit may elect to have the contribution treated as if made ratably over five years. A Form 709, *United States Gift (and Generation-Skipping Transfer) Tax Return,* must be filed with respect to any contribution in excess of the annual gift tax exclusion limit.

    EXAMPLE: In 2015 married parents Max and Lara Ernst contributed $140,000 to a QTP, the designated beneficiary of which is their daughter, Carolina. At Max and Lara's election, the program treats the $140,000 as being paid in ratably over a five-year period at $28,000 per year, as allowed for married donors. Max and Lara must elect the five-year averaging on their Form 709 return.

    If a contributor making a contribution in excess of the gift tax exclusion limit dies during the five-year period, the portion of the contribution that has not been allocated is included in the contributor's gross estate.

    If a beneficiary's interest is rolled over to another beneficiary or there is a change in beneficiary, no gift or GST tax consequences result, provided that the two beneficiaries are of the same generation and members of the same family (the latter clarification was added by Code Sec. 529(c)(5)(B). If a beneficiary's interest is rolled over to a beneficiary in a lower generation (for example, parent to child or aunt to niece), or someone outside the family, the five-year averaging rule may be applied to exempt from generation-skipping transfer tax up to $70,000 for 2013–2015 ($65,000 for 2009–2012) of the transfer.

    The IRS has issued a warning in the form of an advanced notice of proposed rulemaking (Announcement 2008-17 Advance NPRM REG -127127-05) that it is looking at potential abuses or inconsistencies between the rules of Code Sec. 529 and the generally applicable income and transfer tax provisions of the tax code.

¶304

The IRS has indicated that, when issued, proposed rules will cover:

- The liability of an account owner for gift and/or generation-skipping transfer tax imposed on a change of designated beneficiary;

- The liability of an account owner for income taxes imposed where the account owner withdraws funds from a Code Sec. 529 account for the account owner's own benefit or transfers control of the account to a new owner or names himself or a spouse as the designated beneficiary;

- The application of transfer taxes in cases where permissible contributors to a Code Sec. 529 account include persons other than individuals;

- The implications for individuals who contribute to a Code Sec. 529 account for their own benefit;

- Uniform Gifts to Minors Act and Uniform Transfers to Minors Act accounts that contribute to Code Sec. 529 accounts for minor beneficiaries; and

- Circumstances in which a deceased designated beneficiary's account will be distributed and includible in the designated beneficiary's gross estate.

STUDY QUESTION

2. Under Code Sec. 529 rules, the contributor and designated beneficiary of a qualified state tuition program:

   a. Will pay no penalty if they withdraw remaining amounts from an account once the student's education is complete

   b. Cannot direct the investment of the program's contributions and earnings but can select an investment strategy for the account

   c. May not withdraw payments for qualified education expenses if they also make direct payments of some expenses to the educational institution

   d. Cannot claim educational tax credits if any withdrawals are made from qualified state tuition programs during the same tax year

¶ 305 COVERDELL EDUCATIONAL SAVINGS ACCOUNTS

Contributions

The total contributions on behalf of any one beneficiary to Coverdell education savings accounts for the tax year are limited in the aggregate to $2,000. Contributions are nondeductible. (Code Sec. 530). The general contribution limits do not apply to contributions made from a military death gratuity (discussed later).

Contributions to one or more Coverdell ESAs for a beneficiary may not be made after the beneficiary's 18th birthday. However, under EGTRRA, the IRS is authorized to issue regulations allowing contributions to be made beyond that date to Coverdell ESAs with a special needs beneficiary (an individual with a physical, mental, or emotional condition requiring additional time to complete his or her education). The regulations may further disregard the 30-year limit (discussed below) on such accounts for determining when remaining Coverdell ESA balances must be distributed, whether rollover contributions may be made, or whether the designated beneficiary may be changed.

Earnings on contributions are distributed tax free to the extent that they are used to pay the beneficiary's postsecondary education expenses for which the American opportunity tax credit (AOTC) or lifetime learning credit is not claimed. EGTRRA extended this exclusion for distributions used to pay the beneficiary's elementary and secondary education expenses, whether incurred at private, public, or religious institutions. Amounts remaining in a Coverdell ESA may be rolled over into another Coverdell ESA for the education of another beneficiary in the beneficiary's family or distributed to the original beneficiary, who must include the earnings portion of the distribution in income and pay a 10 percent penalty on that portion.

Contributions may be made to a Coverdell educational savings account until the return due date (not including extensions) for the tax year of the contribution, i.e., a calendar year taxpayer would have until April 15, 2016, to make a contribution for the year 2015.

Phaseout of contribution amount. The amount that may be contributed to a Coverdell savings account is gradually phased out for single taxpayers with modified adjusted gross income between $95,000 and $110,000, and for married taxpayers filing jointly with modified AGI (MAGI) between $190,000 and $220,000. These phaseout ranges are not adjusted for inflation. MAGI is determined in the same manner as for the American opportunity tax credit and lifetime learning credit.

The $2,000 maximum annual contribution is reduced using the following formula:

$$\frac{\$2,000 \times \text{MAGI} - \$95,000 \ (\$190,000 \text{ if filing jointly})}{\$15,000 \ (\$30,000 \text{ if filing jointly})}$$

> **PLANNING POINTER:** Anyone may make a contribution to a Coverdell ESA for a child. Thus, if the parents' MAGI precludes their contributing the maximum $2,000 amount to each of their children's ESAs, one or more grandparents or other relatives with lower modified AGI could make up the deficit or contribute the entire amount of up to $2,000 per child.

Military death gratuities contributed to Coverdell ESAs. An individual who receives a military death gratuity or payment under the Service members' Group Life Insurance (SGLI) program may contribute such payments to a Coverdell ESA, notwithstanding the $2,000 annual contribution limit and the phase-out of the limit that would otherwise apply (Code Sec. 530(d)(9), as amended by the *Heroes Earnings Assistance and Relief Tax Act of 2008* (HEART Act)). The contribution of an amount received as a military death gratuity or SGLI payment will be considered to be a rollover contribution to the education savings account if the contribution is made before the end of a one-year period beginning on the date on which the amount is received, and the contribution does not exceed the sum of the gratuity and SGLI payments received, less the amount of such payments that were contributed to a Roth IRA or to another education savings account. The Code Sec. 530(d)(5) rule, which generally limits the number of tax-free rollovers to one per year, will not apply for purposes of rollovers under this provision (Code Sec. 530(d)(9)(B), as added by the HEART Act).

Distributions

A distribution from a Coverdell ESA is excludable from gross income to the extent that it does not exceed the qualified higher education, elementary, and secondary education expenses incurred by the beneficiary during the year in which the distribution is made. Distributions are tax exempt regardless of whether the beneficiary attends an eligible educational institution on a full-time, half-time, or less than half-time basis.

Distributions are treated in a manner similar to that under the Code Sec. 72 annuity rules and are deemed paid from both contributions (which are always tax free) and earnings (which may be excludable). The amount of contributions distributed is determined by multiplying the distribution by the ratio that the aggregate amount of contributions bears to the total balance of the IRA at the time the distribution is made.

EXAMPLE: Kelsey Bryant receives a $1,000 distribution from her Coverdell ESA. On the date the distribution is made, the account balance is $10,000, and contributions made to the account total $6,000. The amount of the distribution considered to come from contributions is $600 ($1,000 × ($6,000 ÷ $10,000 or .6)).

If aggregate distributions exceed qualified education expenses during the tax year, such expenses are deemed to be paid from a pro rata share of both principal and earnings. Thus, the portion of earnings excludable from income is based on the ratio that the qualified education expenses bear to the total amount of the distribution. The remaining portion of earnings is included in the income of the distributee.

EXAMPLE: Kelsey Bryant receives a $1,000 distribution from her education IRA. The distribution consists of $600 of contributions and $400 of earnings. Kelsey pays $750 in qualified education expenses for the year. The amount of earnings excludable from Kelsey's income is $300 ($400 × ($750 ÷ $1,000 or .75)). The remaining $100 is included in her income.

If a student receives distributions from an ESA and a qualified tuition program that exceed his or her education expenses (after reduction for the education credits), the student must allocate the expenses between the distributions (Code Sec. 530(d)(2)(C)(ii)).

Additional tax on taxable distributions. The tax on a distribution from a Coverdell savings account that is includible in gross income is increased by an additional 10 percent, unless the distribution:

- Is made to a beneficiary or the beneficiary's estate after the beneficiary's death;
- Is attributable to the designated beneficiary being disabled (as defined under Code Sec. 72(m)(7));
- Is made on account of a scholarship or allowance (as defined under Code Sec. 25A(g)(2)) received by the account holder to the extent the amount of the distribution does not exceed the amount of the scholarship or allowance; or
- Constitutes the return of excess contributions and earnings thereon (although earnings are includible in income) and a corrective distribution is made no later than May 30th of the year following the contribution (Code Sec. 530(d)(4)(C)(i)).

Rollovers. Amounts held in an ESA may be distributed and put into an ESA for a member of the original beneficiary's family who is younger than age 30 or a special needs person. Such distributions will not be included in the distributee's gross income if the rollover occurs within 60 days of the distribution. Similarly, any change in the beneficiary of a Coverdell ESA does not constitute a distribution if the new beneficiary is a member of the original beneficiary's family, as determined under Code Sec. 529(e)(2). Under this definition of *family,* amounts can be rolled over from education IRAs for the benefit of a beneficiary's children.

Amounts held in an education IRA may also be rolled over into another education IRA for the benefit of the same beneficiary (e.g., to change the investment vehicle).

Qualified higher education expenses. Qualified higher education expenses include tuition, fees, books, supplies, and equipment required for the enrollment of the beneficiary at an eligible educational institution. Room and board expenses (generally the school's posted room and board charge) are also treated as qualified higher education expenses if the beneficiary is enrolled at an eligible institution on at least a half-time basis. The room and board expense limitation is equal to the amount allowed under for calculation of a student's costs of attendance for federal financial aid purposes, which, for students living off-campus and not at home is equal to the amount of expenses reasonably incurred by the student for room and board.

Contributions to a qualified tuition program are qualified education expenses that may be made from a Coverdell ESA. However, when applying the Code Sec. 72 annuity rules to QTPs, contributions made with tax-free earnings from an ESA are not taken into account in determining the investment in the contract (Code Sec. 530(b)(2)(B)).

Qualified higher education expenses are reduced by the amount of any scholarships or other excludable financial aid received. However, any amount used to purchase tuition credits or any amount contributed to a qualified state tuition program for the beneficiary is considered a qualified higher education expense.

Elementary and secondary education expenses. Elementary and secondary education expenses are similar to qualified higher education expenses (tuition, books, room and board), but also include expenses for special needs services, academic tutoring, computer technology and equipment, uniforms, transportation, and extended day programs (Code Sec. 530(b)(3)(A)).

Credits and deductions precluded. Since 2002, beneficiaries no longer need to waive the tax-free treatment of ESA distributions in order to take advantage of the education tax credits for the same year (Code Sec. 530(d)(2)(C)). The beneficiary can claim the education credits and exclude Coverdell ESA distributions from gross income provided that the distribution is not used for the same education expenses as the credits.

No deduction or other credit is allowed for any qualified higher education expenses taken into account in determining the excludable amount of a Coverdell ESA distribution. For example, no Code Sec. 162 business expense deduction would be allowed for expenses taken into account for excluding a Coverdell ESA distribution from income.

> **PLANNING POINTER:** Although the $2,000 annual contribution limit may be considered nominal compared to that for qualified tuition plans, Coverdell ESAs give contributors the advantage of having control over investments within the account.

STUDY QUESTION

---

3. Coverdell education savings accounts are similar to qualified tuition plans in that:

   a. The maximum tax-free annual contribution amounts are the same

   b. They are both subject to a 10 percent penalty if withdrawals are not used for qualified education expenses

   c. The account balances must be used or rolled over to another beneficiary before the student reaches age 30

   d. Both types of incentive enable the taxpayer to direct the types of investments made

---

Gift and estate tax treatment. The *Taxpayer Relief Act of 1997* (TRA '97) extended to Coverdell ESAs the transfer tax treatment of contributions to qualified tuition programs. Thus, any contribution to an ESA is treated as a completed gift of a present interest from the contributor to the beneficiary at the time of the contribution. Annual contributions are eligible for the gift tax exclusion under Code Sec. 2503(b)(1) and are excludable for purposes of the generation-skipping transfer tax.

In addition, distributions from a Coverdell ESA are generally not treated as taxable gifts. Further, if a beneficiary's interest is rolled over to another beneficiary or there is a change in beneficiary, no gift or generation-skipping transfer tax consequences result, provided that two beneficiaries are of the same generation. If a beneficiary's interest is rolled over to a beneficiary in a lower generation (e.g., parent to child or aunt to niece), a five-year averaging rule may be applied to exempt from generation-skipping transfer tax up to $70,000 in 2013 through 2015 ($65,000 in 2009–2012 and $60,000 for transfers in 2006–2008) of the transferred amount.

> **EXAMPLE:** In 2013, when the annual exclusion was $14,000, Phyllis Davies rolled over $70,000 from her daughter's QTP to her granddaughter. Because this transfer would be treated as a taxable gift, she elects to account for the gift ratably over the five-year period beginning with 2013. She is treated as making an excludable gift of $14,000 in each of the years 2013 through 2017.

An interest in a Coverdell ESA is not includible in the estate of any individual except with respect to amounts distributed on account of the death of the designated beneficiary.

Termination of Coverdell educational savings accounts at age 30. As the *IRS Restructuring and Reform Act of 1998* made clear, any balance remaining in a Coverdell ESA must be distributed within 30 days after a beneficiary reaches age 30. The earnings portion of the distribution is includible in the beneficiary's gross income. Before the beneficiary's thirtieth birthday, however, the ESA balance may be transferred or rolled over to another Coverdell ESA for a member of the original beneficiary's family. EGTRRA authorized the IRS to issue regulations that may permit this 30-year age limit to be disregarded in the event the Coverdell ESA has a special needs beneficiary.

¶ 306 U.S. SAVINGS BOND INTEREST

An individual taxpayer who redeems qualified U.S. savings bonds and pays qualified higher educational expenses during the same tax year can exclude from income a limited part of the bond interest received. A qualified bond is a Series EE savings bond issued after December 31, 1989, or a Series I savings bond.

> **COMMENT:** Series I bonds, which were first offered in 1998, are inflation-indexed bonds issued at their face amount, with their face value plus accrued interest payable at maturity. Series EE bonds, were first offered in July 1980, and were issued at a discount until 2011, with their face value payable at maturity. Current Series EE bonds are issued at face value. Both types of bonds have a 30-year maturity period.

> **PLANNING POINTER:** Holders of Series EE bonds have the option of reporting interest as it accrues or deferring it. A taxpayer who plans to use the education-expense exclusion should defer the interest rather than report it as it accrues.

Eligible Taxpayers

For bond interest to be excludable, the taxpayer must have attained the age of 24 before the issue date of the bonds. Qualified bonds must also be issued in the name of the taxpayer as sole owner, or in the name of the taxpayer and the taxpayer's spouse as co-owners. Thus, bonds bought by a parent and issued in the name of a child under the age of 24 do not qualify for the exclusion. However, any individual, including a child, can be designated as the beneficiary of the bonds. Married taxpayers must file a joint return in order to exclude bond interest.

CAUTION: The date that a bond is issued may precede the date the bond is purchased, because bonds are issued as of the first day of the month in which they are purchased.

Qualified Expenses

Higher educational expenses for purposes of the educational bond program are tuition and fees required for enrollment or attendance of the taxpayer, the taxpayer's spouse, or the taxpayer's dependent at any eligible educational institution. Eligible educational institutions include most public and nonprofit colleges, universities, and vocational schools that are eligible for federal assistance. Qualified expenses do not include expenses relating to any course or other education involving sports, games, or hobbies, other than as part of a degree program.

Higher educational expenses also include contributions to QTPs and Coverdell ESAs.

PLANNING POINTER: This allows taxpayers to redeem savings bonds to make contributions to a QTP or ESA without incurring tax consequences. Tax-free QTP and ESA distributions can be used to pay some expenses that cannot be paid with tax-free bond interest (such as books, equipment, and room and board). However, a QTP or ESA contribution funded by excluded bond interest is not treated as a contribution for purposes of determining the taxable portion of a QTP or ESA distribution.

Coordination

The savings bond interest exclusion is coordinated with other education benefits allowed to the taxpayer with respect to the student. The amount of education expenses taken into account for the exclusion is first reduced by the amount of any nontaxable scholarships and grants, educational assistance to veterans, and nontaxable payments that are not gifts, bequests, devises, or inheritances. Qualified expenses are further reduced by the amount of expenses taken into account in determining the AOTC or LLC; the exclusion for distributions from Coverdell ESAs; and the exclusion for distributions from qualified tuition plans.

Excludable Amount

Calculating the exclusion. If the aggregate proceeds of bonds redeemed during the tax year exceed the qualified higher education expense paid by the taxpayer during that tax year, the amount excludable from taxation is limited to a fraction of the proceeds. The amount excludable is determined by multiplying the amount otherwise excludable by a fraction, the numerator of which is the amount of the expenses paid and the denominator of which is the aggregate proceeds of bonds redeemed.

EXAMPLE: Davontae Jackson redeems savings bonds in the amount of $1,500, which includes $750 in interest income. He uses two-thirds of the proceeds, or $1,000, to pay qualified educational expenses during the same tax year. The amount he can exclude is $500 ($750 × ($1,000 ÷ $1,500)).

EXAMPLE: Dion and Kimani Washington, a married couple, have MAGI of $80,000. They cash a qualified Series EE U.S. savings bond for $9,000, which includes $3,000 in interest. They pay $7,650 of their dependent daughter Kheisha's college tuition. They do not claim an AOTC or LLC for that amount, and Kheisha does not receive any tax-free educational assistance. They calculate the excludable portion of their bond interest by multiplying the total interest ($3,000) by the ratio of their total education expenses to their total bond proceeds ($7,650 ÷ $9,000). Thus, Dion and Kimani can exclude $2,550 in bond interest.

¶306

Phaseout. The amount that can be excluded is further limited for taxpayers with AGI above certain levels, which are adjusted each year. For 2015, the phaseout range for single filers will be from $77,200 to $92,200 (up from $76,000 to $91,000 for 2014). For joint filers the 2015 phaseout range will be $115,750 to $145,750 (up from $113,950 to $143,950 for 2014).

MAGI is determined after taking into account:

- The Code Sec. 86 inclusion in income of Social Security benefits;
- The Code Sec. 219 deduction for IRA contributions; and
- The Code Sec. 469 limitation on passive activity losses and credits.

MAGI does not take into account:

- The Code Sec. 137 exclusion for employer-provided adoption assistance;
- The Code Sec. 199 deduction for domestic production activities;
- The Code Sec. 221 deduction for qualified student loan interest;
- The Code Sec. 222 exclusion for QTP distributions;
- The Code Sec. 911 exclusion for foreign earned income and housing costs;
- The Code Sec. 931 exclusion for possession source income by residents of U.S. possessions; and
- The Code Sec. 933 exclusion for Puerto Rican source income excluded by residents of Puerto Rico.

Reporting

Form 8815, *Exclusion of Interest from Series EE and I U.S. Savings Bonds Issued After 1989 (For Filers with Qualified Higher Education Expenses)*, is used to compute the amount of the exclusion. Taxpayers can use Form 8818, *Optional Form to Record Redemption of Series EE and I U.S. Savings Bonds Issued After 1989,* to maintain records that are necessary to substantiate the interest exclusion.

¶ 307 DEDUCTIONS FOR QUALIFIED TUITION AND RELATED EXPENSES

> **COMMENT:** The above-the-line deduction for qualified tuition and fees expired at the end of 2014. The following is provided in case Congress acts to extend the deduction for 2015.

An above-the-line deduction for qualified tuition and related expenses was provided to give taxpayers a greater choice of available education tax benefits (Code Sec. 222). This deduction is allowed for qualifying individuals in tax years beginning after December 31, 2001. As originally enacted by EGTRRA, the provision has been extended through tax year 2014, most recently by the *Tax Increase Prevention Act of 2014* (P.L. 113-295).

The term *qualified tuition and related expenses* is defined in Code Sec. 25A(f) to include tuition and fees required for the enrollment or attendance of the taxpayer, the taxpayer's spouse, or a dependent of the taxpayer, at an eligible institution of higher education for courses of instruction. Expenses connected to meals, lodging, insurance, transportation, and similar living expenses are not eligible for the deduction. The expenses must be incurred in connection with enrollment during the tax year, or within an academic term beginning during the tax year or during the first three months of the next tax year (Code Sec. 222(d)).

The amount of the deduction allowed depends on the taxpayer's AGI and the tax year in which the deduction is claimed. Taxpayers whose AGI (as determined with certain exclusions and additions) does not exceed $65,000 ($130,000 for joint filers) may deduct a maximum of $4,000 for tax years beginning in 2004 through 2014. The tuition and fees deduction expired at the end of 2014 and as of this writing has not been extended. Additionally, for tax years beginning in 2004 through 2014, taxpayers with AGI of more than $65,000 ($130,000 for joint filers), but not in excess of $80,000 ($160,000 for joint filers) may deduct a maximum of $2,000 (Code Sec. 222(b)(2)(B)). These amounts are not adjusted for inflation, and married individuals filing separately may not claim the deduction (Code Sec. 222(d)(4)). No deduction is allowed to any individual with respect to whom a personal exemption deduction may be claimed by another taxpayer for the tax year (Code Sec. 222(c)(3)).

> **PLANNING POINTER:** The taxpayer must include the name and taxpayer identification number (TIN) for the student for whom the expenses were paid on the taxpayer's return in order to claim the deduction. As an above-the-line deduction, it can be taken by taxpayers regardless of whether they itemize deductions.

STUDY QUESTION

---

4. Educational U.S. savings bond interest is excludable from income if:

    a. The bond is issued in the name of the student

    b. The name used for the bond is for a taxpayer younger than age 26

    c. The modified adjusted gross income of the named taxpayer does not exceed $92,200 for single taxpayers and $145,750 for joint filers

    d. The bond was issued before December 31, 1989

¶ 308 AMERICAN OPPORTUNITY TAX CREDIT AND LIFETIME LEARNING CREDIT

HOPE Tax Credit Replaced with American Opportunity Tax Credit

For tax years 2009–2017, the HOPE educational tax credit was modified and entitled the American opportunity tax credit (AOTC) (Code Sec. 25A(i), as added by the *American Recovery and Reinvestment Act of 2009* (ARRA) (P.L. 111-5) and extended by the *American Taxpayer Relief Act of 2012* (P.L. 112-240)). The AOTC applies to the sum of 100 percent of the first $2,000 of qualified tuition and related expenses and 25 percent of the next $2,000, for a total maximum credit of $2,500 per eligible student per year in 2009–2017. In addition, the credit applies to the first four years of a student's postsecondary education for 2009–2017.

The AOTC qualification requirements such as the half-time enrollment requirement, has not completed the first 4 years of college requirement, must be pursuing a program leading to a degree and meets the definitions of an eligible student and an eligible educational institution all must be met. For 2009–2017, the AOTC can be claimed for tuition, fees, and course materials, including the cost of books. The cost of course materials can be claimed with respect to the LLC but must be paid to the educational institution.

Forty percent of the taxpayer's otherwise allowable AOTC is refundable in 2009–2017. However, if the taxpayer claiming the credit is a child who has unearned income subject to the "kiddie tax" under Code Sec. 1(g), none of the credit is refundable. The nonrefundable portion of the credit may be used to offset both regular tax and alternative minimum tax liability (Code Sec. 26(a), as amended by the 2012 Taxpayer Relief Act).

> **EXAMPLE:** In 2015, Sue and Tim McComb have two children and taxable income of $13,100. Their regular tax liability is $1,310 and they have AMT of $100. They paid $5,000 in college tuition for their son, Jim, in 2015. Jim has no unearned income in 2015. Their allowable credit is $2,500 ($2,000 × 1 + $2,000 × .25). Forty percent of $2,500 (.40 × $2,500 = $1,000) is refundable and the remaining $1,500 is nonrefundable, but limited to the total of their regular tax and AMT liabilities, or $1,410. Under prior law (the HOPE scholarship credit), they would have only been entitled to a $1,410 nonrefundable credit, but due to the addition of a refundable portion of the AOTC, they can now claim a credit of $2,410 ($1,410 + $1,000).

Lifetime Learning Credit Availability

The LLC consists of a nonrefundable credit for 20 percent of the first $10,000 of qualified tuition expenses paid by the taxpayer in any year the AOTC credit is not claimed for the same student (i.e., one could claim the AOTC credit with respect to one student and the LLC with respect to another student in the same year) (Code Sec. 25A(c)). The credit is available for expenses paid after June 30, 1998, for academic periods beginning after that date. It is available for the first $5,000 of tuition paid in tax years beginning before 2003 and for the first $10,000 of tuition paid thereafter. These limitations are not adjusted for inflation.

In addition to being available for a taxpayer's dependent, both credits are available for qualified expenses incurred by the taxpayer or the taxpayer's spouse. However, a credit may be claimed by only one person (for example, either a parent or a child may claim a credit for the child's expenses for a particular year). In addition, a credit cannot be claimed for expenses for which another tax benefit is received.

Academic Period

Neither Code Sec. 25A nor its legislative history defines the term *academic period*. Under Reg. § 1.25A-2(c), the term means a quarter, semester, trimester, or other period of study (such as a summer school session). The regulations also provide that if an educational institution uses credit or clock hours, each payment period, as defined in 34 CFR 668.4 as revised July 1, 2002, is treated as an academic period.

Election of the Credits

The final regulations provide that a taxpayer must elect to claim the education credit (Reg. § 1.25A-1(d)). The election must be made by attaching Form 8863, *Education Credits (American Opportunity and Lifetime Learning Credits)*, to the taxpayer's federal income tax return for the tax year in which the credit is claimed. Consistent with the identification requirements in Code Sec. 25A(g)(1), the regulations provide that a taxpayer must include on the federal income tax return the name and TIN of each student for whom the credit is claimed (Reg. § 1.25A-1(e)).

Phaseout of Credits

In general, eligibility for the AOTC and LLC is tied to the taxpayer's MAGI level.

Lifetime learning credit phaseout. The LLC begins to phase out for single taxpayers with MAGI in excess of $55,000 in 2015, and for married taxpayers filing jointly with MAGI in excess of $110,000 in 2015. The credit is completely phased out for single taxpayers with a MAGI of $65,000 in 2015 and for married taxpayers filing jointly with MAGI of $130,000 in 2015 (Rev. Proc. 2014-61, IRB 2014-47, 860).

¶308

In 2014, the phaseout range was $54,000–$64,000 (single filers) and $108,000–$128,000 (married joint filers) (Rev. Proc. 2013-35, IRB 2013-47, 537).

Married taxpayers must file joint returns in order to be eligible for either the AOTC or the lifetime learning credit.

AOTC phaseout. The credit begins to phase out for single taxpayers with modified AGI of $80,000 ($160,000 for joint filers) and completely phases out for taxpayers with modified AGI of $90,000 ($180,000 for joint filers) (Code Sec. 25A(i)(4)).These phaseout ranges are not indexed for inflation.

For purposes of the credits, MAGI is AGI increased by income earned outside the United States, including income earned in Puerto Rico and U.S. possessions that is otherwise excluded from income under Code Sec. 911, 931, or 933.

STUDY QUESTION

5. The lifetime learning credit applies:

  a. To 20 percent of qualified tuition expenses paid during a year the AOTC is not claimed

  b. To tuition as well as the cost of course materials not required by and paid to the educational institution for purposes of enrollment

  c. To taxpayers of any income level

  d. To married taxpayers who file jointly or file separate returns

Determining the Lifetime Learning Credit Amount

To determine the amount of the LLC that may be claimed for a tax year, the maximum amount allowable is reduced by an amount that bears the same ratio to the maximum amount allowable as the excess of the taxpayer's modified AGI over $55,000 in 2015 (or $110,000 in 2015 for a joint return) bears to $10,000 (or $20,000 for a joint return). Thus, for a single taxpayer, the reduction would be determined by the following formula:

$$(\text{MAGI} - \$55{,}000) \div \$10{,}000 = \text{Reduction amount of the LLC}$$

Maximum LLC (qualified paid education expenses up to a maximum of $10,000 × 20%)
–Reduction figured above = LLC allowed

EXAMPLE: Louise Johnson, a single mother, has MAGI of $57,000. In 2015, her daughter, Sonia, begins studying for her bachelor's degree as a part-time student at State University. On August 1, 2015, Louise pays $10,000 in qualified tuition for Sonia's first semester. Without the income limitations, Louise would be entitled to the maximum lifetime learning credit of $2,000 ($10,000 × .20). However, taking into account the income limitations, the allowable lifetime learning credit is reduced to $1,600: [($57,000 – $55,000) ÷ $10,000] × $2,000 = $400; $2,000 – $400 = $1,600.

Determining American Opportunity Tax Credit Amount

For tax years before 2017, the AOTC is ratably reduced by the amount bearing the same ratio to the credit as the excess of the taxpayer's MAGI over $80,000 bears to $10,000. These amounts double to $160,000 and $20,000 for joint filers.

EXAMPLE: Richard Watson was a full-time student in 2015 at a university with tuition and related expenses of $10,000. Richard's unmarried father, Andy, paid for Richard's tuition at the college and wishes to claim an AOTC on behalf of

Richard. Andy's AGI for 2015 was $85,000. Andy's AOTC would be calculated as follows:

(MAGI ($85,000) – $80,000 (beginning of phase out for single filers) ÷ $10,000) × the maximum AOTC that Andy could claim (100% of first $2,000 of eligible expenses plus 25% of the next $2,000 of eligible expenses).

The $2,500 AOTC claimed by Andy is reduced by half, so Andy can only claim a credit of $1,250 ($25,000 – (.5 × $2,500) = $1,250).

Timing Tuition Payments

The AOTC and LLC are available only for qualified tuition and related expenses paid during the tax year for education furnished to the student during an academic period beginning during that tax year. If tuition is paid during one tax year for an academic period that begins during the first three months of the following tax year, that academic period is treated as beginning during the year of payment.

PLANNING POINTER: The combination of the prepayment rule with the four-year limit (through 2017) on the AOTC may provide planning opportunities. Under the four-year (or two-year) cap, the credit is allowed for a tax year if the student has not completed, before the beginning of the tax year, the first four years (the first two years after 2017 if the AOTC is not extended and the tax credit reverts to the HOPE credit) of postsecondary education at an eligible educational institution. For a full-time student who enters college in the fall, that means that the credit is available for five of the first five calendar years (if the AOTC is extended before 2018) the student attends college. In order to use the maximum credit in the earliest tax years possible, a student who enters college in the fall and does not incur sufficient first-semester tuition expenses to use the full credit for that year should be sure to pay second-semester tuition before January 1 of the following year. By paying for two semesters of instruction in the first year, these students can maximize their credit in the first calendar year they attend college.

Dependents

If the student is not the taxpayer or the taxpayer's spouse, the student must be a dependent of the taxpayer under Code Sec. 151 for the tax year for which the AOTC or lifetime learning credit is claimed. If the student is claimed as a dependent by another taxpayer, the student is not allowed to claim either the AOTC or the LLC credit for that year on the student's own return, and any qualified tuition and related expenses paid by the student are treated as paid by the other taxpayer.

PLANNING POINTER: If the parents' MAGI exceeds the credit phaseout levels, it may be more advantageous for the parents not to claim the student as a dependent and forego the dependency exemption for the student (which is phased out for high-income taxpayers) in order for the child to claim the credit.

Doubling of Benefits Not Permitted

Any education assistance paid for the student's benefit reduces the amount of qualified tuition expense. However, creditable tuition expenses are not reduced for expenses paid by gift or inheritance (income excludable under Code Sec. 102). In addition, the AOTC and lifetime learning credit are not available for the following items that are considered to reduce the amount of qualified tuition:

- Employer-paid education expenses that can be excluded from an employee's income under Code Sec. 127;
- Scholarships and fellowships received tax-free under Code Sec. 117;

- Amounts deducted by the student as business expenses under Code Sec. 162;
- Educational assistance excludable from the gross income of either the student or the taxpayer claiming the credit; or
- Payments for an individual's educational expenses or attributable to the individual's enrollment at an institution that are excludable from gross income under any U.S. law.

In addition, for any tax year, a taxpayer is permitted to elect only one of the following with respect to one student:

- The HOPE/AOTC; or
- The LLC.

The American opportunity or lifetime learning credit can be claimed in the same year the beneficiary takes a tax-free distribution from a Coverdell ESA, as long as the same expenses are not used for both benefits. This means the beneficiary must reduce the qualified higher education expenses by the tax-free educational assistance, then further reduce them by any expenses taken into account in determining the AOTC of the LLC.

Third-Party Payments

If someone other than the taxpayer, the taxpayer's spouse, or a claimed dependent makes a payment directly to an eligible educational institution to pay for a student's qualified tuition and related expenses, the student would be treated as receiving the payment from the third party, and, in turn, paying the qualified tuition and related expenses to the institution (Reg. § 1.25A-5(b)). The following example illustrates this rule. For purposes of the example, assume that all the requirements to claim an education credit have been met.

> **EXAMPLE:** Sally Hager's grandmother makes a direct payment to an eligible educational institution for Sally's qualified tuition and related expenses. Sally is not a claimed dependent in 2015. For purposes of claiming an education credit, Sally is treated as receiving the money from her grandmother and, in turn, paying her qualified tuition and related expenses.

Comparison of the Two Credits

Although the AOTC and lifetime learning credits are subject to similar limitations, the credits differ on the following points:

- The AOTC is available on a per-student basis. Thus, the maximum AOTC a taxpayer may claim for a year is $2,500 in years through 2017 multiplied by the number of eligible students in the family. The lifetime learning credit is available on a per-taxpayer basis and does not vary with the number of students in the taxpayer's family.
- The AOTC may be elected for four tax years with respect to one student, whereas the lifetime learning credit is available for an unlimited number of years.
- The AOTC is available only for the first four years of postsecondary education, whereas the lifetime learning credit is available for both undergraduate and graduate or professional degree expenses.
- The AOTC is available only for students who are enrolled in a program leading to a degree, certificate, or other recognized education credential at an eligible institution, and who take at least one-half of a full-time course load for at least

¶308

one academic period. The lifetime learning credit is available for any course at an eligible institution that helps an individual acquire or improve job skills.

- The AOTC may be claimed with respect to course materials, including the cost of books. The cost of course materials may not be claimed under the lifetime learning credit unless required by and paid to the educational institution.

For further clarification of the rules applicable to the AOTC and the lifetime learning credit, see Reg. § 1.25A-3 and Reg. § 1.25A-4, respectively.

Required Information Returns by Institutions

Eligible education institutions that receive qualified tuition and related expenses and scholarship programs that reimburse or refund such expenses must file Form 1098-T, *Tuition Statement,* that reports the payments, reimbursements, or refunds made with respect to a student during a calendar year. In addition, students and persons claiming them as dependents must receive payment statements. The information reporting requirements are outlined in Code Sec. 6050S.

The *Trade Preferences Extension Act of 2015* (P.L. 114-27, June 29, 2015) waives certain penalties for educational institutions that fail to file information returns with accurate taxpayer identification numbers (TINs) of students. The educational institution must certify that it properly requested a TIN but was unable to collect it from the student. The provision is effective for returns required to be made, and statements required to be furnished, after December 31, 2015.

If a person is not an eligible educational institution, such a person must file information returns only if the person is in the business of reimbursing or refunding qualified tuition expenses to individuals under an insurance arrangement. Educational institutions that receive payments for qualified tuition and related expenses on behalf of individuals must report the aggregate amount of grant money received by those individuals.

Reporting Requirements for Individuals

Information in relation to the AOTC and lifetime learning credits that must be reported is limited to the student's name, address, tax identification number, and the aggregate amounts billed or received for qualified tuition and related expenses, grants received by the student, reimbursements paid to the student, and interest received. Taxpayers claiming either the AOTC or the LLC must fill out and attach to their Form 1040 return Form 8863, *Education Credits.* In addition the taxpayer must complete a separate Part III on Form 8863 for each student claiming a credit. The IRS has issued final regulations under Code Sec. 6050S relating to these reporting requirements, as well as provide guidance to eligible educational institutions and insurers that make reimbursements or refunds of qualified tuition and related expenses.

The *Trade Preferences Extension Act of 2015*, for tax year beginning after June 29, 2015, now requires individuals to receive payee statements to be entitled to claim education credits or the tuition and fees deduction on a return. Individuals must show that they possess a valid information return (Form 1098-T, *Tuition Statement*) from the educational institution.

STUDY QUESTION

6. The American opportunity tax credit (AOTC):

   a. Provides a maximum credit of $2,500 per year for qualified tuition and related expenses

   b. Does not apply to the cost of course materials and textbooks

   c. Is automatically available to the taxpayer if the educational institution provides a tuition statement for the year

   d. Is 20 percent refundable for 2015–2017

¶ 309 GIFT TAX EXCLUSION FOR DIRECT PAYMENT OF EDUCATION EXPENSES

Direct payments of tuition to a qualifying educational institution may be made gift-tax free in unlimited amounts without regard to the relationship between the donor and the donee (Code Sec. 2503(e)).

Trusts can also be used to accumulate and manage funds for education, but a discussion of the various Trusts is beyond the scope of this course.

Limitations

For federal gift tax purposes, payments made directly to an educational institution for a student's tuition are not subject to any dollar limit (Code Sec. 2503(e)(2)(A)). The exclusion is limited to the payment of tuition. It does not apply to room and board or other education costs. To qualify for this special treatment, the donor must pay the educational institution directly. This exclusion applies to any tuition. Thus, it applies to primary and secondary school costs. Thus, taxpayers can make these payments in addition to gifts covered by the annual gift tax exclusion ($14,000 in 2015 for single taxpayers, $28,000 for joint filers who "split" gifts).

In Letter Ruling 200602002, the IRS concluded that a grandparent who made nonrefundable prepaid tuition arrangements directly to a school for six grandchildren for their education through grade 12 qualified as exempt for the gift tax under Code Sec. 2503(e) and for the generation-skipping transfer tax under Code Sec. 2611(b)(1).

This provides an opportunity for a wealthy individual to exclude a substantial sum from gift and estate tax. Additionally, the donee need not be related to the donor to use the exclusion.

¶ 310 SCHOLARSHIPS, FELLOWSHIP GRANTS, GRANTS, AND TUITION REDUCTIONS

A *scholarship* is generally an amount paid or allowed to, or for the benefit of, a student (whether an undergraduate or a graduate) at an educational institution to aid in the pursuit of his or her studies. A *fellowship grant* is generally an amount paid for the benefit of an individual to aid in the pursuit of study or research.

Amount of Scholarship or Fellowship Grant

The amount of a scholarship or fellowship grant includes the following:

   • The value of contributed services and accommodations. This includes such services and accommodations as room (lodging), board (meals), laundry service, and similar services or accommodations that are received by an individual as a part of a scholarship or fellowship grant;

   • The amount of tuition, matriculation, and other fees that are paid or remitted to the student to aid the student in pursuing study or research; and

   • Any amount received in the nature of a family allowance as a part of a scholarship or fellowship grant.

Taxation Requirements for Scholarships and Fellowship Grants

A scholarship or fellowship grant is tax free (excludable from gross income) only if the student is a candidate for a degree at an eligible educational institution. A taxpayer may be able to increase the combined value of an education credit and certain educational assistance if the student includes some or all of the educational assistance in income in the year it is received.

A scholarship or fellowship grant is tax free only to the extent:

- It does not exceed expenses;
- It is not designated or earmarked for other purposes (such as room and board) and does not require (by its terms) that it cannot be used for qualified education expenses; and
- It does not represent payment for teaching, research, or other services required as a condition for receiving the scholarship.

Exceptions for payments are described later.

Candidate for a degree. A student is a candidate for a degree if he or she:

- Attends a primary or secondary school or are pursuing a degree at a college or university; or
- Attends an educational institution that

  - Provides a program that is acceptable for full credit toward a bachelor's or higher degree, or offers a program of training to prepare students for gainful employment in a recognized occupation, and

  - Is authorized under federal or state law to provide such a program and is accredited by a nationally recognized accreditation agency.

Eligible educational institution. An eligible educational institution is one whose primary function is the presentation of formal instruction and that normally maintains a regular faculty and curriculum and normally has a regularly enrolled body of students in attendance at the place where it carries on its educational activities.

Qualified education expenses. For purposes of tax-free scholarships and fellowship grants, these are expenses for:

- Tuition and fees required to enroll at or attend an eligible educational institution; and
- Course-related expenses, such as fees, books, supplies, and equipment that are required for the courses at the eligible educational institution.

These items must be required of all students in the course of instruction.

Expenses that do not qualify. Qualified education expenses do not include the cost of:

- Room and board;
- Travel;
- Research;
- Clerical help; or
- Equipment and other expenses that are not required for enrollment in or attendance at an eligible educational institution.

Payment for services. Generally, the taxpayer cannot exclude from gross income the part of any scholarship or fellowship grant that represents payment for teaching, research, or other services required as a condition for receiving the scholarship. This

¶310

applies even if all candidates for a degree must perform the services to receive the degree. (Exceptions are described next.)

Exceptions. The taxpayer does not have to treat as payment for services the part of any scholarship or fellowship grant that represents payment for teaching, research, or other services if he or she receives the amount under:

- The National Health Service Corps Scholarship Program; or
- The Armed Forces Health Professions Scholarship and Financial Assistance Program.

Athletic scholarships. An athletic scholarship is tax free only if and to the extent that it meets the requirements discussed later.

Taxable scholarships and fellowship grants. If and to the extent a scholarship or fellowship grant does not meet the requirements described earlier, it is taxable and must be included in gross income.

Reporting scholarships and fellowship grants. Whether the recipient must report a scholarship or fellowship grant depends on whether he or she must file a return and whether any part of the scholarship or fellowship grant is taxable.

If a student's only income is a completely tax-free scholarship or fellowship grant, he or she does not have to file a tax return and no reporting is necessary. If all or part of the scholarship or fellowship grant is taxable and the student is required to file a tax return, he or she must report the taxable amount as explained below. The student must report the taxable amount regardless of whether he or she received a Form W-2. If the Form W-2 is incorrect, the student should ask the payer for a corrected one.

Information on whether an individual must file a return is provided in Publication 501, *Exemptions, Standard Deduction, and Filing Information,* or the federal and state income tax form instructions.

¶ 311 OTHER TYPES OF EDUCATIONAL ASSISTANCE FOR STUDENTS

The student and family may receive one of the following other common types of educational assistance.

Fulbright Grants

A Fulbright grant is generally treated as a scholarship or fellowship grant in figuring how much of the grant is tax free. A recipient can only exclude the amount from income if the amounts are received for study and research abroad for the benefit of the recipient. If, however, the amount is paid to an individual for teaching and lecturing abroad, then the amount is compensation subject to taxation.

Pell Grants and Other Title IV Need-Based Education Grants

These need-based grants are treated as scholarships for purposes of determining their tax treatment. They are tax free to the extent used for qualified education expenses during the period for which a grant is awarded.

Payment to Service Academy Cadets

An appointment to a United States military academy is not a scholarship or fellowship grant. Payment received as a cadet or midshipman at an armed services academy is pay for personal services and will be reported to the recipient on Form W-2, box 1. This pay is included in income in the year of receipt unless one of the exceptions, discussed earlier regarding payment for services, applies.

Veterans' Benefits

Payments received for education, training, or subsistence under any law administered by the Department of Veterans Affairs (VA) are tax free. These payments are not included as income on a federal tax return.

If the recipient qualifies for one or more other education benefits, the veteran may have to reduce the amount of education expenses qualifying for a specific benefit by part or all of the VA payments. This applies only to the part of VA payments that is required to be used for education expenses.

The Veteran's Administration website at www.gibill.va.gov lists specific information about the various VA benefits for education.

Qualified Tuition Reduction

If an individual is allowed to study tuition free or for a reduced rate of tuition, he or she may not have to pay tax on this *tuition reduction* benefit. A tuition reduction is qualified only if the student receives it from, and uses it at, an eligible educational institution. The student does not have to use the tuition reduction at the eligible educational institution from which he or she received it. In other words, if a student works for an eligible educational institution and the institution arranges for him or her to take courses at another eligible educational institution without paying any tuition, the student may not have to include the value of the free courses in income.

The rules for determining whether a tuition reduction is qualified, and therefore tax free, are different if the education provided is for undergraduate or graduate education.

A student must include in income any tuition reduction received in payment for services, as described for scholarships and grants above.

Education Below the Graduate Level

If a student receives a tuition reduction for education below the graduate level (including primary or secondary), it is a qualified tuition reduction, and therefore tax free, only if the student is:

- An employee of the eligible educational institution;
- An employee of the eligible educational institution, but retired or left on disability;
- A widow or widower of an individual who died while an employee of the eligible educational institution or who retired or left on disability; or
- A dependent child or spouse of an individual described above.

For purposes of the qualified tuition reduction, a child is a dependent child if the child is under age 25 and both parents have died, or is a dependent child of divorced parents is treated as the dependent of both parents.

Graduate Education

A tuition reduction received for graduate education is qualified, and therefore tax free, if both of the following requirements are met:

- It is provided by an eligible educational institution; and
- The recipient is a graduate student who performs teaching or research activities for the educational institution.

The student must include in income any other tuition reductions for graduate education received.

STUDY QUESTION

7. Which of the following types of payments is *not* tax free?

    a. National Health Service Corps Scholarship Program

    b. Payments to service academy cadets

    c. Pell grant amounts applied to qualified education expenses during the academic period

    d. Veterans' benefits

¶ 312 PENALTY-FREE IRA WITHDRAWALS FOR QUALIFIED HIGHER EDUCATION

The 10 percent penalty tax on early withdrawals (taken before age 59½) from an individual retirement account (IRA) does not apply if the amounts withdrawn are used to pay qualified higher education expenses of the taxpayer, the taxpayer's spouse, or any child or grandchild of the taxpayer or the taxpayer's spouse (Code Sec. 72(t)(2)(E)). A child or grandchild need not be a dependent of the taxpayer in order for this exception to apply. Qualified higher education expenses include tuition, fees, books, and supplies. They also include room and board if the student is enrolled at least half-time (Code Sec. 72(t)(7) and Code Sec. 59(e)(3)).Such expenses are reduced by the amounts of any qualified scholarship, educational assistance allowance, or payment (other than a gift or inheritance) for an individual's enrollment that is excludable from income.

The taxpayer must include the distribution from a traditional deductible IRA in income and pay income tax on it. The taxpayer avoids only the 10 percent early distribution penalty that would otherwise apply. (Code Sec. 72(t)(2)(E)).

> **COMMENT:** The waiver of the 10 percent penalty also applies to Roth IRA distributions that meet the above requirements. However if the other requirements for qualified distributions from a Roth IRA are not met, the distribution may be subject to income tax on earnings.

> **PLANNING POINTER:** Grandparents, who are eligible to tap their IRAs to help their grandchildren pay for college, may want to pay the funds directly to the educational institution to avoid using either the annual gift tax exclusion limit ($14,000 per donor per recipient in 2015) or lifetime exclusion amount.

The law strictly limits the timing of withdrawals to pay qualified expenses. The withdrawal from the IRA and the payment of qualified expenses must occur within the same calendar year. In one case, a taxpayer's two distributions from her IRA in 2001 to pay down credit card debt incurred in 1999 and 2000 from paying qualified higher education expenses were not penalty free because the 2001 withdrawal related to 1999 and 2000 education payments (*Lodder-Beckert,* TC Memo 2005-162).

In another case, a 2002 IRA distribution was used to pay qualified expenses for 2003 and 2004 and, therefore, were not penalty free (*Ambata,* TC Summary Opinion 2005-93). Similarly, payment of 2002 educational expenses in 2001 did not qualify for a penalty-free IRA withdrawal in 2002 (*Duronio,* TC Memo 2007-90).

The usual 60-day IRA rollover rule cannot be waived merely because funds are used to cover higher education costs (Letter Ruling 200504037). In this case, a parent took an IRA distribution because of problems processing his Free Application for

Federal Student Aid (FAFSA) and the issues were not resolved within the 60-day rollover period.

STUDY QUESTION

8. When a taxpayer younger than age 59½ withdraws funds from a traditional IRA for qualified higher education expenses of eligible students:

    a. The taxpayer is subject to the 10 percent early withdrawal penalty on the amount distributed

    b. The taxpayer must pay income tax for the amount withdrawn

    c. The 60-day limit on rollovers does not apply if payments of qualified expenses are delayed

    d. The student whose expenses are paid must be a dependent of the taxpayer holding the account

¶ 313 STUDENT LOAN INTEREST DEDUCTION

Generally, personal interest paid, other than certain mortgage interest, is not deductible. However, there is a special deduction of up to $2,500 allowed for paying interest on a student loan (also known as an *education loan*) used for higher education For 2015, the $2,500 student loan interest deduction will phase out for joint filing married couples with MAGI between $130,000 and $160,000, and for single taxpayers, the phaseout range is from $65,000 to $80,000 the same as for 2014.

The student loan interest deduction is claimed as an adjustment to income. This means a taxpayer can claim this deduction even if he or she does not itemize deductions on Schedule A (Form 1040).

Student Loan Interest Defined

Student loan interest is interest paid during the year on a qualified student loan. It includes both required and voluntary interest payments.

Qualified student loan. This is a loan taken solely to pay qualified education expenses that were:

    • For the taxpayer, spouse, or dependent when the loan was initiated;

    • Paid or incurred within a reasonable period of time before or after the loan term; and

    • For education provided during an academic period for an eligible student.

Loans from the following sources are not qualified student loans:

    • A related person; or

    • A qualified employer plan.

Dependent defined. Generally, a dependent is someone who is either a:

    • Qualifying child; or

    • Qualifying relative.

Dependents are further described in IRS Publication 501, *Exemptions, Standard Deduction, and Filing Information.*

Exceptions. For purposes of the student loan interest deduction, the following exceptions apply to the general rules for dependents:

- An individual can be the taxpayer's dependent even if the taxpayer is the dependent of another taxpayer;
- An individual can be the taxpayer's dependent even if that individual files a joint return with a spouse; and
- An individual can be the taxpayer's dependent even if the individual had gross income for the year that was equal to or more than the exemption amount for the year ($4,000 for 2015).

Reasonable period of time. Qualified education expenses are treated as paid or incurred within a reasonable period of time before or after an individual takes out the loan if the expenses are paid with the proceeds of student loans that are part of a federal postsecondary education loan program.

Even if not paid with the proceeds of that type of loan, the expenses are treated as paid or incurred within a reasonable period of time if both of the following requirements are met:

- The expenses relate to a specific academic period; and
- The loan proceeds are disbursed within a period that begins 90 days before the start of that academic period and ends 90 days after the end of that academic period.

If neither of the above situations applies, the reasonable period of time usually is determined based on all the relevant facts and circumstances.

Academic period. An academic period includes a semester, trimester, quarter, or other period of study (such as a summer school session) as reasonably determined by an educational institution. In the case of an educational institution that uses credit hours or clock hours and does not have academic terms, each payment period can be treated as an academic period.

Eligible student. This requirement includes a student who was enrolled at least half-time in a program leading to a degree, certificate, or other recognized educational credential.

Enrolled at least half-time. A student was enrolled at least half-time if the student was taking at least half the normal full-time workload for his or her course of study.

The standard for what is half of the normal full-time workload is determined by each eligible educational institution. However, the standard may not be lower than any of those established by the U.S. Department of Education under the *Higher Education Act of 1965.*

Related person. An individual cannot deduct interest on a loan obtained from a related person. Related persons include the individual's:

- Spouse;
- Brothers and sisters;
- Half brothers and half sisters;
- Ancestors (parents, grandparents, etc.);
- Lineal descendants (children, grandchildren, etc.); and
- Certain corporations, partnerships, trusts, and exempt organizations.

Qualified Education Expenses

For purposes of the student loan interest deduction, the following amounts constitute the total costs of attending an eligible educational institution, including graduate school:

- Tuition and fees;
- Room and board;
- Books, supplies, and equipment; and
- Other necessary expenses (such as transportation).

The cost of room and board qualifies only to the extent that it is not more than the greater of:

- The allowance for room and board, as determined by the eligible educational institution, that was included in the cost of attendance (for federal financial aid purposes) for a particular academic period and living arrangement of the student; or
- The actual amount charged if the student is residing in housing owned or operated by the eligible educational institution.

Eligible educational institution. An eligible educational institution is any college, university, vocational school, or other postsecondary educational institution eligible to participate in a student aid program administered by the U.S. Department of Education. It includes virtually all accredited public, nonprofit, and proprietary (privately owned profit-making) postsecondary institutions.

Certain educational institutions located outside the United States also participate in the U.S. Department of Education's Federal Student Aid (FSA) programs.

For purposes of the student loan interest deduction, an eligible educational institution also includes an institution conducting an internship or residency program leading to a degree or certificate from an institution of higher education, a hospital, or a health care facility that offers postgraduate training. An educational institution must meet the above criteria only during the academic period(s) for which the student loan was incurred. The deductibility of interest on the loan is not affected by the institution's subsequent loss of eligibility.

Adjustments to qualified education expenses. Qualified education expenses must be reduced by the distributions from all qualified educational assistance payments from an employer or accounts such as a Coverdell ESA or prepaid tuition plan, U.S. savings bond interest excluded from income, tax-free part of scholarships and fellowship grants, veterans educational assistance, and other nontaxable payments (other than gifts and inheritances).

Items included as interest. In addition to simple interest on the loan, if all other requirements are met, a loan origination fee and capitalized interest can be considered interest.

Loan origination fee. In general, this is a one-time fee charged by the lender when a loan is made. To be deductible as interest, a loan origination fee must be for the use of money rather than for property or services (such as commitment fees or processing costs) provided by the lender. A loan origination fee treated as interest accrues over the term of the loan.

Loan origination fees were not required to be reported on Form 1098-E, *Student Loan Interest Statement,* for loans made before September 1, 2004. If loan origination fees are not included in the amount reported on Form 1098-E, a taxpayer can use any reasonable method to allocate the loan origination fees over the term of the loan. The method shown here allocates equal portions of the loan origination fee to each payment required under the terms of the loan. A method that results in the double deduction of the same portion of a loan origination fee would not be reasonable.

> **EXAMPLE:** In August 2004, Ken Bacchio took out a student loan for $16,000 to pay the tuition for his senior year of college. The lender charged a 3 percent loan

origination fee ($480) that was withheld from the funds Ken received. Ken began making payments on his student loan in 2014. Because the loan origination fee was not included in his 2014 Form 1098-E, Ken can use any reasonable method to allocate that fee over the term of the loan. Ken's loan is payable in 120 equal monthly payments. He allocates the $480 fee equally over the total number of payments ($480 ÷ 120 months = $4 per month). Ken made 7 payments in 2014, so he paid $28 ($4 × 7) of interest attributable to the loan origination fee. To determine his student loan interest deduction, he will add the $28 to the amount of other interest reported to him on Form 1098-E.

CAUTION: If an individual refinances a qualified student loan for more than the original loan principal and uses the additional amount for any purpose other than qualified education expenses, the individual cannot deduct any interest paid on the refinanced loan.

Voluntary interest payments. Voluntary payments are amounts made on a qualified student loan during a period when interest payments are not required, such as when the borrower has been granted a deferment or the loan has not yet entered repayment status.

EXAMPLE: The payments on Robert Malloy's student loan were scheduled to begin in June 2014, 6 months after he graduated from college. He began making payments as required. In September 2015, Robert enrolled in graduate school on a full-time basis. He applied for and was granted deferment of his loan payments while in graduate school. Wanting to pay down his student loan as much as possible, he made loan payments in October and November 2015. Even though these were voluntary (not required) payments, Robert can deduct the interest paid in October and November.

Capitalized interest. This is unpaid interest on a student loan that is added by the lender to the outstanding principal balance of the loan. Capitalized interest is treated as interest for tax purposes and is deductible as payments of principal are made on the loan. No deduction for capitalized interest is allowed in a year in which no loan payments were made.

Interest on revolving lines of credit. This interest, which includes interest on credit card debt, is student loan interest if the borrower uses the line of credit (credit card) only to pay qualified education expenses.

Interest on refinanced student loans. This includes interest on both:

- Consolidated loans—loans used to refinance more than one student loan of the same borrower, and
- Collapsed loans—two or more loans of the same borrower that are treated by both the lender and the borrower as one loan.

Allocating Payments Between Interest and Principal

The allocation of payments between interest and principal for tax purposes might not be the same as the allocation shown on the Form 1098-E or other statement from the lender or loan servicer. To make the allocation for tax purposes, a payment generally applies first to stated interest that remains unpaid as of the date the payment is due, second to any loan origination fees allocable to the payment, third to any capitalized interest that remains unpaid as of the date the payment is due, and fourth to the outstanding principal.

EXAMPLE: In August 2014 Madison McGregor took out a $10,000 student loan to pay the tuition for her senior year of college. The lender charged a 3 percent loan origination fee ($300) that was withheld from the funds Madison received. The 5 percent simple interest on this loan accrued while she completed her senior year and for 6 months after she graduated. At the end of that period, the lender determined the amount to be repaid by capitalizing all accrued but unpaid interest ($625 interest accrued from August 2014 through October 2015) and adding it to the outstanding principal balance of the loan. The loan is payable over 60 months, with a payment of $200.51 due on the first of each month, beginning November 2015.

Madison did not receive a Form 1098-E for 2015 from her lender because the amount of interest she paid did not require the lender to issue an information return. However, she did receive an account statement from the lender that showed the following 2015 payments on her outstanding loan of $10,625 ($10,000 principal + $625 accrued but unpaid interest).

Payment Date	Payment	Stated Interest	Principal
November 2015	$200.51	$44.27	$156.24
December 2015	$200.51	$43.62	$156.89
Totals	$401.02	$87.89	$313.13

To determine the amount of interest that could be deducted on the loan for 2015, Madison starts with the total amount of stated interest she paid, $87.89. Next, she allocates the loan origination fee over the term of the loan ($300 ÷ 60 months = $5 per month). A total of $10 ($5 of each of the two principal payments) should be treated as interest for tax purposes. Madison then applies the unpaid capitalized interest ($625) to the two principal payments in the order in which they were made, and determines that the remaining amount of principal of both payments is treated as interest for tax purposes. Assuming that Madison qualifies to claim the student loan interest deduction, she can deduct $401.02 ($87.89 + $10 + $303.13).For 2016, Madison will continue to allocate $5 of the loan origination fee to the principal portion of each monthly payment she makes and treat that amount as interest for tax purposes. She also will apply the remaining amount of capitalized interest ($625 – $303.13 = $321.87) to the principal payments in the order in which they are made until the balance is zero, and treat those amounts as interest for tax purposes.

Amounts not considered interest. An individual cannot claim a student loan interest deduction for any of the following items:

- Interest paid on a loan if, under the terms of the loan, the individual is not legally obligated to make interest payments;
- Loan origination fees that are payments for property or services provided by the lender, such as commitment fees or processing costs; and
- Interest paid on a loan to the extent payments were made through participation in the National Health Service Corps Loan Repayment Program or certain other loan repayment assistance programs.

Deductibility of interest. The individual can deduct all interest paid during the year on the student loan, including voluntary payments, until the loan is paid off.

Claiming a deduction for interest. Generally, an individual can claim the deduction if all of the following requirements are met:

- The individual's filing status may be any filing status except married filing separately;
- No one else is claiming an exemption for the individual on his or her tax return;
- The individual is legally obligated to pay interest on a qualified student loan; and
- The individual paid interest on a qualified student loan.

¶313

The student as a dependent. Another taxpayer is claiming an exemption for the student if that taxpayer lists the student's name and other required information on his or her Form 1040 (or Form 1040A), line 6c, or Form 1040NR, line 7c.

> **EXAMPLE:** During 2015, Josh Wosnyk paid $600 interest on his qualified student loan. Only he is legally obligated to make the payments. No one claimed an exemption for Josh for 2015. Assuming all other requirements are met, Josh can deduct the $600 of interest he paid on his 2015 Form 1040 or 1040A.

> **EXAMPLE:** During 2014, Jo McNamara paid $1,100 interest on her qualified student loan. Only she is legally obligated to make the payments. Jo's parents claimed an exemption for her on their 2014 tax return. In this case, neither Jo nor her parents may deduct the student loan interest Jo paid in 2014.

Interest paid by others. If an individual is the person legally obligated to make interest payments and someone else makes a payment of interest on the individual's behalf, he or she is treated as receiving the payments from the other person and, in turn, paying the interest.

> **EXAMPLE:** Darla Buchner obtained a qualified student loan to attend college. After Darla's graduation from college, she worked as an intern for a nonprofit organization. As part of the internship program, the nonprofit organization made an interest payment on Darla's behalf. This payment was treated as additional compensation and reported on her Form W-2, box 1. Assuming all other qualifications are met, Darla can deduct this payment of interest on her tax return.

> **EXAMPLE:** Ethan Masiak obtained a qualified student loan to attend college. After graduating from college, the first monthly payment on his loan was due in December. As a gift, Ethan's mother made this payment for him. No one is claiming a dependency exemption for Ethan on his or her tax return. Assuming all other qualifications are met, Ethan can deduct this payment of interest on his tax return.

No double benefit allowed. The taxpayer cannot deduct as interest on a student loan any amount that is an allowable deduction under any other provision of the tax law (for example, as home mortgage interest).

Form 1098-E. The student should receive Form 1098-E for the previous tax year. Generally, an institution (such as a bank or governmental agency) that received interest payments of $600 or more during 2015 on one or more qualified student loans must send Form 1098-E (or acceptable substitute) to each borrower by January 31, 2016.

Calculating the deduction. Generally, a taxpayer figures the deduction using the Student Loan Interest Deduction Worksheet in the instructions for Form 1040, Form 1040A, or Form 1040NR.

Claiming the deduction. The student loan interest deduction is an adjustment to income entered on line 33 (Form 1040), line 18 (Form 1040A), line 33 (Form 1040NR), or line 9 (Form 1040NR-EZ).

Exclusion for Certain Student Loan Forgiveness

With a great number of graduates facing onerous student debt repayment, some individuals opt to work in jobs that provide for some student loan forgiveness. Usually, the cancellation of student loan debt is taxable income. However, if a loan by a government agency, government-funded loan program of an educational organization, or a qualified hospital is canceled because the borrower works for a certain period in a certain geographical area, then the canceled amount is not taxable. This applies, for

¶313

example, to doctors who work in areas that otherwise lack adequate medical professionals or teachers who work in inner city schools. There is no dollar limit on the amount of student loan debt that can be forgiven on a tax-free basis.

There is also a special exclusion for health care professionals who work in underserved communities with respect to loans forgiven or repaid under:

- The National Health Services Corps Loan Repayment Program;
- State loan repayment programs eligible for funding under the Public Health Service Act; or
- Any state loan repayment or forgiveness program intended to increase the availability of health care services within its borders (the need is determined by the state).

STUDY QUESTION

9. An individual is *not* eligible to claim a student loan interest deduction if:
   a. The individual borrower is not claimed as a dependent on another taxpayer's income tax return
   b. The individual borrower files an income tax return independently from his or her parents
   c. The individual borrower is married and files a separate income tax return for the year
   d. The individual borrower is younger than age 26

MODULE 2: MAXIMIZING INDIVIDUAL BENEFITS—Chapter 4: Same-Sex Marriage

¶ 401 WELCOME

This chapter describes some of the federal tax advantages and disadvantages of married vs. single tax status for same-sex partners. There many additional tax issues, advantages, and disadvantages that are beyond the scope of this chapter, as well as other economic advantages and disadvantages outside of taxation that should be considered. Ultimately, however, the decision of whether or not to marry generally will be based primarily on noneconomic considerations.

¶ 402 LEARNING OBJECTIVES

Upon completion of this chapter, you will be able to:

- Recognize the differences in the tax treatment of married and unmarried couples;
- Identify couples' contribution deductions for traditional IRAs and maximum contributions for traditional and Roth IRAs;
- Recognize how same-sex marriage affects business relationships and transactions for spouses; and
- Identify rules for alimony and child support payments in divorces of same-sex couples.

¶ 403 INTRODUCTION

In its decision concerning *In the matter of Obergefell v. Hodges* (U.S. Supreme Court No. 14–556, decided June 26, 2015,), the U.S. Supreme Court extended the right of same-sex partners to marry to the 14 states that previously had not allowed or recognized same-sex marriages. The ruling effectively nullified Section 2 of the Defense of Marriage Act (DOMA), which allowed states not to recognize same-sex marriages legally performed in other states. Prior to the *Obergefell* decision, the Supreme Court in *E. S. Windsor* (S. Ct. 2013-2, USTC ¶ 50.400) struck down as unconstitutional Section 3 of DOMA, which statutorily defined marriage for purposes of federal law, including tax law, as a legal union between one man and one woman.

¶ 404 FILING STATUS OF SAME-SEX SPOUSES

A taxpayer's filing status generally depends on the taxpayer's marital status and family situation. If a taxpayer is married, his or her filing status is generally married filing jointly or married filing separately. If the taxpayer and his or her spouse lived apart the last six months of the year, head of household status may also be available. If a taxpayer is unmarried, his or her filing status will be single, head of household, or qualifying widow(er). Marital status for federal tax purposes is defined by state law. Same-sex couples who are legally married are treated as married for federal tax purposes.

> **CAUTION:** In states that recognize common-law marriage, a marriage may be recognized without a marriage license or ceremony if the partners "hold themselves out" as married. Common-law marriage is recognized for federal tax purposes if it is recognized by the state in which the taxpayers currently live or the state where the common-law marriage began.

Unmarried couples cannot file as married filing jointly or married filing separately, and cannot claim head of household status if the taxpayer's only dependent is his or her partner.

EXAMPLE: Brian Stuart and Steve Ebersol live together, but are not married, have no children, and do not share the home with any qualifying relatives. Brian and Steve must each file a return using the filing status of single.

If an unmarried same-sex couple has one child, one of the parents may be able to file as a head of household if that individual otherwise qualifies. If the couple has multiple children, it is possible for both parents to file as heads of households on their separate returns.

COMMENT: Head of household status offers more benefits than filing as single. Whether head of household offers more benefits than if the same sex-couple were allowed to file as married, however, depends on the facts and circumstances.

While married taxpayers who previously filed as married filing separate returns may join together and file an amended return jointly, the reverse is not allowed. Married taxpayers who previously filed a joint return cannot retroactively amend their return and file separately. This is because the liability on a joint return is joint and several and the tax code does not release either party from that potential liability.

¶ 405 EXEMPTIONS AND SAME-SEX SPOUSES

Married taxpayers filing a joint return generally may take two personal exemptions—one for each spouse. However, a personal exemption may not be taken for a spouse that is claimed as a dependent on another person's return.

The amount of a taxpayer's total exemptions is reduced when a taxpayer's adjusted gross income (AGI) exceeds certain threshold amounts.

COMMENT: High-income unmarried same-sex couples may be able to claim a higher exemption than would otherwise be allowed because the exemption phaseout amounts apply separately to each taxpayer.

A married taxpayer filing a separate return may take a personal exemption for himself or herself. However, such a taxpayer may not take a personal exemption for his or her spouse unless the spouse had no gross income, is not filing a return, and cannot be claimed as a dependent of another taxpayer.

EXAMPLE: Bonnie Stipek and Connie Stipek are married taxpayers who file a joint return and have AGI of $100,000. Neither spouse may be claimed as a dependent on another person's return. Bonnie and Connie may take two personal exemptions on their 2015 return—one personal exemption for each spouse.

EXAMPLE: Use the same facts, except that Bonnie and Connie file separate returns, and each has AGI of $50,000. Each spouse may take one personal exemption on her 2015 return. Neither spouse may take a personal exemption for the other spouse.

EXAMPLE: Assume the same facts, except that Connie does not have any AGI, does not file a return for the year, and cannot be claimed as a dependent on another person's return for the year. Bonnie may take two personal exemptions on her separate 2015 return—one for herself and one for Connie.

A taxpayer may not claim a spousal exemption for his or her same-sex partner if the couple is not married. A dependency exemption might be available, however, if the spouse meets the qualifications of a qualifying relative.

EXAMPLE: Brian Reklys and Steve Baterio are not married and have no children, and there are no qualifying relatives living with them. Brian can only claim one exemption, for himself, on his return. Likewise, Steve can take one exemption. Neither can claim a spousal exemption.

A taxpayer is allowed one exemption for each person who can be claimed as a dependent. In order to claim a dependent exemption, the person being claimed must be either a "qualifying child" or a "qualifying relative." To be a qualifying child, the child must be the taxpayer's son, daughter, stepchild, adopted child, eligible foster child, brother, sister, stepbrother, stepsister, or a descendant of any such person.

To be a qualifying child, the child must be:

- Under age 19 at the end of the taxpayer's tax year;

- A full-time student under age 24 at the end of the taxpayer's tax year;

- Permanently and totally disabled at any time during the taxpayer's tax year (regardless of age);

- Younger than the taxpayer, unless the child is permanently and totally disabled; or

- Generally, must have lived with the taxpayer for more than half the tax year.

A child is considered to have lived with the taxpayer during periods of time during which the child and/or the taxpayer are temporarily absent from the home due to special circumstances such as illness, education, business, vacation, or military service. There are also exceptions for the birth or death of a child, and for kidnapped children, as well as for the children of divorced or separated parents.

An unmarried same-sex couple with children will find that, as a family, their taxes differ from those of married couples with children. Each same-sex partner must file completely separate returns, and therefore the dependents must be divided between them in claiming exemptions. The parent that claims the exemption for a particular child will be able to claim certain child-related credits.

For unmarried same-sex couples, if one of the same-sex partners is the biological parent of the child, that parent is eligible to claim an exemption for the child. If a same-sex partner is the stepparent of his or her partner's child under the laws of the state in which the partners reside, the same sex-partner is the stepparent of the child for federal income tax purposes. Therefore, because stepparents are able to claim a dependency exemption for the stepchild, an individual in a same-sex relationship who adopts his or her partner's child is eligible to claim an exemption for the child.

Thus, it is possible that either same sex-partner could be eligible to claim a child as a dependent. However, a child can only be claimed as a dependent on one return, and unmarried same-sex parents must file separate returns. Therefore, couples must determine which parent will claim the dependency exemption for a child. The parents are not allowed to claim an exemption for the same child; if both parents claim the same child as a dependent, the IRS will apply certain tie-breaking rules to determine which parent will receive the exemption, and therefore the parent with the higher AGI will normally receive the exemption.

COMMENT: The determination of which parent claims an exemption for a dependent also affects the determination of who can claim certain child-related credits for that dependent.

¶405

¶ 406 CHOICE OF WHETHER TO ITEMIZE OR TAKE THE STANDARD DEDUCTION BY SAME-SEX SPOUSES

Most taxpayers have a choice of either taking the standard deduction or itemizing their deductions. However, a taxpayer is not eligible for the standard deduction if the taxpayer:

- Is married filing a separate return and the taxpayer's spouse itemizes deductions;
- Files a tax return for a short tax year because of a change in his or her annual accounting period; or
- Is a nonresident alien or dual-status alien (i.e., both nonresident and resident alien) during the year.

For the first rule, a legally married taxpayer who qualifies for head of household filing status is treated as unmarried. Thus, such a taxpayer is eligible for the standard deduction even if the taxpayer's spouse itemizes deductions.

An unmarried individual can either itemize or claim the standard deduction, regardless of what his or her partner does. A married taxpayer is prohibited from claiming the standard deduction if his or her spouse itemizes deductions, if filing as married filing separately.

The standard deduction may be limited for a taxpayer who can be claimed as a dependent by another taxpayer.

The choice between taking the standard deduction and itemizing deductions generally should be based on which method results in the highest deduction amount. That method will usually result in the lowest tax.

Itemized deductions are reduced for higher income taxpayers. For 2015, allowable itemized deductions are reduced by the lesser of:

- Three percent of the amount of the taxpayer's AGI in excess of an applicable threshold amount, which is tied to the taxpayer's filing status and is adjusted for inflation; or
- 80 percent of the itemized deductions otherwise allowable for the tax year.

For 2015, the threshold amounts are:

- Joint return or surviving spouse: $309,900;
- Head of household: $284,050;
- Single: $258,250;
- Married filing separately: $154,950.

EXAMPLE: Ellen Washington and Elaine Tarosas are married and file jointly. Each has annual income of $175,000. Their itemized deductions are reduced by the lesser of: $1,203 [($175,000 + $175,000 = $350,000) − $309,900 = $40,100. 40,100 × 3 percent = $1,203)] or 80 percent of the itemized deductions otherwise allowable for the tax year.

EXAMPLE: Assume the same facts in Example 1, except that Ellen and Elaine are not married. Each has income below the $258,250 phaseout threshold; thus, neither is subject to the itemized deduction phaseout.

STUDY QUESTION

---

1. If a married individual files a separate return:

    a. If not a head of household, he or she cannot claim the standard deduction if his or her spouse itemizes deductions

    b. Both the taxpayer and spouse must take the standard deduction

    c. The taxpayer must take the standard deduction if he or she is a nonresident alien or dual-status alien

    d. Must not take either the standard deduction or itemize

---

¶ 407 RETIREMENT PLANS AND SAME-SEX SPOUSES

Retirement plans have been required to treat same-sex spouses as spouses since September 16, 2013. The IRS has not yet provided guidance on periods before that date.

IRA Contributions

There is a general dollar limitation on the amount of annual contributions that can be made to a traditional IRA. Generally, the contribution that a taxpayer may make to a traditional IRA for 2015 is limited to the smaller of:

- $5,500 ($6,500 if age 50 or older); or
- The taxpayer's taxable compensation for the year.

This general limitation applies to the total contributions made to all traditional IRAs during the year, even if some or all of the contributions made to a traditional IRA are nondeductible.

However, for a taxpayer who files a joint return with a spouse and has less compensation than the spouse, the contribution to a traditional IRA is limited to the smaller of:

- $5,500 ($6,500 if age 50 or older) for 2015; or
- The combined compensation of the taxpayer and spouse reduced by (i) the amount of any contribution by the spouse to a traditional IRA, and (ii) the amount of any contribution made on behalf of the spouse to a Roth IRA.

Thus, the total combined contributions that can be made to traditional IRAs of the taxpayer and the taxpayer's spouse are limited to $11,000 ($12,000 if one spouse is age 50 or older and $13,000 if both spouses are age 50 or older) for 2015.

- The contribution limit for Roth IRAs is the same as applies to traditional IRAs. As with traditional IRAs, a married individual filing a joint return may make a Roth IRA contribution by treating the combined income as his or her own, reduced by the amount of any contribution by the spouse to a traditional or Roth IRA.

If the taxpayer makes contributions to both traditional IRAs and Roth IRAs, the contributions that a taxpayer may make to Roth IRAs are subject to that same limitation reduced by all contributions made to all other IRAs other than Roth IRAs (but not reduced by employer contributions under a SEP IRA or a SIMPLE IRA).

    EXAMPLE: During 2015, Jessica Calhoun, a 24-year-old full-time student with no compensation, marries Jennifer Tolbert, a 32-year-old administrative assistant with taxable compensation of $30,000. If Jessica and Jennifer file a joint return for 2015, each can contribute $5,500 to a traditional IRA. Jennifer's contribution limitation is equal to the smaller of $5,500 or her compensation ($30,000). Jessica's contribution limitation is equal to the smaller of $5,500 or their combined compensation less any contribution made by Jennifer to a traditional IRA or a Roth IRA ($30,000 – $5,500 = $24,500).

Generally, a taxpayer can deduct the contributions made to a traditional IRA up to the amount of the contribution limitations. However, the amount of a taxpayer's deduction for contributions to a traditional IRA may be subject to an additional limitation if the taxpayer or spouse was covered by an employer retirement plan at any time during the year for which the contributions were made.

Phaseout of Deductions for IRA Contributions for Employees Covered by Employer Plans

If the taxpayer or spouse was covered by an employer retirement plan at any time during the year for which the contributions were made, and he or she did not receive any Social Security benefits during the year, the taxpayer's deduction for the contributions may be limited based on his or her income and filing status. If a taxpayer was covered by an employer retirement plan, the following are the phaseout ranges for 2015 based on the taxpayer's filing status:

- For a taxpayer with the filing status of married filing jointly or qualifying widow(er), the deduction limits begin to phase out at a modified adjusted gross income (MAGI) of $98,000 and are fully phased out at a MAGI of $118,000;
- For a taxpayer with the filing status of single or head of household, the contribution limits begin to phase out at a MAGI of $61,000 and are fully phased out at a MAGI of $71,000; and
- For a taxpayer with the filing status of married filing separately, the contribution limits begin to phase out at a MAGI of $0 and are fully phased out at a MAGI of $10,000.

If the taxpayer is married and both the taxpayer and the taxpayer's spouse contributed to IRAs during the year, the taxpayer's deduction and the taxpayer's spouse's deduction must be figured separately.

An individual is not considered an active participant in an employer-sponsored plan merely because the individual's spouse is an active participant for any part of a plan year. However, if a taxpayer was not covered by an employer retirement plan but is married and his or her spouse was covered by such a plan, the following are the phaseout ranges for 2015 based on the taxpayer's filing status:

- For a taxpayer with the filing status of married filing jointly, the deduction limits begin to phase out at a MAGI of $183,000 and are fully phased out at a MAGI of $193,000; and
- For a taxpayer with the filing status of married filing separately, the deduction limits begin to phase out at a MAGI of $0 and are fully phased out at a MAGI of $10,000.

Under these rules, MAGI is the taxpayer's AGI modified by adding back:

- The traditional IRA deduction;
- The student loan interest deduction;
- The tuition and fees deduction;
- The domestic production activities deduction;
- The foreign earned income exclusion;
- The foreign housing exclusion or deduction;

- The exclusion of qualified savings bond interest; and
- The exclusion for employer-provided adoption benefits.

The amount by which the deduction limit is reduced is determined by multiplying the deduction limit by the following fraction:

Taxpayer's MAGI – Dollar amount at which the limit begins to phase out

---

$10,000 ($20,000 if married filing jointly or qualifying widow(er) and the taxpayer is covered by an employer retirement plan)

EXAMPLE: Jack Evans and Jim Peterson are 40-year-old married taxpayers who file a joint return. They both work, but only Jack is covered by an employer retirement plan. They each have a MAGI of $60,000 for 2015. Thus, their combined MAGI is $120,000. Each spouse makes a $5,500 contribution to his own traditional IRA for the year. The amount of Jack's contribution that is deductible is determined under the rules for a taxpayer who is covered by an employer retirement plan. Under those rules, a taxpayer who is married filing jointly with MAGI greater than $118,000 is not permitted a deduction for his contributions to a traditional IRA. The amount of Jim's contribution that is deductible is determined under the rules for a taxpayer who is not covered by an employer retirement plan but whose spouse is covered by such a plan. Under those rules, a taxpayer who is married filing jointly with MAGI less than $183,000 is permitted a full deduction for his contributions to a traditional IRA. Thus, Jim may take a $5,500 deduction for his IRA contributions, but Jack may not take any deduction for his IRA contributions.

Inherited Accounts

If a taxpayer inherits a traditional IRA from his or her spouse, the taxpayer generally has three options:

- The taxpayer can make a spousal rollover into a traditional IRA established in the taxpayer's name;
- The taxpayer can choose to treat the inherited IRA as his or her own by designating him- or herself as the account owner; and
- The taxpayer can choose to treat him- or herself as a beneficiary rather than an owner.

COMMENT: If an unmarried individual is the beneficiary of his or her partner's qualified plan, such as a 401(k) plan, the surviving partner can leave the money in the account, roll the account into an IRA in the deceased partner's name for the benefit of the beneficiary, or take a lump-sum distribution. The various annuity options available to spouses are not available to unmarried individuals.

STUDY QUESTION

---

2. The effect of marriage on deductible IRA contributions of joint filing same-sex couple is to:

    a. Reduce the amount of maximum contributions the couple may make to their traditional IRAs

    b. Apply a lower threshold for phasing out contribution deductions for a couple covered by an employer retirement plan than would apply if they were unmarried filers

    c. Require the spouses to file separately in order to deduct their contributions

    d. Restrict the amount of contributions if both spouses are covered by an employer retirement plan

¶ 408 MEDICAL EXPENSES OF SAME-SEX SPOUSES

Expenses paid during the tax year for the medical care of the taxpayer, spouse, and dependents generally are deductible as itemized deductions. Medical expenses are generally deductible only to the extent that they exceed 10 percent of the taxpayer's AGI. However, taxpayers (or their spouses) who are age 65 and older before the close of the tax year are exempt from the increased threshold and continue to be eligible to claim the medical expense deduction if their medical expenses exceed 7.5 percent of AGI for tax years beginning after December 31, 2012, and ending before January 1, 2017. Medical expenses are not deductible to the extent the taxpayer is reimbursed for them by insurance or otherwise.

> **EXAMPLE:** Mary Schroeder was born in July 1951, so she turns 65 in 2016. Her spouse Janine Steiner was born in 1956, so she turns 65 in 2021. For 2014 and 2015, Mary and Janine can deduct medical expenses that exceed 10 percent of AGI. For 2016, they can deduct medical expenses that exceed 7.5 percent of AGI. For 2017 and later years, they can deduct medical expenses that exceed 10 percent of AGI.

> **COMMENT:** The statute does not require the spouses to file a joint return for the temporary exemption from the 10 percent threshold for those 65 and older to apply. For instance, it appears that the 7.5 percent threshold would apply to a 30-year-old taxpayer who is married to a 65-year-old, even if the spouses file separate returns.

A health savings account (HSA) is a tax-exempt trust or custodial account that is created exclusively to pay for the qualified medical expenses of the account beneficiary, spouse, and dependents. It provides a taxpayer with tax-favored treatment for amounts saved to pay medical expenses. Contributions to an HSA are generally deductible as an "above-the-line" deduction, subject to limitations.

For HSAs, the following special rules apply to married individuals if either spouse has family coverage:

- The maximum annual HSA contribution limit for a married couple if one spouse has family high-deductible health plan (HDHP) coverage and the other spouse has self-only HDHP coverage is the Code Sec. 223(b)(2)(B) statutory maximum for family coverage as adjusted for inflation. The contribution limit is divided between the spouses by agreement. This is the result regardless of whether the family HDHP coverage includes the spouse with self-only HDHP coverage;

- If a spouse has HDHP family coverage and the other spouse has non-HDHP self-only coverage, the spouse with the HDHP family coverage is an eligible individual and may contribute to an HSA up to the amount of the annual contribution limit. Because the other spouse is covered by a non-HDHP and is therefore not an eligible individual, the other spouse may not contribute to an HSA; and

- The maximum HSA contribution limit for a married couple when both spouses have family HDHP coverage is the Code Sec. 223(b)(2)(B) statutory maximum $6,650 for 2015. This rule applies regardless of whether each spouse's family coverage covers the other spouse. The contribution limit is divided between the spouses by agreement.

A same-sex married couple is subject to the joint deduction limit for contributions to an HSA. If the combined HSA contributions elected by two same-sex spouses exceed the applicable HSA contribution limit for a married couple, contributions for one or both of the spouses may be reduced for the remaining portion of the tax year to avoid exceeding the limit. To the extent that the combined contributions to the HSAs of the married couple exceed the contribution limit, any excess may be distributed from the HSAs of one or both spouses no later than the tax return due date for the spouses. Any excess contributions that remain undistributed as of the due date for the filing of the spouse's tax return (including extensions) will be subject to excise taxes.

COMMENT: The spouses can divide the annual HSA contribution in any way they want—including allocating nothing to one spouse.

EXAMPLE 1: For 2015, Bill and Karl are married and both 40 years old. They are otherwise eligible individuals. Bill has self-only HDHP coverage. Karl has an HDHP with family coverage for himself and their two children. The combined contribution limit for Bill and Karl is $6,650, which is the statutory contribution limit for 2015. They may divide the $6,650 contribution limit between themselves by agreement.

EXAMPLE 2: In 2015, Jane Culbert, who is 37, and Cynthia Winston, who is 32, are married and have two dependent children. Jane has HDHP family coverage for herself and their two children with an annual deductible of $3,200. Cynthia has HDHP family coverage for herself and their two children with a deductible of $3,900. The combined contribution limit for Jane and Cynthia is $6,650, the maximum annual contribution limit for 2015. They may divide the $6,650 contribution limit between them by agreement.

If an HSA account beneficiary dies and the HSA passes to a surviving spouse, it continues to operate as an HSA with the surviving spouse as the account beneficiary. If the HSA passes to the account beneficiary's estate, the HSA is considered to cease on the date of death and the fair market value of its assets is includible in the gross income of the beneficiary (decedent) for his or her final tax year. If the HSA passes to some other person, it is considered to cease on the date of death, and the fair market value of its assets is includible in the gross income of the person to whom the HSA passes for his tax year that includes the date of the account beneficiary's death.

Health Care Exemption

Normally, if a taxpayer's employer-provided health care covers the taxpayer's spouse, the coverage is exempt from taxation.

EXAMPLE: Jillian Hartley's employer sponsors a group health plan covering eligible employees and their dependents and spouses. Fifty percent of the cost of health coverage elected by employees is paid by the employer. Jillian was married to her same-sex spouse Krista Swenson at all times during the year and had elected coverage for Krista through the health plan at the beginning of the year. Jillian may exclude the value of Krista's employer-funded health coverage from gross income.

¶ 409 APPLICATION OF RENTAL REAL ESTATE LOSS RULES TO SAME-SEX SPOUSES

The deduction of passive activity expenses is generally limited to the amount of income from the passive activity. Passive activities include trade or business activities in which the taxpayer does not materially participate and rental activities. However, passive activity rules governing rental real estate allow up to $25,000 of passive losses to be offset against nonpassive income depending on the taxpayer's marital status and income.

This special deduction for passive activity losses from a rental real estate activity is allowed only if the taxpayer actively participates in the rental real estate activity. Active participation is a lower standard than the material participation. The $25,000 amount is reduced by 50 percent of the amount by which a taxpayer's AGI exceeds $100,000. Thus, the offset is fully phased out if the taxpayer has AGI of $150,000 or more.

The maximum deduction if married filing separately is $12,500 reduced by 50 percent of the amount by which such individual's adjusted gross income exceeds $50,000. This married filing separate deduction is available only if the taxpayer lived apart from his or her spouse for the entire tax year.

> **EXAMPLE:** Jack O'Reilly and John Regan, who are married filing jointly, have a combined AGI of $120,000, none of which is passive income. They have a $45,000 rental real estate loss. Each actively participates in the real estate activity. Because their income exceeds the AGI threshold by $20,000, the $25,000 offset amount that they otherwise would be entitled to deduct is reduced by 50 percent of $20,000, or $10,000. Thus, Jack and John are entitled to deduct $15,000 of the rental real estate loss against nonpassive income, and they carry forward $30,000 ($45,000 – $15,000) of the passive activity loss.

> **EXAMPLE:** Use the same facts, except that Jack and John are not married, each owns a 50 percent interest in the real estate, each actively participates in the real estate activity, and each has AGI of $60,000. Each would be entitled to a deduction of up to $25,000 in rental real estate losses offsetting nonpassive income. Therefore each would be able to deduct their 50 percent share of the loss or $22,500.

A rental real estate activity in which the taxpayer materially participates as a real estate professional is not treated as a passive activity.

¶ 410 OTHER PHASEOUTS, FLOORS, AND CEILINGS

In addition to the phaseouts discussed above, such as those for medical expenses, rental real estate losses, and the general itemized deduction phaseout, the tax code contains other phaseouts that trigger when a taxpayer's income reaches certain amount. Many of these phaseout limitations are designed so that the benefit for married couples begins to phase out at an amount of income that is double the amount at which the phaseout begins for single taxpayers. However, some phaseout limitations are not designed that way, meaning that the phaseout limitation for married couples is lower than twice the amount for single taxpayers.

> **COMMENT:** For these types of phaseout limitations, an unmarried same-sex couple may be able to claim a larger tax deduction than a married couple. The reason is that unmarried same-sex couples are treated as completely separate taxpayers—each separately subject to the phaseout limitation for single taxpayers. When combined, the separate limitations shield more income from tax than the phaseout limitation for married couples. Thus, practitioners should determine which limitations may apply to particular clients and review the potential tax consequences with them. This same logic applies to AGI floors, such as the floor for the medical deduction (discussed above), the casualty deduction, and miscellaneous itemized deductions, as well as for ceilings, such as the $3,000 ceiling on capital losses used to offset ordinary income.

STUDY QUESTION

3. If Baylea Jackson is 65 years old, her spouse Avari Austin is 63, and the couple files jointly:

    a. Baylea must pay income tax for her employer's spousal health plan coverage for Avari

    b. The spouses must file separate returns so Baylea's lower deduction threshold will apply to her expenses

    c. Their medical expenses may be deducted if the amount exceeds 7.5 percent of their AGI

    d. The couple's combined medical expense totals must exceed 10 percent of their AGI to be deductible

¶ 411 APPLICATION OF RELATED-PARTY ANTIABUSE RULES TO SAME-SEX SPOUSES

A taxpayer cannot deduct losses on the sale or exchange of property to any family member or certain other related persons and entities. The purpose of this rule is to avoid abusive transactions that are designed to create tax deductible losses while a family continues to own the property on which the loss is taken. The related-party disallowance rules apply even if the transaction is bona fide and even when the relationship between the family members is clearly hostile. On the other hand, the related-party limitations do not apply to relationships that fall outside the relationships specifically listed—no matter how close the relationship may be.

Married couples are treated as related parties under these rules, but unmarried couples are not.

Certain constructive stock ownership rules apply in determining whether stock ownership by related parties exists (and consequently whether the related party limitations apply). These constructive ownership rules are as follows:

1. Stock owned, directly or indirectly, by or for a corporation, partnership, estate, or trust is considered as being owned proportionately by or for its shareholders, partners, or beneficiaries;

2. An individual is considered as owning the stock owned, directly or indirectly, by or for his or her family;

3. A partner in a partnership owning (other than by the application of rule (2) above) any stock in a corporation is considered as owning the stock owned, directly or indirectly, by or for the other partners in the partnership;

4. The family of an individual includes only his brothers and sisters (whether by whole or half-blood), spouse, ancestors, and lineal descendants (e.g., children, including legally adopted children, and grandchildren); and

5. Stock constructively owned by a person by reason of applying rule 1, above, is treated as actually owned by that person in applying rules 1, 2, or 3, but stock constructively owned by the reason of applying rule 2 or 3 is not treated as owned by that person for again applying either of such rules in order to make another the constructive owner of the stock.

    EXAMPLE: Matthew Jenson's spouse Lars Tiebold owns 30 percent of the stock in Scandifoods Company. Matthew's son owns 40 percent of Scandifoods stock; Matthew does not directly own any Scandifoods stock, but he is considered to constructively own 70 percent of the stock in Scandifoods. Because Matthew is considered as owning more than 50 percent of Scandifoods, he and Scandifoods are related parties. As a result, if Matthew sells property to Scandifoods and incurs a loss, he is not allowed to take a tax deduction for the loss.

If an individual sells property used in a business to a related party at a loss, and the related party purchaser later sells the property to an unrelated party at a gain, the inherited loss can be used to reduce the gain on the subsequent sale (Code Sec. 267(d)).

¶412 QUALIFIED JOINT VENTURE ELECTION FOR SAME-SEX SPOUSES

Generally, absent a qualified joint venture election, if spouses operate a business as a partnership, they report business income and expenses on Form 1065, *U.S. Return of Partnership Income,* and attach separate Schedules K-1 showing each partner's share of the earnings.

A qualified joint venture whose only members are the two spouses filing a joint return can, however, elect not to be treated as a partnership for federal tax purposes. In determining net earnings from self-employment, each spouse's share of income or loss from a qualified joint venture is taken into account in accordance with his or her respective interests in the venture. Each spouse takes into account his or her respective share of these items as a sole proprietor.

> **COMMENT:** The election of qualified joint venture status for a rental real estate business does not convert the income from that business into net earnings from self-employment when the income otherwise would be excluded from net earnings from self-employment.

A qualified joint venture is a joint venture involving the conduct of a trade or business, if:

- The only members of the joint venture are the two spouses;
- Both spouses materially participate in the trade or business; and
- Both spouses elect to have qualified joint venture status apply.

¶413 SAME-SEX SPOUSE AS EMPLOYEE

Services performed by an employee in the employ of his or her spouse are excluded from the definition of employment for purposes of FUTA taxes.

> **COMMENT:** Therefore, for all years for which the period of limitations is open, the employer can claim a refund of the Social Security, Medicare, and FUTA taxes paid on the compensation that the employer paid his or her same-sex spouse as an employee in the business.

¶414 ESTATE AND GIFT TAX ISSUES AFFECTING SAME-SEX SPOUSES

The estate, gift, and generation-skipping transfer (GST) taxes are designed to form a unified transfer tax system on the transfer of property at death (estate tax), during life (gift tax), and on transfers that skip a generation (GST tax). The maximum marginal tax rate is 40 percent for estates of decedents dying and gifts and GSTs made after December 31, 2012. The estate and gift tax exclusion amount and the GST exemption amount are indexed annually for inflation. The exclusion and exemption amounts are $5.43 million for 2015. A decedent's estate may elect to allow the unused portion of the decedent's applicable exclusion amount to be available to his or her surviving spouse or the spouse's estate (referred to as "portability"). As a result, the applicable exclusion amount of a surviving spouse may include the predeceased spouse's unused exclusion amount, allowing the spouse to transfer up to $10.86 million in 2015.

A gift donor is allowed a unified credit against gift tax, equal to (1) the estate tax applicable credit amount in effect for the calendar year of the gift minus (2) the sum of all applicable credits allowable to the donor for gifts made in all prior calendar periods. The applicable credit amount for 2015 is $2,117,800, which effectively shields the first $5.43 million of a donor's lifetime gifts from gift tax. The applicable credit amount might be higher for any year if the donor is a surviving spouse and the estate of his or her predeceased spouse has elected portability of the deceased spouse's unused exclusion amount.

The first $14,000 of gifts of a present interest made by a donor during calendar year 2015 to each donee is not included in the total amount of the donor's taxable gifts during that year. Therefore, these amounts are not taxed and do not use up any of the donor's lifetime gift tax applicable credit amount. Also, spouses who consent to split their gifts may transfer a total of $28,000 per donee in 2015 free of gift and GST taxes. Special rules apply if the donor's spouse is not a U.S. citizen.

A marital deduction is allowed for gifts to the donor's spouse. Thus, property transferred between spouses, other than certain terminable interests, is not subject to the gift tax. The gift tax marital deduction is not available, however, if the donor's spouse is not a U.S. citizen at the time of the gift. Instead, gifts to a noncitizen spouse are eligible for a gift tax annual exclusion of up to $147,000 in 2015.

> **COMMENT:** A gift tax marital deduction is not allowed for transfers of terminable interests in property. A *terminable interest in property* is an interest that will terminate or fail on the lapse of time or on the occurrence or failure to occur of some contingency. For example, terminable interests include life estates, terms for years, and annuities. However, a gift tax marital deduction will be allowed if the donee spouse is given a life estate with a general power of appointment or qualified terminable interest property (QTIP), or if the donor and spouse are named as the only noncharitable beneficiaries of a qualified charitable remainder trust.

Same-sex married couples may take advantage of portability and other benefits previously enjoyed only by opposite-sex married couples such as the estate and gift tax marital deductions and split gifts. These benefits are not available to unmarried couples.

> **EXAMPLE:** Hilda Eisenberg and Henrietta Fisher are married. Hilda adds Henrietta's name to the ownership title of her house. Because they are married, there are no gift tax consequences.

> **EXAMPLE:** Use the same facts, but Hilda and Henrietta are unmarried same-sex partners. In this case, a gift occurs, which may have gift/estate tax consequences for any amount above the annual exclusion.

Other issues may arise in connection with the estate tax for unmarried partners. For example, in a joint tenancy with rights of survivorship, the entire value of the property would be included in the estate of the first to die, unless the surviving partner could prove he or she contributed to the purchase price.

> **COMMENT:** Records should be kept to help identify contributions to jointly held property.

If a lifetime transfer to a surviving spouse is included in the gross estate of the transferor, the marital status of the spouses at the time of the transfer is irrelevant. The deduction is based on the marital status of the couple at the time of the transferor's death.

EXAMPLE: George Bentley transferred a life insurance policy on his life to Gary Roberts on January 5, 2014. At the time of the transfer, George and Gary were not married. George and Gary married in 2015, and George died on January 7, 2016. The policy proceeds payable to Gary were included in George's gross estate as a transfer of life insurance within three years of death. The proceeds paid to George qualify for the marital deduction even though George and Gary were not married at the time of the transfer.

STUDY QUESTION

4. Portability for the purposes of the tax exclusion amount for spouses means:

    a. The unused portion of a decedent's applicable exclusion amount is available to his or her surviving spouse or spouse's estate

    b. The unified credit for the taxes applies only to the surviving spouse, not the decedent's estate

    c. The gift tax marital deduction is available to the donor's spouse who is not a U.S. citizen at the time of the decedent's death

    d. Any lifetime transfer to a surviving spouse is included in the gross estate of the transferor

¶ 415 COMMUNITY PROPERTY ISSUES AFFECTING SAME-SEX SPOUSES

Nine states have mandatory community property laws. Community property may only be held by two married spouses.

COMMENT: Although there are a number of concepts common to all community property jurisdictions, there are significant differences among the laws of the nine states.

The usual rule in community property jurisdictions is that all property acquired during marriage (except property acquired individually by gift, bequest, devise, or inheritance) or derived from the earnings of either spouse while in that marriage is community property or community income. Moreover, the proceeds and earnings of community property are themselves community property or community income. Rents, profits, royalties and income derived from the separate property are considered separate property in five of the nine community property states. Community property retains its character as community property even if the owners have moved out of a community property state.

EXAMPLE: Frances Duschene and Felicia Beauchamp are a married couple in in California, a community property state. Frances' earnings from her employment are community property. Thus, Felicia legally owns one-half of Frances' weekly pay. The royalties Felicia receives from the book she has written during their marriage are also community property, i.e., one-half are Frances'. They deposit Frances' wages and Felicia's royalties in a bank account. The interest earned from this account is community income as well.

All property acquired before the marriage, or after the marriage is over, and all property separately received by either spouse through gift, bequest, devise, or inheritance is separate property. In general, unless commingled, separate or community property retains its respective character. Although separate property may be disposed of by its individual owner, community property gifts or other transfers can only be made with the consent of both owners.

> **COMMENT:** Commingling occurs when separate and community property becomes so mixed and intertwined that its separate origins can no longer be traced. If property can no longer be apportioned, it is commingled, and a presumption arises that it is community property.

An additional category of community property is that of quasi-community property. In a number of community property jurisdictions, quasi-community property is any property (real or personal), but not separate property, wherever situated, that would have been community property had the acquiring spouse or spouses been domiciled in a community property state at the time of the acquisition.

> **EXAMPLE:** Ed Miller and Robert Menlo, spouses, live in New York, a noncommunity property state. Ed purchases a vacation condominium on the New Jersey seashore and places the title in his name only. New Jersey is also not a community property jurisdiction. Ed did not use or in any manner designate separate marital funds for the purchase. Some years later, Ed and Robert move to California, a community property state. On their subsequent divorce, under California law, Robert will seek a one-half interest in the New Jersey condo because it is quasi-community property.

For federal income tax purposes, state community property laws may not apply to an item of community income if one spouse treats the item as if only he or she were entitled to the income from it and does not notify the spouse of the nature and amount of the income by the due date, including extensions, for filing the tax return on which the income should be reported.

In general, one spouse may be entitled to relief from separate return liability for an item of community income if:

- The taxpayer files a separate return for the tax year that does not include the item of community income in gross income;

- The taxpayer can establish that he or she did not know of, and had no reason to know of, the item of community income; and

- Under all the facts and circumstances, it would not be fair to include the item of community income in the taxpayer's gross income.

For federal gift tax purposes, a gift of community property is treated as a gift of one-half the property by each spouse. For federal estate tax purposes, the value of all of a decedent's separate property and one-half of his or her community property is included in the decedent's gross estate.

> **EXAMPLE:** Donna Ralston and Debbie Ward live in a community property jurisdiction. Debbie came into their marriage owning two tracts of land and a stock portfolio. Donna came into the marriage with an office building and substantial investments in tax-free bonds. Over the course of their marriage, Donna and Debbie sold their original separate properties, sometimes purchasing new property, sometimes using the cash proceeds to invest in other business ventures, and sometimes making gifts to each other and to their children. When Donna dies, it is possible to trace (through a series of transactions) one plot of land held for development back to the office building she originally held as separate property. The plot of land is considered Donna's separate property and is included in her gross estate. However, because the couple's other property is so thoroughly commingled that it is not possible to trace its origins, it is deemed community property and one-half of its value is included in Donna's gross estate.

¶415

COMMENT: Because community property rules vary from jurisdiction to jurisdiction, it is not always possible to predict the federal tax consequences with certainty.

Some jurisdictions permit more and some allow less flexibility in a couple's power to designate (usually by a written document) property as community or separate. Several community property states allow the spouses to change the classification of property as separate or community. In some, a pre- or post-nuptial agreement can define the couple's assets as community or separate. It is also possible for one spouse to give the other a gift of a one-half interest in the donor's separate property, which most states treat as intent to make the asset community property.

The division of community property into separate property is not a taxable event. Federal tax law usually respects a designation of property as separate or marital provided state law requirements have been met.

STUDY QUESTION

1. Quasi-community property is:

   a. Property to which one spouse contributed more funds or active participation than the other

   b. Property acquired when the spouses were not domiciled in a community property state

   c. Community property that is sold or exchanged in a noncommunity property state

   d. Separate property bought before marriage, not commingled during the marriage, and sold after the divorce of the spouses

¶ 416 SAME-SEX DIVORCE

No gain or loss is recognized on a transfer of property incidental to a divorce even if a transfer is in exchange for the release of marital rights, for cash or other property, for the assumption of liabilities in excess of basis (except for certain transfers in trust), or for other consideration. In addition, property that was not owned by the transferor-spouse during the marriage may be able to be transferred without recognition of gain or loss.

EXAMPLE: Kevin Kelly and Kenneth Harris divorced. Their marital home had been in Kevin's family for three generations. Rather than sell the house and split the proceeds after the end of the marriage, Kevin buys a house with a value of about half of the marital home and transfers it to Kenneth within one year of the divorce. This transfer results in no gain or loss to Kevin, and Kenneth takes a carryover basis.

This nonrecognition applies to any debt that is discharged. The nonrecognition rules govern regardless of whether the transfer is of separately owned property or community property.

Only transfers of property are governed by the nonrecognition rules. Transfers of services are not.

EXAMPLE: Sally O'Rourke is a physician and is divorced from Sue Black. During the year following the end of their marriage, Sally continues to serve as her former spouse's physician. Sally is taxed on fees paid by her ex-spouse, because the transfer involves services rather than property.

For unmarried couples, the division of property is treated as a taxable transaction between two unrelated parties. Therefore, a taxable gain or loss could arise, or the transfer could be treated as a gift.

Retirement plan benefits are often divided in connection with a divorce or separation. A qualified domestic relations order (QDRO) is a particular type of judgment, decree, or order. It is made under a state's domestic relations or community property law. It requires that retirement plan amounts be distributed to someone other than the participant.

If the division is made in the form of a QDRO, the following special rules apply:

- A spouse or former spouse who receives the interest or benefits under the plan is treated as though he or she were the plan participant;

- The plan participant is not treated as receiving the amount distributed to the spouse or former spouse (but is treated as receiving amounts distributed to any other payee, such as a child);

- The plan can distribute the benefits without violating the antialienation rules that otherwise prevent benefits from going to someone other than the employee or the restrictions on distributions that would otherwise apply; and

- The penalties on early distributions do not apply.

COMMENT: An unmarried couple is not able use a QDRO to keep a qualified plan transaction nontaxable.

QDROs can only attach to benefits payable to a plan participant. Thus, a domestic relations order cannot be a QDRO for benefits that have already vested in a new spouse of the participant.

> **EXAMPLE:** John Walston, a plan participant, divorces Jared Jamal. John remarries and names his new spouse, Jeff Foster, as the beneficiary entitled to receive survivor benefits. When John retires, he begins receiving a joint and survivor annuity. Jared obtains a domestic relations order from state court ordering that he be named as the annuity's alternate payee. The order is not a QDRO for the survivor benefits because QDROs can only attach to benefits payable to a plan participant, and Jeff is a beneficiary with a vested interest in the survivor benefits rather than a plan participant.

Alimony and Child Support in Same-Sex Divorces

When spouses divorce or separate, one spouse is often required to pay alimony to the other spouse. The payee spouse generally must include the amount of alimony received in gross income, whereas the payor spouse generally may take a deduction for the amount of alimony paid. Thus, the rules for determining whether a payment between spouses is an alimony payment are important in determining the proper tax treatment of that payment. There are a number of requirements that must be met for a payment between spouses to be properly classified as an alimony payment.

The payment of alimony by one spouse to another effectively results in a splitting of the payor spouse's income because the amount paid is taxed to the payee spouse rather than the payor spouse. Thus, the alimony rules create a tax planning opportunity to shift income from a high-bracket taxpayer to a low-bracket taxpayer, allowing the spouses to achieve an aggregate tax savings. This favorable tax treatment may tempt some taxpayers to disguise property settlements as alimony payments. The alimony recapture rules are designed to prevent taxpayers from taking this approach. Under those rules, the amount of any excess front-loaded alimony payments must be recaptured by the payor spouse and included in gross income. The payee spouse may take a corresponding deduction for the amount of recaptured alimony.

Alimony payments. A taxpayer who receives alimony or separate maintenance payments from a spouse or former spouse must include the amount received in gross income. The spouse who pays alimony or separate maintenance payments may take a deduction for the amount paid.

An alimony or separate maintenance payment is a payment that meets all of the following requirements:

- The payment is made in cash;
- The payment is made under a divorce or separation instrument;
- The divorce or separation instrument does not designate the payment as nonalimony;
- The payor spouse is not required to make payments (or any substitute for payments) after the death of the payee spouse;
- If legally separated under a decree of divorce or separate maintenance, the spouses are not members of the same household at the time the payment is made; and
- The spouses do not file a joint tax return.

Child support payments (discussed below) do not qualify as alimony or separate maintenance payments.

Only cash payments (including checks and money orders payable on demand) qualify as alimony payments. Payments made in the form of services or properties do not qualify. The issuance of a note or other debt instrument by the payor spouse to the payee spouse does not qualify until principal payments are made on the note.

Payments of cash to a third party on behalf of the payee spouse that are made under the terms of the divorce or separation instrument may qualify as alimony payments. Thus, cash payments of rent, mortgage, tax, or tuition on behalf of the payee spouse may qualify as alimony payments. However, cash payments made to maintain a property that is owned by the payor spouse and used by the payee spouse do not qualify, even if made under the terms of the divorce or separation instrument.

> **EXAMPLE:** Under the terms of their divorce decree, Don Carros must pay the mortgage payments, real estate taxes, and insurance premiums on a home owned by his ex-spouse, Darren MacNeil. Don can deduct these payments as alimony (if they otherwise qualify as alimony). Darren must include the payments in gross income as alimony received. However, Darren can take a deduction for the amounts of mortgage interest and real estate taxes if he itemizes his deductions.

Payments of cash to a third party on behalf of the payee spouse and made at the written request, consent, or ratification of that spouse may also qualify as alimony payments. One example is the payment of cash to a charitable organization at the request of the payee spouse. The written request, consent, or ratification must state that the spouses intend the payment to be treated as an alimony payment.

> **COMMENT:** Life insurance premiums paid by the payor spouse under the terms of the divorce or separation instrument on a policy on his or her own life qualify as alimony payments to the extent that the payee spouse is the owner of the policy.

Child support payments. Child support payments do not qualify as alimony payments.

A *child support payment* is a payment that, under the terms of the divorce or separation instrument, is fixed (or treated as fixed) as payable for the support of a child of the payor spouse. A child support payment is not deductible by the payor spouse and not includible in the gross income of the payee spouse.

A payment is fixed as payable for the support of a child if the divorce or separation instrument specifically designates an amount of money or a part of a payment as payable for the support of the child.

A payment is treated as fixed as payable for the support of a child if the payment is reduced upon the happening of a contingency related to the child or at a time that can clearly be associated with such a contingency.

A contingency relates to a child if it depends on any event relating to the child, regardless of the likelihood that the event will occur. Some examples of events that may relate to a child include the child's dying, marrying, leaving school, leaving the spouse's home, gaining employment, attaining a specific age, or attaining a specific income level.

Payments are treated as reduced at a time that can clearly be associated with such a contingency if:

- The payments are to be reduced not more than six months before or after the date the child turns 18, 21, or the local age of majority; or
- The payments are to be reduced on two or more different occasions that occur not more than one year before or after a different child of the payor spouse turns a specified age between the ages of 18 and 24, inclusive.

However, the presumption that such a time can be clearly associated with a contingency in those two situations may be rebutted by showing that the time the payments are to be reduced was determined independently of any contingencies relating to the children of the payor spouse.

> **EXAMPLE:** Alice Mason and Bernice Tillis are divorced on July 1, 2016, when their children, Charlie (born July 15, 2001) and David (born September 23, 2003), are 14 and 12, respectively. Under the divorce decree, Alice is to make alimony payments to Bernice of $2,000 per month. The payments are to be reduced to $1,500 per month on January 1, 2022, and to $1,000 per month on January 1, 2026. On January 1, 2022, the date of the first reduction in payments, Charlie will be 20 years 5 months and 17 days old. On January 1, 2026, the date of the second reduction in payments, David will be 22 years, 3 months, and 9 days old. Each of the reductions in payments is to occur not more than one year before or after a different child attains the age of 21 years and 4 months. Accordingly, the reductions will be presumed to clearly be associated with the happening of a contingency relating to Charlie and David. Unless this presumption is rebutted, payments under the divorce decree equal to the sum of the reductions ($1,000 per month) will be treated as fixed for the support of Alice's children of and therefore will not qualify as alimony or separate maintenance payments.

STUDY QUESTION

6. When divorcing spouses divide one of their employer's retirement plan accounts under a qualified domestic relations order:

   a. The plan participant is responsible for paying the early distribution penalty for the account

   b. The benefits going to the ex-spouse do not violate the antialienation rules

   c. The participant spouse pays income tax on the distribution regardless of whether it is made to the former spouse or their child

   d. The ex-spouse who receives the plan benefits must take a lump-sum distribution or roll the funds over to his or her own account

¶ 417 CONCLUSION

As can be seen from this discussion, there are both tax advantages and disadvantages for same-sex couples contemplating marriage. Although tax issues will probably not be the primary factors in the decision of whether or not to marry, the tax practitioner can provide valuable planning assistance in explaining these issues to same-sex couple clients by researching their particular circumstances and offering scenarios of tax consequences based on these circumstances. Among the factors that should be taken into account are:

- The advantages and disadvantages of married filing jointly vs. single or head of household status, and any issues that might require married filing separately status;

- The effect of marital status on exemptions and exemption phaseouts and/or the standard deduction;

- The effect of marital status on retirement accounts and IRA contributions and phaseouts;

- The effect of marital status on the medical expense deduction floor, taking into account the projected expenses and ages of the clients;

- Application of the special deduction for rental real estate activities;

- A review of other deduction and credit phaseouts, floors, and ceilings based on the circumstances of the clients;

- Whether situations exist that would give rise to related-party transaction or antiabuse rules in the event of marriage;

- Whether the qualified joint venture rules would be advantageous, or advantageous Social Security, or Medicare rules could apply if couple operates or plans to operate a business;

- Estate and gift tax issues; and

- Community property issues.

MODULE 3: RECENT REPORTING AND COMPLIANCE CHALLENGES—Chapter 5: International Tax Reporting

¶ 501 WELCOME

In their ongoing effort to close the *tax gap,* or the taxable amounts underreported on tax returns, Congress and the Internal Revenue Service (IRS) continue to extend the information reporting requirements for taxpayers and financial institutions domestically and abroad. With the ability to locate and collect excess monies already owed, Congress can, in effect, increase revenues without having to increase taxes. At the same time, information reporting is extremely useful to the IRS because collecting this data enables the agency to verify a taxpayer's income by matching what is reported by one taxpayer with that provided by another and then act upon discrepancies. As a result, these matching efforts are likely to expand even further. In keeping with this trend, this chapter examines the reporting requirements for foreign assets and financial interests imposed by the *Foreign Account Tax Compliance Act* (FATCA) and the FinCEN Form 114, *Report of Foreign Bank and Financial Accounts* (FBAR), and discusses how certain taxpayers may decide to use the Offshore Voluntary Disclosure Program (OVDP) developed by the IRS. The chapter also discusses the base erosion and profit shifting (BEPS) project of the Organisation for Economic Cooperation and Development (OECD).

¶ 502 LEARNING OBJECTIVES

Upon completion of this chapter, you will be able to:

- Recognize the differences between the FBAR and FATCA reporting requirements;
- Recognize the civil and criminal penalties associated with noncompliance with the FATCA and FBAR requirements;
- Identify how the OVDP may be used;
- Recognize the differences between the 2014 OVDP and the Streamlined Compliance Process; and
- Identify the Action Plan items of the Organisation for Economic Cooperation and Development's BEPS project.

¶ 503 INTRODUCTION

U.S. persons with foreign financial interests may be subject to various information reporting requirements. A *U.S. person* includes:

- A citizen or resident of the United States;
- A domestic partnership;
- A domestic corporation;
- Any estate (other than a foreign estate); and

- Any trust, if

    - A court within the United States is able to exercise primary supervision over the administration of the trust, and

    - One or more U.S. persons have the authority to control all substantial decisions of the trust (Code Sec. 7701(a)(30) and Reg. § 1.1471-1T(b)(141)(i)).

COMMENT: The terms of FATCA were codified in Code sections 1471 to 1474 and section 6038D.

First, under FATCA, U.S. citizens, resident aliens, and certain nonresident aliens must file information returns using Form 8938, *Statement of Specified Foreign Financial Assets,* with their annual income tax returns for any year in which their interests in specified foreign assets exceed the applicable reporting threshold.

Second, a U.S. person with financial interests in or signature authority over foreign financial accounts generally must file FinCEN Form 114, *Report of Foreign Bank and Financial Accounts* (FBAR) if, at any point during the calendar year, the aggregate value of the accounts exceeds the reporting threshold.

These reporting requirements may often overlap, but they apply separately. Thus, a person who satisfies both the FATCA and the FBAR filing requirements must file both Form 8938 and FinCEN Form 114. Filing one of the forms does not satisfy the filing requirement for the other form.

Different policy considerations apply to Form 8938 and FinCEN Form 114. In addition to tax administration, FBAR reporting is also used for law enforcement purposes. These differences are reflected in the different categories of persons required to file each form, the different filing thresholds, and the different assets and accompanying information required on each form.

¶ 504 FATCA REQUIREMENTS

As discussed above, FATCA mandates that for some taxpayers a report of foreign financial assets be made. Accordingly, *specified persons* who hold an interest in a "specified foreign financial asset" during the tax year must attach to their tax returns a Form 8938, *Statement of Specified Foreign Financial Assets,* to report certain information for each asset if the total value of all such assets exceeds an applicable reporting threshold amount.

This requirement applies to any U.S. citizen and any individual who is resident alien for any part of the tax year. A nonresident alien who makes the election to be treated as a resident alien for purposes of filing a joint return for the tax year must also file Form 8938, as must a nonresident alien who is a bona fide resident of American Samoa or Puerto Rico.

Form 8938 must also be filed by any domestic entity formed or availed for purposes of holding, directly or indirectly, specified foreign financial assets, in the same manner as if the entity were an individual.

> **COMMENT:** Proposed regulations (Proposed Reg. § 1.6038D-6(a)) have designated specified domestic entities subject to the reporting requirement. They include certain closely held domestic corporations or partnerships, as well as certain domestic trusts. Reporting by specified domestic entities, however, will not be required before the date provided in final regulations. (*See* Notice 2013-10.)

Interests

A specified person has an interest in a specified foreign financial asset if any income, gains, losses, deductions, credits, gross proceeds, or distributions from holding or disposing of the asset are or would be required to be reported, included, or otherwise reflected on the specified person's income tax return. The interest exists even if there are no income, gains, losses, deductions, credits, gross proceeds, or distributions from holding or disposing of the asset included or reflected on the taxpayer's income tax return for that tax year (Treas. Reg. § 1.6038D-2(b)(1)).

> **COMMENT:** Therefore, a specified person must file a Form 8938 despite the fact that none of the specified foreign financial assets that must be reported affects his or her tax liability for the year (Treas. Reg. § 1.6038D-2(a)(8)).

STUDY QUESTION

1. Which of the following is *not* a U.S. person potentially subject to FATCA and/or FBAR requirements?

   a. A foreign estate

   b. A domestic corporation

   c. A domestic trust

   d. A holding company for specified foreign financial assets

Specified Foreign Financial Assets

Specified foreign financial assets include:

- Any financial account maintained by a foreign financial institution; and
- Any of the following assets that are not held in an account maintained by a financial institution

   - Any stock or security issued by a person other than a U.S. person (as defined above),

   - Any financial instrument or contract held for investment that has an issuer or counterparty which is other than a United States person, and

   - Interest in a foreign entity (Treas. Reg. § 1.6038D-3(a), (b)).

Financial accounts. The primary type of specified foreign assets is financial accounts maintained by foreign financial institutions. "Financial account" and "foreign financial institution" are generally defined by reference to the Code Sec. 1471 FATCA rules that require withholding from payments to foreign financial institutions. Thus, a *financial account* is any depository or custodial account maintained by a foreign financial institution, as well as any equity or debt interest in a foreign financial institution (other than interests that are regularly traded on an established securities market) (Treas. Reg. § 1.6038D-1(a)(7), (8)).

A *foreign financial institution* (FFI) is generally any financial institution (other than a U.S. entity) that:

- Accepts deposits in the ordinary course of a banking or similar business;
- Holds financial assets for the account of others as a substantial part of its business; or
- Is engaged (or holds itself out as being engaged) primarily in the business of investing, reinvesting, or trading in securities, partnership interests, commodities, or any interest (including a futures or forward contract or option) in such securities, partnership interests, or commodities (Treas. Reg. § 1.1471-5(d)).

However, for purposes of the FATCA reporting requirements for specified persons, a specified foreign financial asset also includes a financial account maintained by a financial institution organized under the laws of a U.S. territory. As a result, such an account is subject to FATCA unless it is owned by a bona fide resident of the relevant U.S. territory.

FATCA also imposes complex reporting requirements for foreign financial institutions. Under Code Sec. 1471, FFIs are required to report to the IRS certain information about financial accounts held by U.S. taxpayers or by foreign entities in which U.S. taxpayers hold substantial ownership interests. If an FFI fails to meet the FATCA requirements, a U.S. withholding agent must deduct and withhold a tax equal to 30 percent on any "withholdable payment" made to the FFI after June 30, 2014, unless the withholding agent can reasonably rely on documentation that the payment is exempt from withholding. No withholding is required, however, if an FFI enters into an agreement with the IRS to provide the required information (participating FFI). An FFI may also be deemed to meet the requirements of the agreement (deemed-compliant FFI). These agreements encourage reporting by U.S. taxpayers. If the taxpayers fail to comply with the reporting requirements themselves, the FFIs will provide the required information directly to the IRS, which can then use that information to target the noncompliant taxpayer (Notice 2014-33).

> **COMMENT:** The FATCA rules apply to the foreign financial account itself. The assets held in the account do not have to be separately reported on Form 8938, because their value is included in the determination of the account's maximum value.

> **COMMENT:** Foreign deposit and custodial accounts are reported on Part I of Form 8938.

Other assets. The following items are also specified foreign assets if they are held for investment, even if they are not held in an account maintained by a foreign financial institution:

- Any stock or security issued by a person other than a U.S. person;
- Any financial instrument or contract held for investment that has an issuer or counterparty that is not a U.S. person; and
- Any interest in a foreign entity (Treas. Reg. § 1.6038D-3(b)(1)).

> **COMMENT:** The other assets categories are broad and may sometimes overlap, so a single asset may fall into more than one category, for example, stock issued by a foreign corporation is stock that is issued by a person other than a U.S. person and is also an interest in a foreign entity.

> **COMMENT:** The IRS has stated that an interest in a social security, social insurance, or other similar program of a foreign government is not a specified foreign financial asset.

Examples of assets other than financial accounts that may be considered *other specified foreign financial assets* include, but are not limited to:

- Stock issued by a foreign corporation;
- A capital or profits interest in a foreign partnership;
- A note, bond, debenture, or other form of indebtedness issued by a foreign person;
- An interest in a foreign trust;
- An interest rate swap, currency swap, basis swap, interest rate cap, interest rate floor, commodity swap, equity swap, equity index swap, credit default swap, or similar agreement with a foreign counterparty; and

¶504

- Any option or other derivative instrument with respect to any of the items listed as examples in this paragraph or with respect to any currency or commodity that is entered into with a foreign counterparty or issuer (Treas. Reg. § 1.6038D-3(d)).

   COMMENT: Specified foreign financial assets that are not held in deposit and custodial accounts are reported on Part II of Form 8938.

Exceptions. Exceptions to the reporting requirements apply to particular types of foreign financial assets, as well as assets subject to duplicative reporting, assets held by certain types of trusts, and assets held by certain bona fide residents of U.S. possessions.

The following types of assets are not specified foreign financial assets and, therefore, do not have to be reported on Form 8938:

- A financial account (including the assets held in it) that is maintained by a U.S. payer, such as a domestic financial institution. In general, a U.S. payer also includes a domestic branch of a foreign bank or foreign insurance company and a foreign branch or foreign subsidiary of a U.S. financial institution, if subject to the same tax and reporting rules as the U.S. payer;

- A financial account (including the assets held in it) that is maintained by a dealer or trader in securities or commodities, if all of the holdings in the account are subject to the mark-to-market accounting rules for dealers in securities, or a mark-to-market election is made for all of the holdings in the account; and

- Any other financial asset, if the asset is subject to the mark-to-market accounting rules for dealers in securities or commodities or a mark-to-market election is made for the asset (Treas. Reg. § 1.6038D-3(b)).

The rules intend to limit duplicative reporting and provide that specified foreign financial assets do not have to be reported on Form 8938 if they are properly reported on any of the following timely filed forms for the same tax year:

- Form 3520, Annual Return to Report Transactions with Foreign Trusts and Receipt of Certain Foreign Gifts;

- Form 5471, Information Return of U.S. Persons with Respect to Certain Foreign Corporations;

- Form 8621, Information Return by a Shareholder of a Passive Foreign Investment Company or Qualified Electing Fund; and

- Form 8865, Return of U.S. Persons with Respect to Certain Foreign Partnerships (Treas. Reg. § 1.6038D-7(a)(1)).

   COMMENT: The specified person's Form 8938 must identify these other form(s) that reported the specified foreign financial asset and report how many of these forms were filed.

   COMMENT: The value of assets reported on these duplicative forms must be included in determining whether the specified person satisfies the application reporting threshold.

If the grantor trust rules treat a specified person as the owner of one of these trusts or a portion of the trust for income tax purposes, the following assets held by trust (or the owned portion) do not have to be reported on the specified person's Form 8938:

- A domestic trust that is a widely held fixed investment trust;

- A domestic trust that is a liquidating trust created under a court order in a chapter 7 or chapter 11 bankruptcy; or

- A foreign trust, if

  - The specified person reports the trust on a Form 3520 timely filed with the IRS for the tax year,

  - The trust timely files Form 3520-A, Annual Information Return of Foreign Trust With a U.S. Owner, with the IRS, and

  - The specified person's Form 8938 reports the filing of the Form 3520 and Form 3520-A (Treas. Reg. § 1.6038D-7(b)).

Additionally, bona fide residents of U.S. possessions (American Samoa, Guam, the Northern Mariana Islands, Puerto Rico, or the U.S. Virgin Islands) who must file Form 8938 do not have to report the following specified foreign financial assets:

- A financial account maintained by a financial institution organized under the laws of the U.S. possession where the specified person is a bona fide resident;

- A financial account maintained by a branch of a financial institution not organized under the laws of the U.S. possession where the specified person is a bona fide resident, if the branch is subject to the same tax and information reporting requirements that apply to a financial institution organized under the laws of the U.S. possession;

- Stock or securities issued by an entity organized under the laws of the U.S. possession where the specified person is a bona fide resident;

- An interest in an entity organized under the laws of the U.S. possession where the specified person is a bona fide resident;

- A financial instrument or contract held for investment, provided each issuer or counterparty that is not a U.S. person either is an entity organized under the laws of the U.S. possession where the specified person is a bona fide resident or is a bona fide resident of that U.S. possession (Treas. Reg. § 1.6038D-7(c)).

Nonvested property. A specified person who receives nonvested interests in property in connection with the performance of personal services does not need to report those interests until they are substantially vested. However, if the specified person makes a valid election under Code Sec. 83(b) (Election to Include in Gross Income in Year of Transfer), he or she is considered to have an interest in the property on the date of transfer, giving rise to a reporting obligation under Code Sec. 6038D.

STUDY QUESTION

---

2. Which of the following is *not* a reportable specified foreign financial asset?

   a. A financial account maintained by a financial institution organized under U.S. territorial law

   b. A currency swap with a foreign counterparty

   c. Stock issued by an entity under the laws of Guam owned by a bona fide resident there

   d. Any interest in a foreign entity

Reporting Threshold

The FATCA requirements apply when:

- A specified person is required to file an annual return; and

- The aggregate value of the specified person's specified foreign assets exceeds the applicable threshold.

¶504

The applicable reporting thresholds for specified foreign financial assets are shown in Table 1.

Table 1. Reporting Thresholds for Application of FATCA Requirements

Taxpayer Type	Threshold Amount on Last Day of Year Exceeding	or	Threshold Amount at Any Time During the Year Exceeding
Unmarried (or married filing separately) and living in United States	$50,000		$75,000
Joint filers living in United States	$100,000		$150,000
Single (or married filing separately) filers living abroad	$200,000		$300,000
Joint filers living abroad	$400,000		$600,000

These thresholds are not adjusted for inflation (Treas. Reg. § 1.6038D-2(a)(1) through (4)).

> **COMMENT:** The statute requires reporting only when an individual's specified foreign financial assets exceed the threshold dollar amounts (for example $50,000 on the last day of the tax year for unmarried taxpayers). However, the IRS can prescribe a higher dollar amount for the reporting threshold, which was done in T.D. 9567, which increased the reporting threshold for specified individuals who are qualified individuals under Code Sec. 911(d).

> **COMMENT:** Taxpayers generally must include the value of all of their specified foreign financial assets, even if they are also reported on another form.

Valuation. Once the reporting threshold is triggered, specified persons must report the maximum value during the tax year of each specified foreign financial asset reported on Form 8938. Account assets are generally valued at their fair market value (FMV). Thus, the maximum value of a specified foreign financial asset is generally equal to a reasonable estimate of the asset's highest FMV during the tax year. If this amount is less than zero, such as in the case of a foreign mortgage, the value of the asset is treated as zero for the purposes of determining the aggregate value and the maximum value of the specified person's specified foreign financial assets. All values must be determined and reported in U.S. dollars (Treas. Reg. § 1.6038D-5(b)).

Financial accounts. The value of assets held in a financial account maintained by an FFI is included in determining the value of that financial account. A specified person may rely upon periodic account statements provided at least annually to determine a financial account's maximum value, unless the specified person has actual knowledge or reason to know (based on readily accessible information) that the statements do not reflect a reasonable estimate of the maximum account value during the tax year (Treas. Reg. § 1.6038D-5(d)).

> **COMMENT:** The value of particular assets held in a financial account does not have to be separately reported on Form 8938 because that value is included in the value of the account itself.

Other assets. The maximum value of a specified foreign asset that is not held in a financial account maintained by an FFI is generally equal to the value of the asset as of the last day of the tax year. However, this general rule does not apply to a specified person with actual knowledge or reason to know, based on readily accessible information, that the FMV determined as of the last day of the tax year does not reflect a reasonable estimate of the maximum value of the asset during the year—for example, because there is a reason to know that the asset's value declined significantly during the year (Treas. Reg. § 1.6038D-5(c)(4)).

¶504

An interest in a foreign pension or deferred compensation plan is reported if the value of the specified foreign financial assets is greater than the reporting threshold that applies. In general, the value of an interest in the foreign pension plan or deferred compensation plan is the FMV of the taxpayer's beneficial interest in the plan on the last day of the year. However, if the taxpayer does not know or have reason to know based on readily accessible information the FMV of his or her beneficial interest in the pension or deferred compensation plan on the last day of the year, the maximum value is the value of the cash and/or other property distributed to the taxpayer during the year. This same value is used in determining whether the reporting threshold has been met (Treas. Reg. § 1.6038D-5(f)(3)).

> **EXAMPLE:** James Chatley, an individual taxpayer, has publicly traded foreign stock not held in a financial account, with a fair market value as of the last day of the tax year of $100,000. However, based on daily price information that is readily available, the 52-week high trading price for the stock results in a maximum value of the stock during the tax year of $150,000. If James satisfies the applicable reporting threshold, he must report the maximum value of the foreign stock as $150,000, based on readily available information of the stock's maximum value during the tax year.

Trusts. If the specified person is a beneficiary of a foreign trust, the maximum value of the specified person's interest in the trust is the sum of the FMV, determined as of the last day of the tax year, of all of the currency or other property distributed from the foreign trust during the tax year to the specified person as a beneficiary; plus the value as of the last day of the tax year of the specified person's right as a beneficiary to receive mandatory distributions from the foreign trust. This amount is also used to determine the aggregate value of the specified person's specified foreign financial assets, if the specified person does not know or have reason to know based on readily accessible information the FMV of his or her interest in a foreign trust during the tax year (Treas. Reg. § 1.6038D-5(f)(2)).

Estates, pension plans, and deferred compensation plans. The maximum value of a specified person's interest in a foreign estate, foreign pension plan, or a foreign deferred compensation plan is the FMV, determined as of the last day of the tax year, of the specified person's beneficial interest in the assets of the estate, pension plan, or deferred compensation plan. If the specified person does not know or have reason to know (based on readily accessible information) that value, then the maximum value to be reported, and the value to be included in determining the aggregate value of the specified foreign financial assets, is the FMV, determined as of the last day of the tax year, of the currency and other property distributed during the tax year to the specified person as a beneficiary or participant. If the specified person received no distributions during the tax year and does not know or have reason to know (based on readily accessible information) the FMV of the interest as of the last day of the tax year, the maximum value of the asset is equal to the amount of currency or property distributed to the beneficiary or participant during the taxable year (i.e., zero if no distributions are made) (Treas. Reg. § 1.6038D-5(f)(3)).

Jointly owned interests. The treatment of jointly owned interests depends on the specified person's relationship to the other owner. If the owners are married to each other and one spouse is not a specified person, each spouse includes the entire value of the jointly owned asset to determine the total value of his or her specified foreign financial assets.

If both owners are spouses who file jointly (and, therefore, file a single Form 8938), the total value of the jointly owned asset is taken into account only once in determining the total value of the couple's specified foreign financial assets. If the spouses also file

Form 8814, *Parents' Election to Report Child's Interest and Dividends,* to include a child's unearned income on their own return, they also must include the maximum value of the child's specified foreign financial assets in the calculation of their own specified foreign financial assets (Treas. Reg. § 1.6038D-2(b)(3)).

If both owners are spouses who do not file jointly, each includes one-half of the value of the jointly owned assets in his or her own specified foreign financial assets. A spouse who files Form 8814 to include a child's unearned income on his or her own return must include the maximum value of the child's specified foreign financial assets in his or her own specified foreign financial assets.

If the owners are not married to each other, each owner includes the entire value of the jointly owned asset to determine the total value of his or her specified foreign financial assets.

Foreign currency. As mentioned above, all values must be determined and reported in U.S. dollars. The value of a specified foreign financial asset that is denominated in a foreign currency is first determined in the foreign currency prior to conversion into U.S. dollars (that is, independently of exchange rate fluctuations during the year). The asset's foreign currency value is then converted into U.S. dollars at the tax year-end spot rate for converting the foreign currency into U.S. dollars (that is, the rate to purchase U.S. dollars). The U.S. Treasury Department's Financial Management Service foreign currency exchange rate is used to convert the value of a specified foreign financial asset into U.S. dollars. If no such rate is available, another publicly available foreign currency exchange rate may be used to determine an asset's maximum value, but the use of such rate must be disclosed on Form 8938.

STUDY QUESTION

3. Co-owners of a jointly owned interest should list the entire value of the interest on Form 8938 *unless* they are:

    a. Married filing separately

    b. Owners not married to each other

    c. Co-owners who are a parent and minor child using Form 8814

    d. Married owners when one spouse is not a specified person

Penalties

Failure to disclose. A $10,000 penalty applies to any failure to properly furnish the required information. If the failure is not corrected within 90 days after the IRS mails notice of it to the taxpayer, an additional $10,000 penalty applies for each 30-day period (or portion thereof) in which the failure continues after that 90-day period expires. This additional penalty with respect to any failure is limited to $50,000. Married taxpayers who file a joint return are treated as one taxpayer for purposes of the penalty, and their liability for the penalty is joint and several (Treas. Reg. § 1.6038D-8(a), (b), (c)).

For purposes of assessing the penalty, if an individual with multiple financial assets does not provide sufficient information to determine their aggregate value, the IRS presumes that the aggregate value exceeds the reporting threshold. In other words, the IRS presumes that the individual was required to file Form 8938 and, therefore, is liable for penalties for failing to do so (Treas. Reg. § 1.6038D-8(d)).

The penalty is not imposed on any specified person that can show that the failure is due to reasonable cause and not willful neglect. The determination of whether a failure to disclose a specified foreign financial asset on Form 8938 was due to reasonable cause and not due to willful neglect is made on a case-by-case basis, taking into account all pertinent facts and circumstances. The specified person must make an affirmative showing of all the facts alleged as reasonable cause for the failure to disclose (Treas. Reg. § 1.6038D-8(e)).

Accuracy-related penalty. A 40 percent accuracy-related penalty applies to underpayments attributable to transactions involving undisclosed foreign financial assets. *Undisclosed foreign financial assets* are foreign financial assets that are subject to information reporting under various provisions, but for which the required information was not provided by the taxpayer (Treas. Reg. § 1.6038D-8(f)).

Limitations. Reporting failures can also affect the limitations period for assessments. The statute of limitations on tax assessment does not begin to run until the taxpayer provides the required information. In addition, although the IRS normally has a *maximum* of three years to assess tax, it has a *minimum* of three years to assess tax arising from improperly reported specified foreign financial assets. These rules generally apply to the taxpayer's entire tax liability; however, if the taxpayer has reasonable cause for the reporting failures, these rules apply only to items related to the unreported specified foreign financial assets.

Finally, the normal three-year limitations period for assessments is extended to six years for any substantial omission of gross income in excess of $5,000 that is attributable to a specified foreign financial asset. This extension applies even if the taxpayer's specified foreign financial assets:

- Are properly reported;
- Fall below the reporting threshold; or
- Are included in classes of assets that the IRS has excepted from the reporting requirements.

STUDY QUESTION

---

4. The IRS statute of limitations for assessments may *not* be extended if:

    a. The assets that increase gross income more than $5,000 fall in the classes of excepted assets

    b. The specified foreign financial assets with values of more than $5,000 are properly reported

    c. The omitted income amount in question is less than $5,000

    d. The value of the specified foreign financial assets that increase gross income by more than $5,000 falls below the reporting threshold

---

¶ 505 FBAR REQUIREMENTS

Under the terms of the FBAR requirements, a U.S. person with financial interests in or signature authority over foreign financial accounts generally must file FinCEN Form 114, *Report of Foreign Bank and Financial Accounts* (FBAR) if, at any point during the calendar year, the aggregate value of the accounts exceeds the reporting threshold of $10,000. Under terms of the *Bank Secrecy Act* (BSA), FBARs must be electronically filed through the BSA e-filing system for each calendar year on or before June 30 of the succeeding year. The June 30 deadline may not be extended.

Those subject to FBAR reporting are:

- U.S. citizens;
- Resident aliens; and
- Entities created, organized, or formed under U.S. laws, including, but not limited to
  - Domestic corporations,
  - Partnerships,
  - Limited liability companies (LLCs),
  - Trusts, and
  - Estates.

The federal tax treatment of a person or entity does not determine whether an FBAR filing is required.

> **COMMENT:** An entity disregarded for federal tax purposes must still file an FBAR if filing is otherwise required.

> **EXAMPLE:** FBARs are required under Title 31 and not under any provisions of the Internal Revenue Code. Thus, a single-member LLC, which is a disregarded entity for U.S. tax purposes, must file an FBAR if one is otherwise required.

Interest

A U.S. person can have a financial interest in a foreign account in three situations.

Owner of record or the holder of legal title. A U.S. person has a financial interest in each bank, securities, or other financial account in a foreign country for which that person is the owner of record or holds legal title, regardless of whether the account is maintained for that person's own benefit or for the benefit of others. If an account is maintained in the name of more than one person, each U.S. person in whose name the account is maintained has a financial interest in that account.

Constructive owner. A U.S. person has a financial interest in each bank, securities, or other financial account in a foreign country if the owner of record or holder of legal title is a person acting on behalf of the U.S. person, such as an attorney, agent, or nominee with respect to the account.

Deemed owner. A U.S. person is deemed to have a financial interest in a bank, securities, or other financial account in a foreign country if the owner of record of holder of legal title is:

- A corporation in which the U.S. person owns, directly or indirectly, more than 50 percent of the voting power or the total value of the shares;
- A partnership in which the U.S. person owns, directly or indirectly, more than 50 percent of the profits or capital interest;
- Any other entity, other than a trust, in which the U.S. person owns, directly or indirectly, more than 50 percent of the voting power, total value of the equity interest or assets, or profits interest;
- A trust, if the U.S. person is the trust grantor and has an ownership interest for U.S. federal tax purposes; or
- A trust, if the U.S. person
  - Has a present beneficial interest in more than 50 percent of the assets, or
  - Receives more than 50 percent of the trust's current income (based on the calendar year).

However, a U.S. person does not have a financial interest in a discretionary trust merely because of the person's status as a discretionary beneficiary. Similarly, a remainder interest in a trust is not a present beneficial interest in the trust.

Signature Authority

Qualification of an individual. An individual has *signature or other authority* over an account if the individual has the authority, alone or in conjunction with another, to control the disposition of money, funds, or other assets held in a financial account by direct communication, written or otherwise, to the person with whom the financial account is maintained. An individual also has signature or other authority over an account if the FFI will act upon a direct communication from that individual regarding the disposition of assets in that account. Additionally, an individual has signature or other authority in conjunction with another if the FFI requires a direct communication from more than one individual regarding the disposition of assets in the account.

Exceptions. Exceptions to the FBAR requirements apply to officers and employees of financial institutions that have a federal functional regulator, certain entities that are publicly traded on a U.S. national securities exchange, and certain entities that are otherwise required to register their equity securities with the Securities and Exchange Commission (SEC). These exceptions apply, however, only when the officer or employee has no financial interest in the reportable account.

The exceptions to the FBAR requirements include:

- Bank officers and employees need not report that they have signature or other authority over a foreign financial account if

   - The account is owned or maintained by the bank,

   - The officer or employee has no financial interest in the account, and

   - The bank is examined by the Office of the Comptroller of the Currency, the Board of Governors of the Federal Reserve System, the Federal Deposit Insurance Corporation, the Office of Thrift Supervision, or the National Credit Union Administration;

- Officers and employees of a financial institution that is registered with and examined by the SEC or Commodity Futures Trading Commission (CFTC) need not report that they have signature or other authority over a foreign financial account if

   - The account is owned or maintained by the financial institution, and

   - The officer or employee has no financial interest in the account;

- Officers and employees of an authorized service provider (ASP) need not report that they have signature or other authority over a foreign financial account if

   - The account is owned or maintained by an investment company that is registered with the SEC, and

   - The officer or employee has no financial interest in the account. An ASP is an SEC-registered entity that provides services to a regulated investment company (RIC). Because mutual funds do not have employees of their own, they can use ASPs, such as investment advisors, to conduct their day-to-day operations. Thus, this exception can apply to persons who do not qualify for the exception for RICs, discussed above, but it is limited to the reportable accounts of RICs that are managed by the ASP;

- Officers and employees of an entity with a class of equity securities (or American depository receipts) listed on any U.S. national securities exchange need not report their signature or other authority over the entity's foreign financial accounts if the officer or employee has no financial interest in the accounts. This exception also applies if the American depository receipts are listed on the designated offshore market. In addition, if the entity is a U.S. entity, the officers and employees of any U.S. subsidiary need not report that they have signature or other authority over a foreign financial account of the subsidiary if

- The officer or employee has no financial interest in the account, and

- The U.S. subsidiary is named in a consolidated FBAR filed by the parent; and

- Officers and employees of an entity that has a class of equity securities (or American depository receipts in respect of equity securities) registered under Section 12(g) of the *Securities Exchange Act* need not report their signature or other authority over the entity's foreign financial accounts if the officer or employee has no financial interest in the accounts. This exception applies when corporations must register their stock with the SEC and comply with related reporting requirements because of their size in terms of assets and shareholders (currently more than $10 million in assets and more than 500 shareholders of record).

Accounts

An *account* is a formal relationship with a person to provide regular services, dealings, and other financial transactions. The length of the time the service is provided does not affect the fact that a formal account relationship has been established. For example, an escrow arrangement can qualify as an account, even if it exists for only a short period of time. However, an account is not established simply by conducting transactions like wiring money or purchasing a money order.

Bank accounts, securities accounts, and other financial accounts are all reportable accounts. *Bank accounts* include savings deposit, demand deposit, checking, and other accounts maintained with persons engaged in a banking business. This includes time deposits such as certificate of deposit accounts (CDs) that allow individuals to deposit funds with a banking institution and redeem the initial amount (along with interest earned) after a prescribed period of time. *Securities accounts* are accounts with persons engaged in the business of buying, selling, holding, or trading stock or other securities.

Other financial accounts include:

- Accounts with persons in the business of accepting deposits as a financial agency;

- Insurance or annuity policies with cash value;

- Accounts with persons who act as brokers or dealers for futures or options transactions in commodities that are on or subject to the rules of a commodity exchange or association;

- Accounts with mutual funds or similar pooled funds that issue shares that are available to the general public and have a regular net asset value determination and regular redemptions; and

- Other investment funds.

   COMMENT: The inclusion of "accounts with persons in the business of accepting deposits as a financial agency" is intended to ensure that deposit accounts and similar arrangements are covered by the reporting requirements, despite international differences in terminology, financial institution operations, and legal frameworks.

¶505

COMMENT: When a reportable account is an insurance policy with cash value, the owner of the policy, not the beneficiary, is responsible for filing the FBAR.

COMMENT: A federal district court (**U.S. v. J.C. Hom,** DC Calif., 2014-1 USTC ¶ 50,307) has held that because foreign poker websites functioned for a U.S. poker player as banks, his online accounts with them were reportable.

Exceptions. Certain accounts are specifically exempted from the reporting requirements. For example, no reporting is required with respect to correspondent accounts that are maintained by banks and used solely for bank-to-bank settlements.

Several other types of accounts are excluded from the reporting requirements based on the governmental status and functions of the entities and agencies involved.

The reporting requirements do not apply to:

- Accounts of an international financial institution that includes the United States as a member;
- Accounts in a U.S. military banking facility or U.S. military finance facility operated by a U.S. financial institution designated by the U.S. government to serve U.S. government installations abroad;
- Accounts of a department or agency of the United States, an Indian tribe, or any state or its political subdivisions, or a wholly owned entity, agency or instrumentality of any of the foregoing, including

  - An employee retirement or welfare benefit plan of a governmental entity, and

  - A college or university that is an agency of, an instrumentality of, owned by, or operated by a governmental entity; and

- Accounts of an entity that is established under the laws of, and exercises governmental authority on behalf of, the United States, an Indian tribe, any state or its political subdivision, or any intergovernmental compact among states and/or Indian tribes. An entity generally exercises governmental authority only if it has taxing, police, and/or eminent domain powers.

Foreign accounts. A *foreign country* is any area outside the geographical boundaries of the United States; and a *foreign financial account* is a reportable account located outside the United States. For instance, an account with a U.S. bank is a foreign financial account if it is maintained in a branch of the bank that is physically located outside the United States. Conversely, an account with a foreign bank is not a foreign account if it is maintained in a bank branch that is physically located in the United States. The mere fact that an account may contain holdings or assets of foreign entities does not mean the account is foreign, as long as the account is maintained with a financial institution in the United States.

EXAMPLE: Joshua Bloom, a U.S. citizen, has an account with a securities broker located in New York. He occasionally uses this account to purchase securities of foreign companies. Because Joshua maintains his securities account with a financial institution in the United States, the account is not a foreign account even though it contains foreign securities.

COMMENT: A federal district court (**U.S, v. J.C. Hom,** DC Calif., 2014-1 USTC ¶ 50,307) has held that digital online accounts with poker websites were located in the foreign countries where the websites that created and managed the accounts were located, not the geographic location of the funds. Thus, it was irrelevant where the poker websites opened their own accounts.

¶505

In an omnibus account, a U.S. institution acts as the global custodian for a U.S. person's foreign assets, and creates pooled cash and securities accounts in the non-U.S. market to hold assets for multiple investors. The omnibus account is in the name of the global custodian. When the U.S. person has no legal right to the account and cannot directly reach the foreign assets in it, the U.S. person is treated as maintaining an account with a financial institution located in the United States.

An omnibus account with a financial institution located in the United States is not a reportable foreign account if the U.S. person:

- Does not have any legal right to the account; and

- Can access foreign holdings in the account only through the U.S. institution.

> **COMMENT:** A custodial arrangement that permits the U.S. person to have direct access to foreign assets maintained at a foreign institution is a reportable foreign financial account.

Valuation

An account's maximum value is a reasonable approximation of the greatest value of currency or nonmonetary assets in the account during the year. Periodic account statements can establish the maximum value of an account, as long as the statements fairly reflect that value during the calendar year. This includes a statement that provides the account value at the end of the statement period, as long as it is a bona fide statement prepared in the ordinary course of business.

Account value is determined in the currency of the account. Any value stated in foreign currency must be translated into U.S. currency by using the Treasury's Financial Management Service Rate from the last day of the calendar year. If no such rate is available, the FBAR filer must use another verifiable exchange rate and identify its source. If the currency is of a country that uses multiple exchange rates, the filer must use the one that would apply if the currency in the account were converted into U.S. dollars on the last day of the calendar year.

Penalties

The civil penalty for *willfully* failing to file an FBAR may be as high as the greater of $100,000 or 50 percent of the total balance of the foreign account per violation. *Nonwillful* violations that the IRS determines were not due to reasonable cause are subject to a $10,000 penalty per violation.

The criminal penalties are also harsh. For example, a person who fails to file a tax return is subject to a prison term of up to one year and a fine of up to $100,000. Willfully failing to file an FBAR and willfully filing a false FBAR are both violations that are subject to criminal penalties under U.S. tax law.

Possible criminal charges related to tax matters include tax evasion (Code Sec. 7201), filing a false return (Code Sec. 7206(1)), and failure to file an income tax return (Code Sec. 7203). Willfully failing to file an FBAR and willfully filing a false FBAR are both violations that are subject to criminal penalties under 31 U.S.C. § 5322. Additional possible criminal charges include conspiracy to defraud the government with respect to claims (18 U.S.C. § 286) and conspiracy to commit offense or to defraud the United States (18 U.S.C. § 371).

Table 2 summarizes penalties associated with the criminal charges under FBAR requirements.

Table 2. Comparative Prison Terms and Fines for Violating Tax Laws and FBAR Requirements

Violation	Maximum Prison Term	Maximum Fine
Tax evasion	5 years	$250,000
Filing false return	3 years	$250,000
Failing to file an FBAR	10 years	$500,000
Conspiracy to defraud government for claims	10 years	$250,000
Defrauding government	5 years	$250,000

STUDY QUESTION

5. Which individual violation of the tax reporting laws potentially carries the highest maximum fine?

    a. Tax evasion

    b. Filing a false return

    c. Failing to file an FBAR

    d. Defrauding the government

¶ 506 OFFSHORE VOLUNTARY DISCLOSURE PROGRAM

Taxpayers who have failed to previously to report their taxable income—including failing to disclose their interests in foreign accounts (and failing to file the applicable FBARs)—but who have not been contacted by the IRS may consider filing delinquent or amended income tax returns or otherwise notifying the IRS of the reason for their noncompliance.

Historically, voluntary disclosure programs were put in place by the IRS in order to give those taxpayers who had not been fully compliant a method of coming forward without fear of criminal prosecution. The theory behind the voluntary disclosure programs makes sense as it would be impossible for the IRS to catch every taxpayer who is noncompliant; the better approach is to entice them to come forward voluntarily. Their incentive, as stated, is no criminal prosecution and perhaps a promise of reduced taxes and related penalties/interest if the noncompliant taxpayer agrees to come forward and file all delinquent returns.

2014 Offshore Voluntary Disclosure Program

For 2015, it appears the IRS is again offering an Offshore Voluntary Disclosure Program (OVDP). The objective remains the same as the with previous OVDPs from 2009, 2010, 2012, and 2014, which is to bring taxpayers that have used undisclosed foreign accounts and undisclosed foreign entities to avoid or evade tax into compliance with the U.S. tax laws. The 2012 OVDP established a procedure to encourage U.S. taxpayers to come forward and avoid criminal prosecution while agreeing to provide detailed information about their offshore assets and activities; file corrected tax forms; and pay tax, interest, and penalties under a specified framework. The 2014 OVDP is a continuation of that program. The 2014 OVDP has no set deadlines; however, taxpayers must be aware that the terms of the program can change at any time. The IRS has disclosed that since the launch of the first program more than 45,000 taxpayers have become compliant voluntarily, paying about $6.5 billion in taxes, interest, and penalties.

Because the purpose of the 2014 OVDP is to provide a way for taxpayers who did not report taxable income in the past to come forward voluntarily and resolve their tax matters, a taxpayer who has properly reported all of his or her taxable income but not filed FBARs is not eligible for the 2014 OVDP. These taxpayers should consider making a quiet disclosure by filing their FBARs and may follow the delinquent FBAR submission procedures provided by the IRS on its website. The IRS will not impose a penalty for the failure to file the delinquent FBARs if the taxpayer properly reported on U.S. tax returns, and paid all tax on, the income from the foreign financial accounts reported on the delinquent FBARs, and the taxpayer had not previously been contacted regarding an income tax examination or a request for delinquent returns for the years for which the delinquent FBARs are submitted.

Voluntary disclosure is required to be complete, accurate, and truthful. Consequently, in addition to disclosing all items relating to foreign financial accounts, OVDP submissions must correct any previously unreported income from domestic sources; inappropriate deductions or credits claimed; or other incomplete, inaccurate, or untruthful items on the originally filed returns. The offshore penalty structure only resolves liabilities and penalties related to offshore noncompliance. Domestic portions of a voluntary disclosure are subject to examination.

The 2014 OVDP penalty framework requires participants to:

- Provide all required documents;
- File both amended returns (or original tax returns if delinquent) and FBARs for the past eight years;
- Pay the appropriate tax and interest;
- Pay a 20 percent accuracy-related penalty on such tax;
- Cooperate in the voluntary disclosure process, including

   - Providing information on foreign accounts and assets, institutions, and facilitators, and

   - Assigning agreements to extend the period of time for assessing Title 26 liabilities and FBAR penalties;

- Pay a failure-to-file penalty and/or failure-to-pay penalty, if applicable; and
- Pay, in lieu of all other penalties that may apply to the undisclosed foreign accounts, assets and entities, including FBAR and offshore-related information return penalties and tax liabilities for years prior to the voluntary disclosure period, a miscellaneous Title 26 offshore penalty equal to 27.5 percent (or 50 percent in some circumstances) of the highest aggregate value of OVDP assets as defined (in FAQ 35) during the period covered by the voluntary disclosure.

Beginning on August 4, 2014, the 27.5 percent offshore penalty percentage has been increased to 50 percent if, before the taxpayer's OVDP preclearance request is submitted, it becomes public that a financial institution where the taxpayer holds an account or another party facilitating the taxpayer's offshore arrangement is under investigation by the IRS or the Department of Justice (DOJ).

In fact, the IRS has pointed out that, balanced against the modified OVDP program, the government change will bolster its continued effort to combat the misuse of offshore assets. Working closely with the DOJ, the IRS will continue to investigate FFIs that may have assisted US taxpayers in avoiding their tax filing and payment obligations, whereas, on July 1, 2014, the new information reporting regime resulting from

¶506

FATCA went into effect, and FFIs will begin to report to the IRS the foreign accounts held by U.S. persons.

Streamlined Procedure. Effective as of September 1, 2012, a special procedure for U.S. citizens living abroad was put into place, known as "Streamlined Procedure." The procedure was launched with the objective of bringing U.S. citizens living overseas into compliance with tax obligations. This procedure was only applicable to U.S. taxpayers living abroad who represent a low risk of tax evasion ($1,500 liability threshold) and who have not filed tax returns since 2009.

In 2014, the streamlined filing compliance procedures were expanded to include U.S. taxpayers whose failure to disclose their offshore assets was "nonwillful." To participate in the Streamlined Procedure, taxpayers must now certify that previous failures to comply were due to nonwillful conduct. The low-risk threshold, as well as the $1,500 liability threshold, is no longer required.

The expanded streamlined procedures are available to a greater number of U.S. taxpayers living outside the United States who have unreported foreign financial accounts and, for the first time, to certain American taxpayers residing in the United States. Taxpayers who choose the Streamlined Procedure must file information returns for the last three years (and six years of FBARs) as well as the payment of income tax and interest for each such tax year.

For eligible American taxpayers residing outside the United States, all penalties are to be waived. For eligible U.S. taxpayers residing in the United States, the only penalty will be a miscellaneous offshore penalty equal to 5 percent of the foreign financial assets that gave rise to the tax compliance issue.

STUDY QUESTION

6. A change in the Streamlined Procedure for tax compliance in 2014 was:

   a. Eliminating all penalties for U.S. taxpayers currently living in the United States

   b. Replacing the "low risk" of tax evasion requirement with "nonwillful" failure to disclose offshore assets

   c. Narrowing the scope of the procedure so it applies to fewer taxpayers

   d. Raising the amount of liability threshold for eligibility

¶ 507 BEPS PROJECT

The Organisation for Economic Cooperation and Development (OECD) originated in 1960 when 18 European countries plus the United States and Canada joined forces to create an organization dedicated to economic development. Currently, 34 member countries worldwide regularly turn to one another to identify problems, discuss and analyze them, and promote policies to solve them.

The OECD base erosion and profit shifting (BEPS) project came into being on February 12, 2013, when the OECD's first formal report on the subject, "Addressing Base Erosion and Profit Shifting," was published. It was noted in that report that due to imperfect interaction between nations' tax regimes, multinationals had been permitted to legitimately structure their tax affairs using profit-shifting arrangements to pay minimal rates of tax, limiting their exposure to corporate tax rates as high as 30 percent, faced by fiscally immobile businesses in some OECD member states. The report was for all intents and purposes a call for the world's governments to come together and tackle the issue of aggressive corporate tax avoidance once and for all.

In July 2013, the OECD released the BEPS Action Plan, consisting of 15 specific actions designed to give governments the domestic and international mechanisms to effectively close loopholes in the international tax system. They included:

- Action 1: Address the challenges of the digital economy
- Action 2: Neutralize the effects of hybrid mismatch arrangements
- Action 3: Strengthen controlled foreign company rules
- Action 4: Limit base erosion via interest deductions and other financial payments
- Action 5: Counter harmful tax practices more effectively, taking into account transparency and substance
- Action 6: Prevent treaty abuse
- Action 7: Prevent the artificial avoidance of PE status
- Action 8: Assure that transfer pricing outcomes are in line with value creation/ intangibles
- Action 9: Assure that transfer pricing outcomes are in line with value creation/ risks and capital
- Action 10: Assure that transfer pricing outcomes are in line with value creation/ other high-risk transactions
- Action 11: Establish methodologies to collect and analyze data on BEPS and the actions to address it
- Action 12: Require taxpayers to disclose their aggressive tax planning arrangements
- Action 13: Re-examine transfer pricing documentation
- Action 14: Make dispute resolution mechanisms more effective
- Action 15: Develop a multilateral instrument

This then called for the delivery of seven actions by September 2014 and included proposals regarding Action 1, Action 2, Action 5, Action 6, Action 8, Action 13, and Action 15. The September 2014 BEPS "outputs," as the OECD termed these series of reports, were delivered in an interim form and, while agreed to, were not finalized as they may be impacted by some of the decisions to be taken with respect to the 2015 "deliverables," with which they interact. It is intended that the 2014 outputs will be consolidated with the remaining 2015 deliverables to ensure a coherent package, scheduled to be delivered to the G20 Finance Ministers in October 2015, together with a plan for follow-up work and a timetable for their implementation.

The 2015 deliverables include measures regarding Action 3, Action 4, Action 7, Action 9, Action 10, Action 11, Action 12, and Action 14.

In February 2015, OECD and G20 countries agreed on three key elements that will enable implementation of the BEPS project, including:

- A mandate to launch negotiations on a multilateral instrument to streamline implementation of tax treaty-related BEPS measures (Action 15);
- An implementation package for country-by-country reporting in 2016 and a related government-to-government exchange mechanism to start in 2017 (Action 13); and
- Criteria to assess whether preferential treatment regimes for intellectual property (patent boxes) are harmful or not (Action 5).

If the BEPS project is to be successful, the recommendations will have to be implemented in all countries, not just the advanced economies that are members of the

OECD. The problem is that many emerging and developing economies lack the resources and technical and administrative capacity to make the necessary changes. So-called toolkits have been developed by the OECD to assist developing economies to implement BEPS action items, in cooperation with other international bodies and regional tax organizations. These toolkits contain reports, guidance, model legislation, "train the trainers" materials, and other tools to support capacity building.

When the OECD announced the ambitious timetables for the BEPS project, many observers must have wondered whether it had bitten off far more than it can chew because it is attempting to rewrite a body of international tax rules built up in incoherent fashion largely from the middle of the 20th century, in less than two years.

> **COMMENT:** The effect of the BEPS project on the U.S. tax revenues and jobs remain to be seen. The Congressional Research Service published a report, "Corporate Tax Base Erosion and Profit Shifting: An Examination of the Data," on the impact of BEPS on U.S. tax revenues. The report notes implications for American corporations even if the U.S. does not adopt the OECD's recommendations.

Regardless of whether the OECD fails to meet its objectives—it looks on course to complete the project on time—change in international business and taxation is coming one way or another. Indeed, with some governments preempting the final results of the BEPS work, change is already happening.

STUDY QUESTION

---

7. Which of the following is **not** an action item of the OECD's BEPS project?

    a. Preventing treaty abuse

    b. Making dispute resolution mechanisms more effective

    c. Strengthening controlled foreign company rules

    d. Preventing the permanent establishment status

¶ 508 CONCLUSION

As Congress and the IRS continue to focus on the reporting of income and assets held abroad, taxpayers must carefully examine the different reporting requirements set forth above to determine whether the rules apply to the taxpayers' foreign assets and financial interests and then take the necessary steps to comply in order to avoid the penalties.

FATCA generally requires certain U.S. taxpayers (specified individuals) holding foreign financial assets with an aggregate value exceeding $50,000 to report certain information about those assets on a Form 8938. This form must be attached to the taxpayer's annual tax return. Reporting applies for assets held in taxable years beginning after March 18, 2010. Failure to report foreign financial assets on Form 8938 may result in a penalty of $10,000 (and an additional penalty up to $50,000 for continued failure after IRS notification). Additionally, underpayments of tax attributable to undisclosed foreign financial assets will be subject to an additional substantial understatement penalty of up to 40 percent for certain transactions that should have been reported under the applicable code sections.

In addition to the complying with the FATCA reporting requirements, taxpayers also may be required to file FinCEN Form 114 (FBAR). The FATCA requirements may overlap with and affect the same assets as the FBAR requirements, but they apply separately. The reporting threshold for FBAR is lower than that for FATCA. For FBAR purposes, if at any point during the calendar year, the aggregate value of the accounts exceeds $10,000 an FBAR must be filed. Willfully failing to file an FBAR may result in civil penalties as high as the greater of $100,000 or 50 percent of the total balance of the foreign account per violation. Nonwillful violations that the IRS determines were not due to reasonable cause are subject to a $10,000 penalty per violation. Criminal penalties, including fines and jail time, may also apply.

Moreover, taxpayers that were not previously in compliance must examine the options available to them, such as the 2014 OVDP, and make a determination regarding coming into compliance. Based on recent changes and continual enforcement efforts, it is clear that both the IRS and Congress will continue to maintain their focus on using these new reporting requirements to locate and collect monies owed by U.S. taxpayers.

Finally, the impact of the BEPS project on international business and taxation remains to be seen. There may be implications for American corporations even if the United States does not adopt the OECD's recommendations.

MODULE 3: RECENT REPORTING AND COMPLIANCE CHALLENGES—Chapter 6: Repair and Capitalization Guidance—What Now?

¶ 601 WELCOME

With the close of 2014 filing season, most taxpayers will have completed filing accounting method changes on Form 3115, *Application for Change in Accounting Method,* for the 2014 tax year under the automatic change procedures of Rev. Proc. 2015-13 and Rev. Proc. 2015-14 to change to accounting methods required by the Code Sec. 263 repair regulations (T.D. 9636). Last-minute relief provided qualifying small taxpayers the opportunity to change their accounting methods without filing Form 3115 or computing a Code Sec. 481 adjustment (Rev. Proc. 2015-20). It appears that the vast majority of qualifying small taxpayers accepted this relief.

The story, however, is far from over.

¶ 602 LEARNING OBJECTIVES

Upon completion of this chapter, you will be able to:

- Recognize how taxpayers that did not file changes in accounting method on Form 3115 for the 2014 tax year may file them in 2015;
- Identify how building lessors may deduct expenditures traditionally treated as capitalized leasehold improvements;
- Identify various annual elections that are allowed by the repair regulations, including the *de minimis* safe harbor expensing election; and
- Learn how the MACRS general asset account election can bypass the Code Sec. 280B rule requiring the basis of a demolished building to be capitalized into the land.

¶ 603 INTRODUCTION

Opportunities remain for taxpayers who did not file Form 3115 for the 2014 tax year to file Form 3115 for the 2015 tax year. This includes a qualifying small business taxpayer who formally rejected the Rev. Proc. 2015-20 relief by attaching a rejection statement to its 2014 return. Taxpayers who did file Form 3115 for 2014 could use the automatic method procedure again in 2015 to change to a method in the repair regulations provided the particular change was not filed for 2014. The "eligibility" limitations for automatic changes prevent a taxpayer from filing the same method change twice within a five-year period. The advance consent procedure applies if the eligibility limitation prevents a taxpayer from filing under the automatic procedure.

For the 2015 tax year (and all future tax years) expenditures relating to repairs and improvements will now need to be analyzed applying the principles of the repair regulations to determine whether or not capitalization is required.

Also, for 2015, taxpayers must also be aware of significant elections provided by the repair regulations that are required to be made on an annual basis. Each taxpayer's situation should be reviewed in 2015 (and annually thereafter) to determine which elections are appropriate. Care must be taken to timely file any required election statements in the manner required by the regulations.

Significant annual elections include:

- The de minimis safe harbor election;
- The election to deduct improvements to buildings costing $1 million or less;
- The election to capitalize in accordance with books;
- The partial disposition election to claim retirement losses on structural components; and
- The MACRS general asset account election (for the purposes of avoiding capitalization of demolition losses to land).

A particularly "hot topic" area under the repair regulations is the treatment of lessor improvements. An unintended consequence of the repair regulations is to allow the current deduction of amounts that have been traditionally capitalized as leasehold improvements in situations where the lessor makes the "improvements" to a relatively small portion of a leased building owned by the lessor. Recent informal Internal Revenue Service (IRS) guidance confirms this treatment subject to some important exceptions.

> **COMMENT:** This chapter will make occasional reference to the opinions of "IRS representatives" or "informal IRS guidance." The terms refer to informal opinions expressed by IRS representatives during the Capital Recovery and Leasing panel discussion held on May 8, 2015, as part of the American Bar Association's (ABA's) Section of Taxation May meeting held in Washington, D.C. These opinions are not binding on the IRS.

¶ 604 2015 ACCOUNTING METHOD CHANGES

Taxpayers, other than qualifying small business taxpayers, were required to file Form 3115, *Application for Change in Accounting Method,* for no later than their 2014 tax year to:

- Change accounting methods required by the Code Sec. 263 repair regulations; and
- Compute a Code Sec. 481(a) adjustment with respect to the treatment of prior-year transactions that conflicted with the treatment provided under the repair regulations.

However, there may still be opportunities to file changes on Form 3115 for the 2015 tax year.

Small Business Taxpayers

On February 13, 2015, the IRS provided significant last-minute relief to "small business taxpayers," granting them a reprieve from filing accounting method changes on Form 3115, which was required to be filed with 2014 tax returns in order to meet the filing deadline (Rev. Proc. 2015-20). A small business taxpayer that accepted the relief was deemed to have changed to the methods required by the Code Sec. 263 repair regulations on a cut-off basis without a Code Sec. 481(a) adjustment.

A small business taxpayer is a taxpayer with total assets of less than $10 million as of the first day of the tax year, or average annual gross receipts of $10 million or less for the prior three tax years. This test is applied to each separate trade or business of the taxpayer. A business that maintains separate books and records is generally considered a separate trade or business.

A small business taxpayer would be treated as if it had accepted this relief unless it either: (i) filed Form 3115 for its 2014 tax year to change to the required Code Sec. 263 repair regulations methods; or (ii) attached a rejection statement to its 2014 tax return without filing Form 3115. It was not necessary to affirmatively attach a statement to the 2014 income tax return in order to accept the relief.

COMMENT: IRS representatives reiterated that, in accordance with earlier guidance contained in an FAQ (Tangible Property Regulations), a small business taxpayer who did not File Form 3115 for 2014 could reject the relief by attaching a rejection statement to its 2014 return. This approach, although not mentioned in Rev. Proc. 2015-20, enables a small business taxpayer to file Form 3115 for the 2015 tax year to change accounting methods and claim a Code Sec. 481(a) adjustment using the automatic consent procedures. However, if such a taxpayer is audited prior to filing Form 3115 for the 2015 tax year, the taxpayer may be treated as using an impermissible accounting method.

CAUTION: The ability of taxpayers who accepted Form 3115 filing relief either by attaching an acceptance statement to their 2014 return or by taking no action to file Form 3115 for the 2015 year will need to be clarified by the IRS. Informally, the IRS representatives indicated that such a taxpayer should be able to file under the advance consent procedures in 2015 noting that the 5-year limitations/scope period would prevent a change from being filed under the automatic consent procedure. Some practitioners, however, hope that the IRS will provide additional guidance allowing the change to be made under the automatic consent procedure.

A small business taxpayer accepting the relief loses the benefit of a possible overall net negative (favorable) Code Sec. 481(a) adjustment (e.g., when prior amounts that were capitalized could be deducted as a repair expense under the repair regulations). A taxpayer that accepted relief for 2014 may not:

- File an accounting method change request in an effort to make a late partial disposition election under Sec. 6.33 of Rev. Proc. 2015-14 and claim retirement losses on any components of an asset (generally, structural components of a building) retired in a pre-2014 tax year; or

- File an accounting method change request under Sec. 6.37, 6.38, or 6.39 in an effort to claim a loss on "phantom" assets that were disposed in a pre-2014 tax year but that remain carried and depreciated on the books.

Significantly, taxpayers accepting relief will receive no audit protection with respect to amounts paid or incurred in tax years beginning before January 1, 2014. This means, for example, that if an amount was claimed as a repair deduction in a tax year that began before January 1, 2014, and that amount should be capitalized under the repair regulations, the IRS in an audit may require the taxpayer to capitalize that amount and impose any applicable penalty and interest charges.

Taxpayers Other Than Small Business Taxpayers

A taxpayer who was not eligible for 2014 Form 3115 filing relief (or was eligible and formally rejected the relief) and for some reason did not file Form 3115 for the 2014 tax year may file Form 3115 for the 2015 tax year using the automatic procedures. A taxpayer, however, risks lack of audit protection until the form is filed. Accordingly, the Form 3115 should be filed with the National Office as soon as possible (no sooner than the first day of the tax year of change). The form must also be filed with the taxpayer's 2015 tax return but audit protection will begin when it is filed with the National Office.

¶604

Some taxpayers may have filed Form 3115 for 2014 without making all the required accounting method changes. A Form 3115 could also be filed for 2015 to make additional changes under the automatic method procedure so long as the change does not violate the five-year eligibility limitation. The "eligibility limitations" (formally referred to as the "scope limitations") prevent a taxpayer from using the automatic consent procedure if a taxpayer is changing the same overall method of accounting or changing an accounting method for the same item a second time within a five-year period (Rev. Proc. 2015-13, Section 5).

CAUTION: The late partial disposition election provided as an accounting method change in Section 6.33 of Rev. Proc. 2015-14 had to be made no later than the 2014 tax year. Taxpayers filing Form 3115 in 2015 under the automatic or advance consent procedures of Rev. Proc. 2015-13 cannot make this election or any other election with a 2014 filing deadline, such as the election to revoke a prior general asset account election that is provided as an accounting method change in Section 6.34 of Rev. Proc. 2015-14.

Incomplete or Improper Form 3115: Second Chance Offered

It is well known that the IRS lacks the resources to review the vast majority of automatic accounting method change submissions. However, if an accounting method change made under the repair regulations is reviewed, in most cases the IRS will not simply reject the submission. Instead, it will usually offer the taxpayer a chance to correct or otherwise explain the submission.

First, IRS guidance provides that if the National Office determines that the Form 3115 is incomplete or improperly completed, it will notify the taxpayer and allow a 30-day period to provide required additional information. Extensions of the 30-day period may be requested. If the required information is not provided, the IRS will notify the taxpayer that the automatic change request is rejected (Section 11.01 of Rev. Proc. 2015-13).

If the National Office tentatively determines that the taxpayer's request for change in method of accounting filed under the automatic change procedure does not comply with all the applicable provisions for an automatic change (for example, the taxpayer changed to a method of accounting that varies from the applicable accounting method described in the list of automatic changes or the taxpayer is not eligible to use the automatic change procedures for the requested change), the National Office will notify the taxpayer of its tentative adverse determination and will offer the taxpayer a conference if the taxpayer requested one by checking box 16 on Form 3115 (Sec. 11.03(1) of Rev. Proc. 2015-13).

COMMENT: Box 16 of Form 3115 states: "Does the applicant request a conference with the IRS National Office if the IRS proposes an adverse response?" This box should have been checked by taxpayers filing changes under the repair regulations.

If box 16 was not checked, the National Office, in its discretion, may allow the taxpayer to (a) make appropriate adjustments to conform its Form 3115 to comply with all the applicable provisions, and (b) make conforming amendments to any federal income tax returns filed for the year of change and subsequent taxable years (Section 11.03(3) of Rev. Proc. 2015-13).

COMMENT: Because multiple accounting method changes were usually filed on a single Form 3115 to comply with the repair regulations, the National Office would presumably only reject particular requested changes that it deemed defective if the taxpayer does not make necessary corrections.

STUDY QUESTIONS

---

1. A taxpayer who did *not* qualify for filing relief under Rev. Proc. 2015-20 and did not file Form 3115 for the 2014 tax year to change to methods required by the repair regulations:

  a. May file Form 3115 for the 2015 tax year under the advance consent procedures

  b. May file Form 3115 for the 2015 tax year under the automatic consent procedures

  c. May make a late partial disposition election for pre-2014 dispositions

  d. May revoke a prior year general asset account election

2. The last-minute relief provided in Rev. Proc. 2015-20 allowed small business taxpayers:

  a. To change to accounting methods required by the repair regulations without filing Form 3115

  b. To file Form 3115 retroactively for 2014 when their 2015 returns are submitted

  c. To claim a Code Sec. 481(a) adjustment

  d. To selectively choose which repair regulations to adopt without filing Form 3115

¶ 605 2015 LESSOR IMPROVEMENTS

Going forward, lessors of buildings need to be aware that expenditures traditionally treated as capitalized leasehold improvements may in fact be deductible under the repair regulations. Central to the analysis is the rule that a lessor treats the entire building as the unit of property (assuming the lessor owns the entire building) (Reg. § 1. 263(a)-3(e)(2)(i)). This means, for example, if the *lessor's* expenditures only relate to a relatively small portion of a building unit of property, such as the first floor of a 10-story building or an office on the first floor, those expenditures will generally not improve the building by bettering, restoring, or adapting it to a new or different use. However, the same expenditures made by the *lessee* of the first floor of a 10-story building or a leased office space on the first floor would likely result in a capital expenditure because the applicable unit of property for the lessee is limited to the leased portion of the building (Reg. § 1.263(a)-3(e)(2)(v)).

Informal IRS Guidance

IRS representatives at the 2015 May meeting of the ABA's Section of Taxation shed some light and caveats on the treatment of lessor improvements. The opinions expressed were those of the representatives and are not binding on the IRS.

First, the representatives pointed out that the regulations do not allow a lessor (or lessee) to deduct the cost of Section 1245 property that is a separate unit of property. Items of Section 1245 property installed in a building are generally separate units of property in addition to being separately depreciable assets. In effect, a taxpayer is simply acquiring a new unit of Section 1245 property that must be separately capitalized and depreciated. The repair regulations require the acquisition costs of a unit of property to be capitalized (Reg. § 1.263(a)-2(d)(1)).

EXAMPLE: A lessor installs a cabinet in a leased office space as part of the reconfiguration required by the lessee. If the cabinet is a separate unit of Section 1245 property (the typical situation) and not a structural component of the building unit of property, the acquisition costs and other related costs (e.g., installation costs) must be capitalized.

CAUTION: The representatives noted that some taxpayers have suggested they can avoid the rule by treating the unit of Section 1245 property as a Section 1250 structural component of the building unit. The IRS cautioned, however, that a taxpayer may not simply choose to classify property as Section 1245 property or Section 1250 property. A property's classification is based on regulatory and court standards that generally require items related to the operation and maintenance of a building to be treated as Section 1250 structural components of the building unit of property and require other items to be treated as separately depreciable section 1245 property if they are easily removable under the **Whiteco** rules (**Whiteco Indus., Inc.,** 65 TC 664, Dec. 333,594). Choosing the wrong classification results in an improper accounting method.

Second, the representatives cautioned that expenditures made in connection with the initial build-out of leased space prior to the time that the building is placed in service must be capitalized as part of the acquisition costs of the building unit of property over 39 years (or a shorter period in the case of section 1245 property installed in the building) (Reg. § 1.263(a)-2(d)(1)).

Finally, the representatives pointed out that if a lessor claims a loss on a structural building component retired in the course of reconfiguring or updating the space for a tenant, the cost of a new component that replaces an old component is a restoration that must be capitalized. Reg. § 1.263(a)-3(k)(1)(i)) provides that a taxpayer must capitalize as a restoration an amount paid for the replacement of a component of a unit of property if the taxpayer deducted a loss on the replaced component.

COMMENT: The MACRS disposition rules allow a taxpayer to claim a loss on the retirement of an original structural component of a building by making a partial disposition election (Reg. § 1.168(i)-8(d)). The recognition of loss, however, is mandatory if the retired component of the building is a separately depreciated asset because it was placed in service after the building was placed in service (Reg. § 1.168(i)-8(c)(4)(ii)(D) and (e)). For example, if an original floor is replaced, loss is recognized only if the partial disposition election is made because the floor is depreciated as part of the building's basis. The new replacement floor, however, is a separately depreciated asset. If the new floor is later replaced, loss recognition is mandatory because an entire asset has been retired. If only part of the new floor is replaced, the partial disposition election may be made because only part of an asset is retired.

EXAMPLE: A lessor made structural leasehold improvements to an office space in 2010 and depreciated the improvements as a single asset. In 2015, all of the improvements are retired in the course of reconfiguring the space for a new tenant. Because the taxpayer retired the entire original leasehold improvement asset, the taxpayer will recognize a loss in an amount equal to the remaining undepreciated basis of the leasehold improvements. If the taxpayer claims the loss, some or all of the cost of the new leasehold improvements must be capitalized as a "restoration" even though the expenditures may otherwise be deductible under the repair regulations. If the taxpayer retires a portion of the prior leasehold improvements, a loss will only be recognized if a partial disposition election is made since the entire leasehold improvement asset has not been retired.

COMMENT: The IRS representatives noted that although a taxpayer is not required to claim a loss on the retirement of a separately depreciated asset, the taxpayer must reduce the basis of the retired asset by the amount of the allowable loss and will lose the benefit of depreciating the remaining basis of the asset. Generally, this course of action would be unfavorable to the taxpayer.

COMMENT: Portions of a leasehold reconfiguration project may be unrelated to removed structural components for which a lessor claims a loss and should not be treated as restorations. For example, if additional walls are added to an office space and no old walls are removed, the cost of the new walls should not be a restoration expense because they do not replace existing walls for which a loss is claimed. On the other hand, the cost of replacing the floor of an office space with a new floor would clearly relate to the replacement of the same component, and the cost of the new floor would need to be capitalized as a restoration if a loss deduction was claimed on the remaining basis of the old floor.

Leasehold improvements made by a lessor are depreciated as a separate asset unless made as part of the initial build-out before the building is placed in service (Reg. § 1.168(i)-8(c)(4)(ii)(D)). However, leasehold improvements made by the lessor are not treated as separate units of property even if made after the building is placed in service. They remain part of the building unit of property (Reg. § 1.263(a)-3(f)(3)(ii)).

EXAMPLE: A taxpayer purchases a 10-story building and places it in service in January 2015 by offering to rent office space. A lessee agrees to rent an office space provided that the taxpayer reconfigures the space. The reconfiguration involves tearing down permanent walls, adding new permanent walls, replacing existing windows and adding new windows, and replacing the carpeting. No loss is deducted with respect to the basis of removed building components. The costs of reconfiguration are not capital improvements because they do not result in a betterment, restoration, or adaption to the building unit of property. Assuming that the carpeting in the entire building was treated by the taxpayer as a single unit of separately depreciable Section 1245 property, the cost of the new carpeting is also deductible because only a small portion of the carpeting unit of property was replaced. However, in the unlikely event a partial disposition election is made to claim a loss on the old carpeting, the replacement carpeting is capitalized as a separately depreciable section 1245 asset but remains part of the carpeting unit of property consisting of all carpeting in the building.

CAUTION: One IRS representative suggested that in some circumstances it is possible that the Code Sec. 263A uniform capitalization rules could require a lessor to capitalize leasehold expenditures which are not considered improvements under the tangible property regulations and which do not constitute repairs or maintenance. Under the UNICAP rules, the direct and indirect costs of production paid or incurred before, during, and after the production period are subject to capitalization (Reg. § 1.263A-2(a)(3)(i)). For purposes of section 263A, *produce* includes the following: construct, build, install, manufacture, develop, improve, create, raise, or grow (Reg. § 1.263A-2(a)(1)(i)). The representative speculated that certain lessor expenditures could constitute construction, building, or installation expenditures for UNICAP purposes. The representative indicated the application of 263A is "an interesting issue which is not overly clear" and that additional guidance ought to be issued. The main IRS concern, according to the representative, is the application of 263A to the "big" projects, for example, where the cost of remodeling/reconfiguring several floors of a building for a lessee are deducted and are not repair expenditures.

COMMENT: In the past, lessor expenditures of the type no longer categorized as improvements under the repair regulations were capitalized as improvements and, therefore, also subject to the UNICAP rules by reason of the definition of production as including "improvements." The IRS did not need to use the "construction" or "building" definitions in the context of lessor expenditures to trigger the UNICAP rules.

STUDY QUESTION

---

3. If a lessor replaces the hardwood floor of a leased office space, the cost of the new floor is:

   a. Deducted as an ordinary expense if the lessor claimed a loss on the old floor's remaining basis

   b. Capitalized as a restoration if the lessor claims a loss on the old floor's remaining basis

   c. Treated as section 1245 property

   d. Treated as a separate unit of property

¶ 606 2015 ELECTIONS

De Minimis Safe Harbor Expensing Election

One of the most important and well known provisions in the repair regulations is the *de minimis* safe harbor election to expense materials and supplies and units of property costing no more than $5,000 for a taxpayer with an applicable financial statement (AFS) or no more than $500 for taxpayers without an AFS (Reg. § 1.263(a)-1(f)).

COMMENT: But for the *de minimis* safe harbor election, nonincidental materials and supplies are deducted in the year used or consumed. Under the *de minimis* safe harbor, materials and supplies are deducted in the year paid or incurred. Incidental materials and supplies (materials and supplies for which no record of consumption or use are kept) are deductible in the year paid or incurred whether or not the *de minimis* safe harbor is elected.

Materials and supplies are defined as (Reg. § 1.162-3(c)(1):

- A component acquired (or produced) to maintain, repair, or improve a unit of tangible property owned, leased, or serviced by the taxpayer and that is not acquired as part of any single unit of tangible property;

- Fuel, lubricants, water, and similar items, reasonably expected to be consumed in 12 months or less, beginning when used in the taxpayer's operations;

- A unit of property that has an economic useful life of 12 months or less, beginning when the property is used or consumed in the taxpayer's operations;

- A unit of property that has an acquisition cost or production cost (as determined under the uniform capitalization rules of Code Sec. 263A) of $200 or less; or

- Property identified in published guidance by the IRS as materials and supplies

The *de minimis* safe harbor does not apply to any of the following:

- Any amounts that are paid for property that is, or will be included in, inventory;

- Amounts that are paid for land;

- Amounts that are paid for rotable, temporary, and standby emergency spare parts (if the taxpayer elects to capitalize and depreciate them); and

- Amounts paid for rotable and temporary spare parts if the taxpayer accounts for them using the optional method of accounting for rotable parts (Reg. § 1.263(a)-1(f)(2)).

The $5,000 or $500 limitation applies by reference to the amount paid for the property as evidenced by: (i) the invoice total; or (ii) each invoiced item so long as the cost of each individual item is substantiated by the invoice (i.e., the invoice is itemized) (Reg. § 1.263(a)-1(f)(2)(i)(D) and Reg. § 1.263(a)-1(f)(2)(ii)(D)).

> **EXAMPLE:** A taxpayer without an AFS pays $800 for four printers. The invoice is itemized and reflects the taxpayer's purchase of four identical printers, at $200 each, for a total sales price of $800. Because the invoice is itemized and shows that each individual printer was $200 (i.e., less than the $500 limitation under the *de minimis* safe harbor), the taxpayer is not required to capitalize the $800. Instead, the $800 total may be expensed and currently deducted (Reg. § 1.263(a)-1(f)(7), Ex. 1).

Although a unit of property costing more than $200 is not a material or supply, the *de minimis* safe harbor allows the expensing of units of property that cost not more than the $500 or $5,000 limit.

> **EXAMPLE:** A taxpayer without an AFS purchases a computer (a unit of property) that cost $500. Although the computer is not a material or supply because it is a unit of property costing more than $200, it is still deductible under the safe harbor because the safe harbor applies to units of property costing $500 or less for a taxpayer without an AFS.

> **COMMENT:** A unit of property generally consists of a group of functionally interdependent components that perform a particular function.

> **COMMENT:** In Revenue Procedure 2015-20, the Treasury Department requests comments on the *de minimis* safe harbor limits of $5,000 and $500 per invoice or per item substantiated by the invoice. The IRS observed, "The *de minimis* safe harbor does not limit a taxpayer's ability to deduct otherwise deductible repair or maintenance costs that exceed the amount subject to the safe harbor." The deadline for submitting comments was April 21, 2014.

Accounting Policy Required. A taxpayer with an AFS may only elect the safe harbor if, at the beginning of the taxable year, it has written accounting procedures that treat as an expense for nontax purposes: (i) amounts paid for property costing less than a specified dollar amount that does not exceed $5,000; or (ii) amounts paid for property with an economic useful life of 12 months or less (Reg. § 1.263(a)-1(f)(1)(i)(B)). The taxpayer must treat the amount paid for the property as an expense on its applicable financial statement in accordance with its written accounting procedures.

A taxpayer without an AFS needs an accounting procedure, but it does not need to be written. The specified dollar amount may not exceed $500 (Reg. § 1.263(a)-1(f)(1)(ii)(B)).

> **COMMENT:** A taxpayer's accounting policy may set a *de minimis* expensing threshold that is less than $500 or $5000. These are upper thresholds. The policy can also set different thresholds for different types of property provided the thresholds set do not exceed the applicable $500 or $5,000 upper limit.

> **COMMENT:** If the taxpayer's financial or book policy sets expensing limits that are higher than the applicable $5,000 or $500 limit, only items that cost $5,000 or $500 or less, as applicable, may be expensed for tax purposes and remain

protected by the safe harbor. If lower per-item limits are set for financial or book accounting purposes, then the tax deduction under the safe harbor is limited to the lower amount. The IRS will allow a taxpayer to expense amounts in excess of the applicable safe harbor threshold if the expensed amount does not cause a material distortion of taxable income. The burden of proof is with the taxpayer. For larger companies, the higher threshold is often agreed upon with an IRS auditor.

Applicable financial statement defined. An *applicable financial statement* is defined as (Reg. § 1.263(a)-1(f)(4)):

- A financial statement required to be filed with the Securities and Exchange Commission (SEC) (the Form 10-K or the Annual Statement to Shareholders);

- A certified audited financial statement that is accompanied by the report of an independent certified public accountant (or in the case of a foreign entity, by the report of a similarly qualified independent professional) that is used for credit purposes; reporting to shareholders, partners, or similar persons; or any other substantial nontax purpose; or

- A financial statement (other than a tax return) required to be provided to the federal or a state government or any federal or state agency (other than the SEC or the Internal Revenue Service).

> **PLANNING TIP:** Property expensed under the *de minimis* rule is not treated upon sale or other disposition as a capital asset under Code Sec. 1221 or as property used in the trade or business under Code Sec. 1231 (Reg. § 1.263(a)-1(f)(3)(iii)). Therefore, the entire amount of gain is treated as ordinary income.

Interaction with UNICAP. The uniform capitalization rules (UNICAP) of Code Sec. 263A trump the *de minimis* safe harbor (Reg. § 1.263(a)-1(f)(3)(v)). Consequently, any amount that is otherwise deductible under the *de minimis* safe harbor may not be deducted but instead must be capitalized if the amount is a direct or indirect cost of property produced by the taxpayer (for the taxpayer's own use or resale) or property acquired for resale (Reg. § 1.263(a)-1(f)(3)(v)). The term *produce* includes construct, build, install, manufacture, develop, or improve (Code Sec. 263A(g)(1)). Thus, an amount paid for a component that improves a unit of property is not deductible under the *de minimis* safe harbor (Reg. § 1.263(a)-1(f)(1), last sentence; Reg. § 1.263(a)-3(c)(2)).

Procedure for Making the *de Minimis* Safe Harbor election. The *de minimis* safe harbor is elected annually by the extended due date of the income return. A statement described in Reg. § 1.263(a)-1(f)(5) must be attached to the return. The election is irrevocable (Reg.§ 1.263(a)-1(f)(5)). The *de minimis* safe harbor election is not an accounting method. Therefore, taxpayers who elect it do not file Form 3115 (Reg.§ 1.263(a)-1(g)).

> **CAUTION:** A taxpayer is not required to attach a copy of its accounting policy to the return or otherwise provide specifics concerning the policy and, therefore, should not do so. The accounting policy only needs to be in place as of the beginning of the tax year of the election.

Election to Deduct Limited Improvements to Buildings Costing $1 Million or Less

An elective safe harbor allows qualifying small taxpayers with relatively minor repair and improvement expenditures for a building to elect on an annual basis to deduct rather than capitalize the improvements (Reg. § 1.263(a)-3(h)).

Specifically, a taxpayer with average annual gross receipts of $10 million or less in the three preceding tax years may make an annual election to deduct amounts with respect to a building with an unadjusted basis of $1 million or less that would otherwise be capitalized as an improvement (Reg. § 1.263(a)-3(h)(3)(i)).

This safe harbor only applies if the total amount paid during the tax year for repairs, maintenance, improvements, and similar activities does not exceed the lesser of $10,000 or 2 percent of the unadjusted basis of the building. Amounts deducted under the *de minimis* safe harbor or the safe harbor for routine maintenance are counted toward the $10,000 limit (Reg. § 1.263(a)-3(h)(2)).

COMMENT: The unadjusted basis of a building is generally its cost.

The IRS may adjust the $10,000, 2 percent, and $1 million amounts in the future through published guidance.

PLANNING TIP: A taxpayer making the election does not need to apply it to all of its qualifying buildings. The election statement should only identify those buildings that the taxpayer wants to apply the election to.

EXAMPLE: A taxpayer owns two rental properties, each with an unadjusted basis of $300,000. The taxpayer pays $5,000 of repair and improvement expenses in 2015 on building A. Because this amount does not exceed the lesser of $10,0000 or $6,000 ($300,000 × 2%), the taxpayer may elect to apply the safe harbor to building A. If the taxpayer pays $7,000 for repairs and maintenance on building B, the election may not be made for building B because $7,000 is greater than 2 percent of building B's unadjusted basis (Reg. § 1.263(a)-3(h)(10), Ex. 3).

COMMENT: The election only benefits taxpayers with relatively minor amounts of repair and improvement expenses because it may not be made if the total spent for repairs and improvements for the tax year exceeds $10,000 or, if less, 2 percent of the cost of the building. For the maximum $10,000 cap to apply, the building must cost at least $500,000 ($500,000 × 2% = $10,000) but no more than $1 million because buildings costing more than $1 million are ineligible. If the building cost less than $500,000, the cap is limited to 2 percent of the cost.

Lessees

A lessee of a building or a portion of a building may also make the election. The unadjusted basis of the building or portion of the building for purposes of the $1 million cost cap is deemed to equal the total amount of undiscounted rent paid or expected to be paid under the lease for the entire term of the lease. The term of the lease includes renewal periods if all of the facts and circumstances in existence during the tax year in which the lease is entered into indicate a reasonable expectancy of renewal.

EXAMPLE: A taxpayer enters into a 20-year lease of a building in which it operates a retail store. If the monthly rent is $4,000, the unadjusted basis of the building is $960,000 ($4,000 × 12 months × 20 years). The safe harbor may be elected if the taxpayer satisfies the gross receipts test (Reg. § 1.263(a)-3(h)(10), Ex. 4).

Making the election. A taxpayer makes the election by attaching a statement to the timely filed original federal tax return (including extensions) for the tax year in which amounts are paid for repairs, maintenance, improvements, and similar activities performed on the eligible building property, provided that the amounts paid qualify under the safe harbor. The statement must be titled "Section 1.263(a)-3(h) Election," and must include:

- The taxpayer's name;
- The taxpayer's address;
- The taxpayer's taxpayer identification number (TIN); and
- A description of each eligible building property to which the taxpayer is applying the election.

The election may not be made on an amended return unless permission to file a late election on an amended return is first obtained. The election is irrevocable (Reg. § 1.263(a)-3(h)(6)).

STUDY QUESTIONS

4. The UNICAP rules under Code Sec. 263A provide that an otherwise deductible amount under the *de minimis* safe harbor of the repair regulations must capitalized if:

   a. The amount is for property acquired or produced abroad
   b. The amount is for property that cost $100 or less
   c. The taxpayer uses the amount to produce property for its own use or resale or to acquire property for resale
   d. The amount is for property that becomes totally worthless during the tax year

5. The election to deduct limited improvements to buildings whose unadjusted basis is $1 million or less applies when taxpayers:

   a. Have annual gross receipts of $10 million or less for the current tax year
   b. Have average annual gross receipts of $10 million or less in the three preceding tax years
   c. Make the election on an amended return without IRS permission
   d. The costs of repairs, maintenance, improvements, and similar activities total less than $1 million in a single tax year

---

Election to Capitalize in Accordance with Books

Rather than going through a potentially complicated analysis to determine whether a trade or business expenditure is a currently deductible repair or a capitalized improvement, a taxpayer may make an annual election to capitalize and depreciate as a separate asset any expenditure for repair and maintenance if the taxpayer capitalizes the expenditure on the books and records it regularly uses to compute its trade or business income (Reg. § 1.263(a)-3(n)).

The election applies to all amounts paid for repair and maintenance of tangible property that are treated as capital expenditures on the taxpayer's books and records for the tax year that is covered by the election. These amounts are not treated as amounts paid for repair or maintenance and, thus, are not currently deductible (Reg. § 1.263(a)-3(n)(1)).

    PLANNING TIP: In effect, the election is a safe harbor because the IRS cannot challenge an electing taxpayer's characterization of a repair expense as a capital expenditure. However, a taxpayer that does not make this election is adopting an improper accounting method when it improperly capitalizes a repair expense (see, for example, Chief Counsel Advice 201231004, April 18, 2012).

    CAUTION: The election works in only one direction. Amounts that are expensed as repairs on the taxpayer's books may not be deducted as repairs for tax purposes under the protection of the book capitalization safe harbor. Repair deductions claimed for tax purposes must be allowable under the standards set forth in the repair regulations.

> **EXAMPLE:** RentProp replaces the shingles on a roof of a rental property and capitalizes the expenditure on its books and records. RentProp also claims a repair expense for replacing the sole chiller on a heating, ventilation, and air conditioning unit. If RentProp makes the election, RentProp may capitalize the cost of replacing the shingles (even though the replacement is a repair under the tax rules). However, RentProp may not claim a repair deduction for the cost of replacing the chiller even though the cost is deducted on the books unless such costs are a repair under the tax rules. Because the cost of replacing a major component of a building system is not a repair under the tax rules (Reg. § 1.263(a)-3(k)(1)(vi)), the chiller replacement cost must be capitalized.

Making the election. The election is made by attaching a statement to the taxpayer's timely filed original tax return (including extensions) for the tax year to which the election applies (Reg. § 1.263(a)-3(n)(2)).

The statement must be titled "Section 1.263(a)-3(n) Election" and include the taxpayer's name, address, TIN, and a statement that the taxpayer is making the election to capitalize repair and maintenance costs under § 1.263(a)-3(n).

Partial Disposition Election to Claim Retirement Loss on Structural Components

Another annual election, the *partial disposition election,* allows a deduction for the remaining undepreciated basis of a retired structural component of a building (or a component of a section 1245 property, such as a machine) (Reg. § 1.168(i)-8(d)).

Prior to issuance of the MACRS disposition regulations (T.D. 9689) (which were issued in conjunction with the Code Sec. 263 repair regulations (T.D. 9636)), a taxpayer who retired a structural component of a building was generally required to continue to depreciate the retired component. No gain or loss was realized because the retirement was not treated as a disposition. For example, if the roof of a commercial building was replaced (i.e., retired), the new roof was depreciated as 39-year MACRS real property and the taxpayer continued to depreciate the old roof.

The MACRS disposition regulations now allow a taxpayer to make a partial disposition election to claim a loss on the retired structural component equal to the remaining basis of the component that has not been depreciated. The election can also be made for replaced components of property other than buildings.

A retirement of a portion of an asset is treated as a disposition on which gain or loss is recognized only if the partial disposition election is made, except that the following dispositions of a portion of an asset are dispositions (upon which gain or loss is recognized) without making a partial disposition election:

- Sale of a portion of an asset:
- Disposition of a portion of an asset as the result of a casualty;
- Disposition of a portion of an asset for which gain (determined without regard to depreciation recapture) is not recognized in a like kind exchange or involuntary conversion;
- Transfer of a portion of an asset in a "step-in-the-shoes" nonrecognition transaction described in Code Sec. 168(i)(7)(B) (Reg. § 1.168(i)-8(c)(4)(ii)(D))

> **PLANNING POINTER:** This election should only be made if the cost of replacing the retired component must be capitalized. If the replacement cost is a repair and the election is made, the otherwise deductible repair costs must be

capitalized. The repair regulations treat an expenditure as a capitalized restoration if the expenditure is paid or incurred to replace a retired component on which a loss deduction is claimed (Reg. § 1.263(a)-3(k)(1)(ii)).

> **EXAMPLE:** Garett McDonnell, business taxpayer, replaces the shingles on the roof of one building and the entire roof on another building. Generally, the replacement of shingles is considered a repair expense because the shingles are not a major component of the building structure. However, if Garett makes the partial disposition election and claims a loss equal to the remaining undepreciated basis of the replaced shingles, he must capitalize the entire cost of the replacement shingles as a restoration. The cost of replacing an entire roof must be capitalized whether or not he makes the partial disposition election to claim a loss on the remaining undepreciated basis of the roof because the replacement of a major component of a building, such as an entire roof, is a capitalized restoration. Therefore, Garett should make the partial disposition election only if the entire roof is replaced.

Retroactive Partial Disposition Election Based on Adverse Audit

If the IRS audits a taxpayer and determines that an amount previously claimed as a repair deduction should have been capitalized, the taxpayer may make a retroactive partial disposition election by filing an accounting method change (Section 6.35 of Rev. Proc. 2015-14) on Form 3115 to claim a loss through a Code Sec. 481 adjustment on the portion of the asset that was disposed of. The taxpayer, however, must own the asset as of the beginning of the tax year of change (Reg. § 1.168(i)-8(d)(2)(iii)).

> **EXAMPLE:** Hot Cakes Inc., replaced the roof of its restaurant in 2014 and claimed a repair expense. It did not make a partial disposition election because if it had claimed a loss on the old roof, the replacement costs would have been required to be capitalized as a restoration. In 2018, the IRS audits Hot Cakes and requires Hot Cakes to capitalize the roof replacement cost even though no loss was claimed because it replaced a major component of the building (i.e., the roof of the building). Hot Cakes may make a retroactive partial disposition election to claim a loss on the undepreciated basis of the original roof by filing Form 3115.

Partial disposition election procedure. The partial disposition election must be made by the due date (including extensions) of the original federal tax return for the tax year in which the portion of the asset is disposed of (unless the audit exception above applies). No formal election statement is required. The taxpayer simply reports the gain or loss on the disposed portion of the asset on the return (i.e., Form 4797, *Sales of Business Property*) (Reg. § 1.168(i)-8(d)(2)(ii)). The election may be made for some or all retired components.

The election may be revoked only with IRS consent obtained by filing a private letter ruling request (Reg. § 1.168(i)-8(d)(2)(v)).

> **PLANNING TIP:** A taxpayer may deduct removal costs if a partial disposition election is made or an entire asset is replaced. If a portion of an asset is replaced, the removal costs are capitalized if the retirement costs relate to a capital improvement and deducted if the costs relate to a repair (Reg. § 1.263(a)-3(g)).

General Asset Account Election to Avoid Capitalization of Demolition Loss

Taxpayers may make an election in the tax year a building is placed in service to place the building in a general account account (GAA) (Reg. § 1.168(i)-1). Generally, this should not be done, however, because a taxpayer may not make a partial disposition election to recognize loss on the retirement of a structural component, such as a roof, if the building is in a GAA.

However, if a taxpayer purchases a building with the intent of demolishing the structure at some point in the future, electing to place the building in a single asset GAA account may bypass the demolition rule of Code Sec. 280B which prohibits a loss deduction and requires the undepreciated adjusted basis of the building to be added to the basis of the land.

Under the final regulations, a taxpayer may continue to depreciate a building placed in service in a single asset GAA account after its demolition rather than increasing the basis of the land by the undepreciated adjusted basis of the building as otherwise required by Code Sec. 280B. There is no requirement that the taxpayer must terminate the GAA upon the disposition of the building and capitalize the loss under Code Sec. 280B (Reg.§ 1.168(i)-1(e)(3)(ii)(A)). However, an asset may not be placed in a GAA if it is acquired and disposed of in the same tax year (Reg.§ 1.168(i)-1(c)(1)(i)). Consequently, this planning tip, which allows a taxpayer to continue to depreciate the demolished building until its basis is fully recovered, will not work if the building is acquired and demolished in the same tax year.

> **CAUTION:** Demolitions for purposes of Code Sec. 280B also include rehabilitations of portions of a building. A modification or rehabilitation of a building will not be considered a demolition if the following conditions are satisfied (Rev. Proc. 95-27, 1995-1 CB 704):
>
> - 75 percent or more of the existing external walls of the building are retained in place as internal or **external** walls; and
> - 75 percent or more of the existing internal structural framework of the building is retained in place.

The effect of the antiabuse rule (Reg.§ 1.168(i)-1(e)(3)(vii)) may also need to be considered. Under the antiabuse rule, a GAA account terminates on the first day of the disposition of an asset in an "abusive transaction." An *abusive transaction* is a transaction entered into, or made, with a principal purpose of achieving a tax benefit or result that would not be available absent an election. For example, an abusive transaction includes a transaction entered into with a principal purpose of shifting income or deductions among taxpayers in a manner that would not be possible absent the GAA election in order take advantage of differing effective tax rates among the taxpayers. The other example provided in the regulations concerns GAA elections made with a principal purpose of disposing of an asset from the GAA to use an expiring net operating loss or credit where the transaction is not a bona fide disposition.

Making the GAA election. The GAA election for any asset is made by following the Form 4562 instructions, which simply require a taxpayer to check a box on the form (line 18) to indicate that certain assets placed in service during the year will be placed in a GAA account. It is not necessary to identify the particular assets to which the election does or does not apply on Form 4562. However, records identifying the property placed in the GAA and its unadjusted depreciable basis, as well as the depreciation reserve of the GAA must be maintained.

STUDY QUESTION

6. The partial disposition election:

    a. applies to the retirement of a structural component of a building or a component of section 1245 property

    b. requires the taxpayer to attach an election statement to its return

    c. applies to the retirement of an entire asset

    d. applies to the sale of a portion of an asset

¶ 607 CONCLUSION

The IRS repair regulations project may be officially ended, but unanswered questions remain. Although written in black and white, the regulations have some "grey areas" that need to be fleshed out with official guidance. One important area of controversy that the IRS will address through its Industry Issue Resolution Program is capitalization issues in the retail and restaurant industry. IRS representatives at the May ABA Tax Section meeting indicated this guidance should be completed and issued by May 2016, if not sooner.

MODULE 4: ENTITY CONCERNS—Chapter 7: Tax-Exempt Hospitals

¶ 701 WELCOME

This chapter explores recent legislative and IRS requirements for hospitals to obtain and maintain tax-exempt status. The chapter examines new requirements imposed under the *Patient Protection and Affordable Care Act* (PPACA) as well as the excise tax imposed on exempt hospitals that fail to meet Code Sec. 501(r) exemption requirements. IRS Form 990 reporting specifics for tax-exempt hospitals also are described.

¶ 702 LEARNING OBJECTIVES

Upon completion of this chapter, you will be able to:

- Identify factors considered under the community benefit standard applied to tax-exempt hospitals;

- Identify the community health needs assessment requirements established for tax-exempt hospitals under the PPACA;

- Recognize major features of the IRS regulations under the PPACA for financial assistance policies, reporting, and noncompliance penalties; and

- Recognize the tax issues associated with regional health information organizations, group purchasing organizations, and joint ventures between tax-exempt and for-profit health entities.

¶ 703 INTRODUCTION

To be tax-exempt for federal purposes, a hospital must meet certain Internal Revenue Code requirements and a community benefit standard. The term *community benefit*—for state and federal law—describes a combination of hospital services and activities that contribute to the well-being of the community. The community benefit standard applies to other healthcare provider organizations under Code Sec. 501(c)(3), such as clinics or HMOs, as well as traditional hospitals. The community benefit standard focuses on a number of factors to determine whether a healthcare provider operates to benefit the community as a whole (see *IRS Technical Instruction Program for Fiscal Year 2002*, Topic D, "Update on Health Care").

The PPACA (2010) imposed additional requirements that charitable hospitals must satisfy to maintain their tax-exempt status:

- Conducting a community health needs assessment: Code Sec. 501(r)(3);

- Establishing and disclosing financial assistance policies: Code Sec. 501(r)(4);

- Limiting charges to needy individuals: Code Sec. 501(r)(5); and

- Following reasonable billing and collection practices: Code Sec. 501(r)(6).

The IRS issued final regulations under Code Sec. 501(r) at the end of 2014 (T.D. 9708). The final regulations are effective for the hospital's first tax year beginning after December 29, 2015. For prior years, a hospital may rely on a reasonable good faith interpretation of the statutory requirements.

¶ 704 APPLYING THE COMMUNITY BENEFIT STANDARD

The following factors are considered in determining whether the community benefit standard has been met:

- Whether the hospital has a governing board composed of civic leaders rather than hospital administrators or physicians;
- If the hospital is part of a multientity hospital system, whether the minutes reflect corporate separateness;
- Whether admission to the medical staff is open to all qualified physicians in the area;
- Whether the hospital operates a full-time emergency room open to everyone; and
- Whether the hospital provides nonemergency care to everyone in the community who is able to pay (Announcement 92-83).

> **COMMENT:** An open medical staff, participation in Medicare and Medicaid, and treating all emergency patients without regard to ability to pay are characteristics now shared by tax-exempt and for-profit hospitals. "So, although they remain factors in assessing whether a nonprofit hospital is entitled to tax-exemption, they no longer meaningfully distinguish one type of hospital from another," said Steven T. Miller, former IRS commissioner, Tax Exempt and Government Entities, in remarks before the Office of the Attorney General of Texas in 2009. "Some distinguishing features do remain, however. One is obvious: Where do the profits go? That, along with a community board designed to ensure that the hospital is accountable to the broader community it serves, are two of the most significant distinguishing characteristics that have survived 40 years of change in the sector. And, of course, charity care and other uncompensated care remain relevant."

In order for a hospital to establish that it is exempt under Code Sec. 501(c)(3) it need not provide free medical care to indigents or provide care to needy persons at reduced rates (Rev. Rul. 69-545). Rev. Rul. 69-545 expressly removed the requirements of Rev. Rul. 56-185 to care for indigent patients without charge or at rates below cost. Thus, providing charity care to patients outside of an emergency setting is not a requirement under Rev. Rul. 69-545. See Rev. Rul. 68-376 for a definition of *patient*.

> **PLANNING NOTE:** A hospital should not send bills to patients it knows cannot pay and should advertise the availability of charity care.

> **PRACTICAL ANALYSIS:** The value of charity care includes direct care provided to uninsured and underinsured patients, unprofitable service lines and facilities that are part of the hospital's charitable mission, and bad or forgiven debt writeoffs. The valuation of tax-exempt status analyzes federal tax liability, state and local tax liability, and nontax costs. Nontax costs may include no longer being able to benefit from the lower interest rates of tax-exempt bond financing, loss of fundraising, higher postage, and loss of volunteer labor.

> **COMMENT:** "The tax policy and tax administration question that needs to be addressed is: How does one meaningfully differentiate a taxpaying, for-profit hospital from a nonprofit hospital that enjoys exemption from federal and state tax, exemption from property tax, and eligibility for favorable bond financing?" asked former IRS Tax Exempt & Government Entities (TE/GE) Division Commissioner Steven Miller. "That is where the community benefit standard comes in—to help one make that distinction. And the question then becomes, how good a job does it do?"

In a suit brought by a group of health and welfare organizations and by indigent persons to have Rev. Rul. 69-545 declared invalid, the U.S. Supreme Court ruled that the suit should have been dismissed by the lower court because the organizations showed no injury to themselves and the indigents failed to show that the hospitals had their tax status in mind when they refused to admit them (*Eastern Ky. Welfare Rights Organization,* 76-1 USTC ¶ 9439).

Under Rev. Rul. 83-157, failure of a nonprofit hospital to operate an emergency room available to all members of the community regardless of their ability to pay did not disqualify it for tax exemption. A state health planning agency had determined that the community was already well-served by neighboring emergency room facilities. In addition, IRS guidelines provide that specialized facilities, such as cancer hospitals, do not need to have emergency rooms. See Announcement 92-83.

Whether an activity creates a community benefit is a fact-driven inquiry. Generally, courts inquire whether the taxpayer's activities promote health on a community-wide basis. Health maintenance organizations (HMOs) can be viewed as either promoting health for a particular, narrow community—the enrollees—or promoting health for a wide community. The court in the *IHC* cases (*IHC Health Plans,* CA-10, 2003-1 USTC ¶ 50,368) below found that the taxpayer's activities failed to promote health community-wide. Its healthcare plans were available only to certain individuals and employers. Its HMO and related plans were marketed primarily to employers with more than 100 employees. Although the taxpayer had offered Medicare participants the opportunity to enroll in its HMO operations, it terminated this option after a limited period. The court further observed that the taxpayer was unable to provide any free medical care to individuals. The taxpayer did not own or operate its medical facilities or employ its own physicians and healthcare professionals. Without these, it could not give any actual health care to individuals. Further, the taxpayer did not offer any free education programs to the public or conduct research that would have a possible public benefit. Its activities, the court concluded, focused on the enrollees in the HMOs and not the community at large.

COMMENT: For purposes of research conducted by a hospital (see Form 990, *Return of Organization Exempt From Income Tax,* Schedule H, Hospitals), research means any study or investigation that receives funding from a tax-exempt or government entity of which the goal is to generate generalizable knowledge that is made available to the public, such as about underlying biological mechanisms of health and disease; natural processes or principles affecting health or illness; evaluation of safety and efficacy of interventions for disease such as clinical trials and studies of therapeutic protocols; laboratory-based studies; epidemiology, health outcomes and effectiveness; behavioral or sociological studies related to health, delivery of care, or prevention; studies related to changes in the health care delivery system; and communication of findings and observations (including publication in a medical journal).

PLANNING NOTE: Kathy Pitts, Ernst & Young, Birmingham, Ala., said that when community benefit costs fluctuate from year to year, in an IRS audit the organization can point to other years. However, there is no evidence that the IRS looks at an organization's cost trends.

CAUTION: Many states have adopted written standards involving community benefit. Although state requirements may be similar to the federal standard in some respects, they may be broader than it in others.

In addition, the IRS will consider private inurement and private benefit in determining whether the hospital is exempt. Joint ventures between taxable and tax-exempt organizations or individuals are to be examined for possible private inurement and private benefit (see General Counsel's Memorandum 39862).

Provider-Sponsored Organization

A hospital, or other Code Sec. 501(c)(3) organization, will not fail to be treated as organized and operated solely for a charitable purpose based solely on its participation in a provider-sponsored organization (PSO), as defined in Section 1855(d) of the *Social Security Act* (Code Sec. 501(o)). A PSO is an entity established or organized and operated by a healthcare provider (or group of providers) that provides a substantial proportion of the required services under a contract directly through the provider (or group of providers). In addition, the affiliated providers share substantial financial risk with respect to the provision of health services and have at least a majority stake in the PSO entity (Section 1855(d) of the *Social Security Act*).

Code Sec. 501(o) applies whether or not the PSO itself is a tax-exempt organization. In determining whether there has been private inurement or benefit to any individual, any person who has a material financial interest in the PSO will be treated as a private shareholder with respect to the hospital. Each PSO arrangement will be evaluated upon the individual facts and circumstances (see the House Committee Report to P.L. 105-33).

> **COMMENT:** A pattern of violating the antidumping provisions of the *Consolidated Omnibus Reconciliation Act of 1985* (P.L. 99-272) can result in revocation of an organization's tax exemption. The antidumping provision requires hospitals who participate in the Medicare program to accept all persons who require emergency medical care, regardless of the persons' ability to pay.

STUDY QUESTION

---

1. Providers in a provider-sponsored organization:

    a. May not qualify as Code Sec. 501(c)(3) organizations

    b. Are subject to Code Sec. 501(o) rules only if they operate as a for-profit organization

    c. Are treated as private shareholders for the hospital if they have a financial interest in the PSO

    d. Are not subject to provisions of P.L. 99-272 antidumping rules for Medicare participants

---

¶705 INTERNAL REVENUE CODE REQUIREMENTS

The *Patient Protection and Affordable Care Act* established four new requirements applicable to Code Sec. 501(c)(3) hospitals (Code Sec. 501(r)(1)). The requirements are in addition to, and not in lieu of, the requirements otherwise applicable to an organization described in Code Sec. 501(c)(3). The requirements generally apply to any Code Sec. 501(c)(3) organization that operates at least one hospital facility (Code Sec. 501(r)(2)(A)). A hospital facility generally includes:

- Any facility that is, or is required to be, licensed, registered, or similarly recognized by a state as a hospital; and

- Any other facility or organization the Secretary of the Treasury determines has the provision of hospital care as its principal purpose. An organization is required to comply with the following requirements with respect to each hospital facility operated by such organization (Code Sec. 501(r)(2)(B)).

COMMENT: The requirements appear to reflect concerns that have arisen in recent years about whether nonprofit hospitals are providing adequate public benefits to justify their tax-exempt status, according to the Congressional Research Service ("501(c)(3) Hospitals and the Community Benefit Standard" (November 10, 2009)).

PRACTICAL ANALYSIS: For a hospital financing, the borrower's counsel and bond counsel should determine whether the Code Sec. 501(r) requirements apply to the Code Sec. 501(c)(3) hospital borrower, as well as each of its facilities, and if the actions taken by the hospital up to the time of the financing are sufficient to meet the requirements so that exempt status is maintained.

The requirements generally apply to any Code Sec. 501(c)(3) organization that operates at least one hospital facility (Code Sec. 501(r)(2)(A)). A "hospital facility" is a facility that is required by a state to be licensed, registered, or similarly recognized as a hospital (Reg. § 1.501(r)-1(b)(17)). Multiple buildings operated by a hospital organization under a single state license are a single hospital facility.

An organization is required to comply with the following requirements with respect to each hospital facility operated by such organization (Code Sec. 501(r)(2)(B)).

Community Health Needs Assessment

First, each hospital facility is required to conduct a community health needs assessment (CHNA) at least once every three tax years and adopt an implementation strategy (IS) to meet the community needs identified through such an assessment (Code Sec. 501(r)(3)). The assessment process must take into account input from persons who represent the broad interests of the community served by the hospital, including those with special knowledge or expertise of public health issues. Each hospital facility is required to make the assessment widely available.

COMMENT: The assessment may be conducted with one or more other organizations, including related organizations. Apparently, the other organizations do not have to be hospitals, but may be other healthcare providers.

COMMENT: "It is a changing environment for hospitals," Nancy Ortmeyer Kuhn, director, Jackson & Campbell, Washington, D.C., told CCH. "Sec. 501(r) is a sea-change in how hospitals have operated. Hospital processes have never been public. CHNAs are one way [for the IRS and the public] to lift the veil and see what hospitals are doing" (*Federal Tax Weekly,* July 21, 2011).

CHNAs are required of "hospital organizations," which include (1) an organization that operates a facility required by a state to be licensed, registered, or similarly recognized as a hospital ("a state-licensed hospital facility"), and (2) any other organization that the IRS determines has the provision of hospital care as its principal function or purpose under Code Sec. 501(c)(3). Code Sec. 501(r) requires that each hospital facility must separately comply with the requirements for a CHNA and an IS. The rules do not apply to hospitals outside the United States.

For a hospital facility with multiple locations, the community served is the aggregate of such areas or populations (Reg. § 1.501(r)-3(b)(3)). However, a hospital facility consisting of multiple buildings may assess the health needs of the different geographic areas or populations served by the different buildings separately and document the assessments in separate chapters or sections of the hospital facility's CHNA report and implementation strategy.

The IRS requires a hospital organization to document a CHNA for each hospital facility in a written report. The CHNA must describe the community served by the facility, the methods used to conduct the assessment and sources of information, organizations the hospital collaborated with on the CHNA, and how the organization obtained input from the community and from experts. In defining its community, a hospital organization may take into account all relevant facts and circumstances. Although the IRS expects the community to be based on geography, it could also take into account target populations (e.g., children or the aged) or the facility's principal functions (e.g., a specialty or a targeted disease). The CHNA cannot exclude medically underserved populations, minorities and low-income groups, and those with chronic diseases.

> **COMMENT:** "The requirements are well spelled-out," Kuhn said. However, "it will be a burden and expensive for hospitals to conduct the CHNA or hire another party" to provide it," she indicated. Moreover, collaboration may not always be possible.

A hospital organization must document the CHNA for all hospital facilities in separate written reports. The CHNA must be made widely available to the public, which an organization can accomplish by posting the CHNA on the hospital facility's website, the hospital organization's website, or a website maintained by another organization.

The implementation strategy must be adopted separately for each hospital facility. A strategy is a written plan that either describes how the facility plans to meet a health need identified through the CHNA or explains why the facility does not intend to meet the health need. An organization may develop strategies in collaboration with other organizations, including related organizations, other hospital organizations, government hospitals, and government agencies, such as public health departments. The implementation strategy must be adopted by the hospital organization's governing body, by the end of the same tax year in which the organization conducts the CHNA.

One aspect of conducting a CHNA is defining the community served. A health system might define "community" as the zip codes that make up 80 percent of the inpatient population, with some exceptions. However, they could also use a regional approach instead of viewing each hospital individually. At first there was not much guidance, but practitioners hope that over time the CHNA approaches used by health-care systems will become more consistent.

STUDY QUESTION

---

2. To prepare a community health needs assessment (CHNA), a hospital facility:

    a. Must define what community it is serving

    b. Prepares one report aggregating all the facilities' assessments and one umbrella implementation strategy

    c. Uses input only from its own experts and medical staff

    d. Generates a written report at least once every five years

---

Financial Assistance Policy

Second, each hospital facility is required to adopt, implement, and widely publicize a written financial assistance policy (FAP) (Code Sec. 501(r)(4)(A)). The financial assistance policy must indicate the eligibility criteria for financial assistance and whether such assistance includes free or discounted care. For those eligible for discounted care, the policy must indicate the basis for calculating the amounts that will be billed to such patients. The policy must also indicate how to apply for such assistance. If a hospital does not have a separate billing and collections policy, the financial assistance policy must also indicate what actions the hospital may take in the event of nonpayment, including collections action and reporting to credit agencies.

Each hospital facility is required to adopt and implement a written policy to provide, without discrimination, emergency medical treatment to individuals regardless of their eligibility under the financial assistance policy (Code Sec. 501(r)(4)(B)).

A plain language summary is required to be included with one post-discharge communication. A hospital has the flexibility to send one plain language summary only to the subset of patients against whom the hospital actually intends to engage in extraordinary collection actions. This is intended to maintain the frequent reminders to patients of the availability of financial aid while reducing the burden and cost of mailing multiple copies of a plain language summary of the financial aid policy (FAP) (T.D. 9708).

The threshold for translating the FAP and related documents into the primary language of any populations with limited English proficiency is 5 percent of the residents of the community served by the hospital (Reg. § 1.501(r)-4(b)(5)(ii)).

Limitation on Charges

Third, each hospital facility is permitted to bill patients who qualify for financial assistance no more than the amount generally billed to insured patients (Code Sec. 501(r)(5)). A hospital facility may not use gross charges (i.e., "chargemaster" rates) when billing individuals who qualify for financial assistance.

> **COMMENT:** The limitation on what could be charged by a charitable hospital for emergency or other medically necessary care was originally "the lowest amounts charged." Americans for Tax Reform has said that the change to "the amount generally billed" makes the limitation less onerous on hospitals.

> **COMMENT:** It is intended that amounts billed to those who qualify for financial assistance may be based on either the best, or an average of the three best, negotiated commercial rates, or Medicare rates.

> **PRACTICAL ANALYSIS:** Melinda Hatton, general counsel for the American Hospital Association, has suggested, among other efforts, including on patient bills a statement such as "If you believe you qualify for financial aid, please contact us." This way the organization demonstrates an awareness and gives a patient the opportunity to contact the hospital to ask "If I qualify, what should my bill be?"

Billing and Collection Requirements

Fourth, a hospital facility may not undertake certain extraordinary collection actions (even if otherwise permitted by law) against a patient without first making reasonable efforts to inform the patient about the hospital's financial assistance policy and to determine whether the patient is eligible for assistance under the policy (Code Sec. 501(r)(6)).

> **COMMENT:** Such extraordinary collection actions include lawsuits, liens on residences, arrests, body attachments, or other similar collection processes (Committee Report for Senate Finance Healthcare Reform, *America's Healthy Future Act of 2009* (October 19, 2009)).

> **COMMENT:** It is intended that, for this purpose, reasonable efforts include notification by the hospital of its financial assistance policy upon admission and in written and oral communications with the patient regarding the patient's bill, including invoices and telephone calls, before collection action or reporting to credit rating agencies is initiated (Committee Report for Senate Finance Health-care Reform, *America's Healthy Future Act of 2009* (October 19, 2009)).

Excise Tax for Failure to Meet Hospital Exemption Requirements

If a hospital organization must meet the additional requirements under Code Sec. 501(r) and fails to meet the community health needs assessments requirements under Code Sec. 501(r)(3), a $50,000 excise tax is imposed on the hospital for any year (Code Sec. 4959).

Mandatory Review of Tax Exemption for Hospitals

The Secretary of the Treasury will review at least once, every three years, the community benefit activities of each hospital organization to which Code Sec. 501(r) applies (Act Sec. 9007(c) of PPACA).

> **COMMENT:** Former IRS Commissioner, Tax Exempt and Government Entities Division (TE/GE), Sarah Hall Ingram has observed that this process is not an audit but rather is a no-contact review. The IRS would not contact a tax-exempt unless it found an issue of potential noncompliance with a hospital. At this point, she noted, the review could become a compliance check.

Additional Reporting Requirements

A hospital must disclose, in its annual information report to the IRS (Form 990, *Return of Organization Exempt From Income Tax,* and related schedules), how it is addressing the needs identified in the CHNA and, if all identified needs are not addressed, the reasons why (for example, lack of financial or human resources) (Code Sec. 6033(b)(15)(A)).

PPACA also requires each organization to which Code Sec. 501(r)(3) applies to file with its annual information return a copy of its audited financial statements (or, in the case of an organization the financial statements of which are included in a consolidated financial statement with other organizations, such consolidated financial statements) (Code Sec. 6033(b)(15)(B)).

Reports. PPACA requires the IRS, in consultation with the Secretary of Health and Human Services, to report annually to Congress the levels of charity care, bad debt expenses, unreimbursed costs of means-tested government programs, and unreimbursed costs of nonmeans-tested government programs incurred by private tax-exempt, taxable, and governmental hospitals, as well as the cost of community benefit activities incurred by private tax-exempt hospitals (Act Sec. 9007(e)(1) of PPACA).

In addition, the IRS, in consultation with the Secretary of Health and Human Services, must conduct a study of the trends in these amounts with the results of the study provided to Congress five years from March 23, 2010 (Act Sec. 9007(e)(2) of PPACA).

> **PRACTICAL ANALYSIS:** Charles Goulding, president and founder of Energy Tax Savers, observes that in recent years there has been concern that certain charitable or not-for-profit hospitals have not been providing the charitable medical services that their privileged not-for-profit status was predicated on, particularly if they are perceived not to be serving the local community. Not-for-profit status typically impacts numerous taxes, including federal, state, and city incomes taxes; property taxes; and sales taxes. In certain localities, a not-for-profit hospital may be

the largest enterprise, employer, and landowner. With the budget constraints impacting all levels of government, there are multiple tax authorities interested in the tax status of these hospitals.

Not-for-profit hospitals will need to establish tax documentation processes to substantiate their continuing right to not-for-profit status. This documentation should be aimed at supporting both federal tax-exempt status and local law-exempt status based on their state charter and state not-for-profit law requirements. Internal control processes should be aimed at achieving perfect reporting compliance so that any inadvertent omission or late filing is not used to put tax status at issue.

There are some large hospital organizations with a mix of for-profit and not-for-profit organizations. When serving overlapping communities, these organizations may have the flexibility to rebalance patient services to ensure compliance with the developing hospital not-for-profit status compliance requirements.

¶ 706 IRS ISSUES FINAL REGULATIONS ON PPACA REQUIREMENTS FOR TAX-EXEMPT HOSPITALS

The IRS has issued final regulations under Code Sec. 501(r) on the additional requirements for charitable hospital organizations to maintain their tax-exempt status under Code Sec. 501(c)(3) (T.D. 9708). The regulations address the requirements for hospitals to conduct a CHNA every three years, to adopt an implementation strategy to meet these needs, and to adopt financial policies that benefit needy individuals.

> **COMMENT:** "The final regulations are well conceived and well written," Nancy Ortmeyer Kuhn, director, Jackson and Campbell, P.C., Washington, D.C., told Wolters Kluwer when they were first released. "They follow the legislative intent and give hospitals the tools they need to objectively satisfy the CHNA and financial policy requirements. I was concerned that the regulations would include a lot of facts and circumstances tests that allow for subjective determinations by the IRS, but they didn't do that."

Effective Dates

The CHNA requirement first applied to tax years beginning after March 23, 2012. The other requirements first applied to tax years beginning after March 23, 2010. The final regulations, to the extent they impose new requirements, generally will not take effect until the hospital's first tax year beginning after December 29, 2015. For tax years beginning on or before that date, a hospital may rely on a reasonable good faith interpretation of the statutory requirements. Complying with either the proposed regulations or the final regulations will satisfy the good faith requirement.

> **COMMENT:** "The rules provide charitable hospitals with adequate time to fully update their policies and programming to implement the changes," Emily McMahon, the Deputy Assistant Secretary for Tax Policy at the U.S. Department of the Treasury, said.

However, the regulations on CHNA reporting violations and excise taxes, which merely clarified or confirmed requirements already in effect, went into effect December 29, 2014.

Hospital Defined

A *hospital organization* is an organization recognized, or seeking to be recognized, under Code Sec. 501(c)(3), that operates one or more hospital facilities. A *hospital facility* is a facility that is required by a state to be licensed, registered, or similarly recognized as a hospital.

The final regulations provide that multiple buildings operated by a hospital organization under a single state license are a single hospital facility. The final regulations also clarify that for a hospital facility with multiple locations the community served is the aggregate of such areas or populations. However, a hospital facility consisting of multiple buildings may assess the health needs of the different geographic areas or populations served by the different buildings separately and document the assessments in separate chapters or sections of the hospital facility's community health needs assessment report and implementation strategy.

Financial Assistance Policies

One concern for hospitals was the requirement to adequately communicate their FAPs to patients. According to Treasury, the regulations revise the notification requirements to protect patients while easing the burden on hospitals. General notifications must appear on bills and conspicuously in the hospital. However, individual notifications are only required when a hospital plans to use extraordinary collection actions, such as reporting a debt to a credit bureau, selling the debt to a third party, or garnishing wages.

Additionally, the final regulations only require a plain language summary to be included with one post-discharge communication and give a hospital the flexibility to send this one plain language summary only to the subset of patients against whom the hospital actually intends to engage in extraordinary collection actions. These changes are intended to maintain the frequent reminders to patients of the availability of financial aid while reducing the burden and cost of mailing multiple copies of a plain language summary of the financial aid policy.

The final regulations also include a threshold for translating the FAP and related documents into the primary language of any populations with limited English proficiency of 5 percent of the residents of the community served by the hospital. This may increase the overall number of translations that hospital organizations will be required to make.

> **COMMENT:** Kuhn expressed a concern that there are no minimum standards for financial assistance policies. "There is nothing in the statute or regulations," Kuhn said. "A hospital could provide a narrow standard. The requirements don't accomplish anything for middle-income people; hospitals can still bill at high rates and take aggressive financial collection actions. But you can't expect the IRS to draft regulations that are tougher than the statute."

Reporting and Penalties

If a hospital fails to meet the consumer protection standards, the IRS could revoke its tax-exempt status. If a hospital fails to properly conduct a CHNA and adopt an implementation strategy, a $50,000 excise tax will apply. If a hospital's failure is neither willful nor egregious, the hospital can correct and disclose the error. This will avoid revocation, but the excise tax will still apply to CHNA violations. The final regulations also require that a hospital disclose its FAPs, its CHNA, and its implementation strategy for the CHNA. Revocation of exempt status may be endangered for failures to meet the requirements that are material, continuous, and not corrected.

A hospital facility's failure to meet a Code Sec. 501(r) requirement that is neither willful nor egregious will be excused if the organization corrects the failure and, if required, makes proper disclosure. If a hospital facility is not sure whether its failure is willful or egregious, the organization probably should correct and disclose, Jeanne Schuster, Ernst & Young LLP, Boston, said in December 2014. This will "help you and be an indicator that it was not willful and egregious. But you will not get a presumption that you have done everything right, so you may still suffer penalties and possibly, depending on the facts, have your exempt status revoked."

She also said a hospital should look at practices and procedures the organization should implement or change to prevent future occurrences.

COMMENT: "The CHNA and the FAP are both public documents," Kuhn said. "The information provided will assist the IRS and nonprofits involved in 'policing' hospitals, to see if they are really charitable. Public involvement will help the IRS's enforcement efforts."

The regulations impose a facility-level income tax on hospital organizations that operate more than one hospital facility when one of its facilities fails to satisfy Code Sec. 501(r). The overall organization would retain its tax-exempt status but would have to pay taxes on its income in noncompliant years.

COMMENT: Kuhn said it is unusual for regulations to impose a tax that is not in the statute.

STUDY QUESTION

---

3. If a hospital's failure to meet Code Sec. 501(r) requirements is neither willful nor egregious, which of the following is **not** a possible consequence?

    a. To avoid revocation of its tax-exempt status, the facility can correct and properly disclose the failure

    b. An income tax is imposed on multifacility hospital organizations with a facility failing to satisfy Code Sec. 501(r)

    c. A $50,000 excise tax will apply for failure to conduct a CHNA and adopt an implementation strategy

    d. The hospital's tax-exempt status can be revoked

¶ 707 IRS FINALIZES PROCEDURES FOR NONPROFIT HOSPITALS TO CORRECT NONWILLFUL VIOLATIONS UNDER CODE SEC. 501(r)

The IRS has finalized a revenue procedure that allows tax-exempt hospitals to correct and disclose violations that are not willful or egregious for purposes of Code Sec. 501(r) (Rev. Proc. 2015-21). The IRS explained that it will not treat the violations that are corrected and disclosed as a failure to comply with the additional requirements for hospitals to qualify as tax-exempt organizations under Code Sec. 501(c)(3).

COMMENT: "There is always a transition period to figure out what will comply with the rules," Nancy Ortmeyer Kuhn, director, Jackson & Campbell, P.C., Washington, D.C., told Wolters Kluwer after the new procedure was finalized in March 2015. "The examples in Section 6 [of Rev. Proc. 2015-21] seem to give hospitals a longer grace period and a second chance to comply with Code Sec. 501(r), assuming the hospital adopted a report or policy. This will be helpful to hospitals," she said.

COMMENT: "The requirements of Section 501(r) are onerous. This procedure allows some wiggle room and gives more comfort to hospitals that inadvertent violations will not subject them to an excise tax or to revocation," Kuhn said.

Procedures

The regulations provided for two categories of correction:

- Under Reg. § 1.501(r)-2(b) an error or omission will be excused that is (1) minor and either inadvertent or due to reasonable cause and (2) corrected by the hospital promptly after discovery. Correction must include establishing or revising procedures to promote overall compliance with Code Sec. 501(r).

- Under Reg. § 1.501(r)-2(c), a failure that is neither willful nor egregious will be excused if the hospital corrects and makes disclosure in accordance with IRS guidance.

In Notice 2014-3, the IRS provided a draft revenue procedure that provided correction and disclosure procedures under which certain failures to meet the requirements of Code Sec. 501(r) would be excused. The IRS finalized the correction procedures in Rev. Proc. 2015-21, effective March 10, 2015.

Rev. Proc. 2015-21 provides that minor omissions and errors in the first category will not be considered failures to comply with Code Sec. 501(r). Hospitals do not need to follow the correction and disclosure procedures that apply to the second category of failures.

> **COMMENT:** "Even though the examples of minor and inadvertent violations are trivial, the concept is still helpful," Kuhn said.

The revenue procedure defines a willful failure as a failure due to gross negligence, reckless disregard, or willful neglect. An egregious failure is a very serious failure, based on the impact and the number of persons affected. Willfulness or egregiousness will depend on all the facts and circumstances. Correction and disclosure of a failure will indicate that the failure was not willful, a change from Notice 2014-3.

> **COMMENT:** "The IRS stated several times that timely correction and disclosure is a factor in determining willfulness," Kuhn said. "The IRS strongly implied that disclosure would protect an organization from a finding that its violations were willful; I doubt that the IRS would find a violation willful if it were corrected early. The penalty for a willful violation would be revocation," she said.

Correction and Disclosure

Rev. Proc. 2015-21 sets out several correction principles and provides examples of violations that may be corrected. All affected individuals should be restored to their appropriate position, even if the violation occurred in a prior year or a closed year, taking into account the seriousness and impact of such failure. Correction should be reasonable and appropriate, and should occur promptly after discovery. The hospital should establish practices and procedures to facilitate overall compliance and should revise existing procedures if needed.

Disclosure requires reporting particular information on a timely Form 990 for the year that the failure is discovered. An organization that does not file a Form 990 can still report the information on the form or provide the information on a website. Disclosure requires:

- A description of the failure, its cause, location, date, number of occurrences, number of persons affected, and dollars involved;

- A description of the correction, including how affected individuals were restored to their appropriate position; and

- A description of the practices or procedures established or revised, or an explanation why no changes were needed.

If a hospital organization is contacted by the IRS regarding an examination, the organization may use the procedures described in the guidance provided that, at the time the hospital is first contacted by the IRS, (a) the hospital has corrected or is in the process of correcting the failure, and (b) if the due date (including all extensions) for the annual return for the tax year in which the failure was discovered has passed (or would have passed, in the case of a hospital organization that is not required to file an annual return), the hospital organization has already disclosed the failure.

Multiple errors of the same type should be reported in the aggregate in a summary. In the case of errors involving the operational requirements described in Reg. §§ 1.501(r)-5 or § 1.501(r)-6, an estimate of the number of individuals affected and the dollar amounts involved is also required.

STUDY QUESTION

4. Under the IRS final procedures for correction by nonprofit hospitals, which of the following is **not** an error or omission that may be excused?

    a. A minor violation that is inadvertent or due to reasonable cause

    b. A failure due to gross negligence

    c. A minor omission as described in Rev. Proc. 2015-21

    d. A failure that is neither willful nor egregious that is corrected and disclosed properly

¶ 708 JOINT VENTURES

Joint ventures between tax-exempt and for-profit health entities are increasingly common and they have generated difficult tax questions. For example, the definition of licensed hospital under state law brings up many questions. In the state of Texas for instance, Code Sec. 501(r) generally does not apply to ambulatory surgery centers. However, in other states the centers may be considered licensed facilities. Health systems should work with the organization's general counsel and others who understand the hospital licensing process and what facilities are included in that license.

That controversy was raised another level in a case for a tax refund after the IRS revoked a hospital's tax-exempt status because it had partnered with a for-profit healthcare company (**St. David's Health Care System Inc.,** CA-5, 2003-2 USTC ¶ 50,713). The Fifth Circuit found that the IRS raised material issues of fact regarding whether the partnership interfered with the hospital's ability to operate exclusively for exempt purposes. Historically, the IRS had held that a tax-exempt organization's participation in a joint venture with a for-profit entity was a per se violation of Code Sec. 501. Now, although such joint ventures are allowable, the nonprofit's level of control is highly scrutinized.

St. David's operated for many years as a nonprofit. For most of its existence, it was recognized as tax-exempt under Code Sec. 501(c)(3). Due to financial difficulties in the healthcare industry in the 1990s, the hospital decided to consolidate with a for-profit healthcare organization (Columbia/HCA Healthcare Corporation (HCA)). The IRS audited the hospital and determined that it no longer qualified for tax-exempt status because it had ceded control over its operations to the for-profit entity. Both the hospital and the IRS filed motions for summary judgment in district court, which granted the hospital's motion and ordered a tax refund. The IRS appealed to the Fifth Circuit.

To qualify for Code Sec. 501(c)(3) tax-exempt status, the hospital was required to show that it was organized and operated exclusively for a charitable purpose. The hospital met the organizational test in that it was created for an exempt purpose. To pass the operational test, the hospital had to show that it:

- Engaged primarily in activities that accomplished its exempt purpose;
- Did not have net earnings that inured to the benefit of private shareholders or individuals;
- Did not expend a substantial part of its resources attempting to influence legislation or political campaigns; and
- Served a valid purpose and conferred a public benefit.

The IRS argued that the hospital failed the first prong of the operational test because, since partnering with a for-profit company, its primary purpose was no longer charitable. The IRS did not contend that tax-exempt status is automatically lost when a partnership is formed with a for-profit entity. Rather, the IRS argued that a nonprofit loses its tax exemption if it gives control over the partnership to a for-profit entity. In the IRS's view, when a nonprofit cedes control, it can no longer ensure that its partnership activities primarily further its charitable purpose.

The hospital asserted that the issue in determining tax-exempt status is not which entity controls the partnership, but rather the partnership's function. The hospital argued that it passed the operational test because its activities, via the partnership, contributed to its charitable purpose of providing healthcare to all persons. Disagreeing with the hospital, the appellate court observed that even if the hospital performed charitable services, it would not qualify for Code Sec. 501(c)(3) status if its activities substantially furthered the profit-seeking interests of its partner. The key issue, in the appellate court's opinion, was whether the partnership with a for-profit company interfered with the hospital's ability to operate exclusively for exempt purposes.

The Fifth Circuit looked to Rev. Rul. 98-15 as the starting point of its analysis. Rev. Rul. 98-15 addresses how a charitable hospital can retain its tax-exempt status when it forms a partnership with a for-profit entity. A nonprofit can demonstrate control by showing that:

- The partnership's founding documents expressly state that it has a charitable purpose and it will take priority over all other concerns;
- The partnership agreement gives the nonprofit organization a majority vote on the partnership's board of directors; and
- The partnership is managed by an independent company not affiliated with the for-profit entity.

In vacating summary judgment, the Fifth Circuit ruled that there were outstanding issues of material fact concerning the nonprofit's level of control in the joint venture. The court cited:

- Flaws in the partnership agreement;
- The nonprofit's level of power (or lack thereof) within the partnership; and
- Conflict of interest between the for-profit partner and a management service that had a long-term contract at the hospital and the for-profit company.

The appellate court observed that even if the hospital performed charitable services, it would not qualify for Code Sec. 501(c)(3) status if its activities substantially furthered the profit-seeking interests of its partner. The key issue, in the appellate court's opinion, was whether the partnership with a for-profit company interfered with the hospital's ability to operate exclusively for exempt purposes. Until those issues of fact were explored, the question of control, which was at the heart of a finding a whether tax-exempt status had been lost, could not be resolved.

COMMENT: An IRS official has commented that the IRS's view would be more in line with the Fifth Circuit's ruling and noted that the original district court's summary judgment "was more of an aberration." He said that the IRS is concerned that joint ventures with a tax-exempt organization are operated for a charitable purpose and noted that the Fifth Circuit makes the point to analyze the structure and management of the joint venture.

The issues of fact were explored when the Fifth Circuit sent the case back to the district court to retry the case. In remanding the case, the appellate court ruled that there were outstanding issues regarding the hospital's level of control in the joint venture. The hospital had the burden of proving that it was entitled to the tax exemption. The hospital had to show, by a preponderance of the evidence, that the operations with the partnership primarily furthered charitable purposes and only incidentally benefited the for-profit healthcare organization. The jury decided that the hospital proved that it was entitled to a tax exemption (***St. David's Health Care System, Inc.,*** DC Tex., Civil Action No. JN, March 12, 2004). The hospital had originally argued that the issue relevant to its tax-exempt status was the partnership's continued charitable function, not which entity controlled the partnership. Nevertheless, it convinced the jury that it had sufficient control in the partnership.

The instructions given to the jury offer some insight as to how similar nonprofit/for-profit joint ventures may be viewed in the future. Jury instructions included the following:

- *Charitable purposes.* Providing free or below-cost healthcare services to eligible individuals in the community is a charitable and exempt purpose under the tax code.
- *Profit.* Operating the partnership at a profit does not preclude a finding that the partnership's operations primarily further charitable purposes.
- *HCA's profit share.* The fact that the for-profit partner received a pro rata share of the capital and profits of the partnership is not an impermissible benefit to the for-profit partner and is not to be considered in determining whether the partnership's operations were more than an incidental benefit to it.
- *"Sufficient" control.* The jury also was instructed to consider whether the hospital had "sufficient" control in the partnership, not necessarily total control. Control may be demonstrated by (1) majority voting power on the governing board or (2) through the exercise of the hospital's rights and powers under the partnership agreement.

PLANNING NOTE: When the practitioner drafts a joint venture agreement, it is important that the parties consider how they will ultimately enforce their rights. To demonstrate sufficient control, the nonprofit should be able to initiate action without the for-profit's consent. In addition, a community-member board requirement may be helpful. However, a nonprofit could show that it had not ceded control to the for-profit partner even if there is no community board.

¶ 709 ELECTRONIC HEALTH RECORD SUBSIDIES

The IRS released a directive explaining that the IRS will not treat the benefits that a hospital provides to its medical staff physicians as impermissible private benefit or inurement in violation of Code Sec. 501(c)(3) if the benefit falls within the range of health IT items and services allowed by the Department of Health and Human Services' electronic health record (EHR) regulations, and the hospital operates in accordance with the conditions set forth in the IRS directive (**www.irs.gov/pub/irs-tege/ehrdirective.pdf**, May 11, 2007). Providers of such systems work with exempt health-care organizations to implement their products, often at substantially reduced fees.

Six questions and answers, which can be found on the IRS website (**www.irs.gov/pub/irs-tege/ehr_qa_062007.pdf**), clarify the following:

- *Financial assistance and subsidies.* The terms "financial assistance" and "subsidies" used in the directive refer to arrangements in which the hospital provides a physician with EHR-related software, information technology or training services, and the physician contributes a portion of the cost. The terms are consistent with the Department of Health and Human Services (HHS) regulations and do not refer to cash payments from hospitals to physicians.

- *Consistent conditions.* If a hospital's EHR subsidy arrangement is not entirely consistent with the conditions set forth in the IRS's directive, the arrangement will not be covered by the safe harbor described in the directive. However, this does not necessarily mean that the arrangement will produce impermissible private benefit or inurement. An IRS agent will look at "all the facts and circumstances" surrounding the arrangement.

- *Disqualified persons.* Assuming that a hospital meets all the conditions set forth in the IRS's directive, an IRS agent will not treat a health IT subsidy arrangement provided to a Code Sec. 4958 "disqualified person" as an excess benefit transaction.

- *Inurement outside EHR arrangements.* If an IRS agent finds that the net earnings of a hospital have inured to the benefit of one or more staff physicians outside the context of an EHR arrangement, the hospital will not be covered by the directive's safe harbor provision. However, a determination of whether the arrangement itself produces impermissible private benefit or inurement will require inquiry into all the facts and circumstances surrounding the arrangement.

- *Access restrictions.* A staff physician may deny a hospital access to patient records if the access would violate federal and state privacy laws or a physician's contractual obligations to patients. Also, a hospital and staff physician may establish "reasonable conditions" relating to the hospital's access.

- *Access availability.* A hospital may provide access to its health IT items and services to various groups of physicians at different times according to criteria related to meeting the healthcare needs of the community.

STUDY QUESTION

---

5. Which of the following circumstances makes EHR subsidies ineligible for the safe harbor under the 2007 IRS directive?

    a. Provision of financial assistance to physicians for software, information technology, or training

    b. Inurement of staff physicians outside of the context of the EHR arrangement with the hospital

    c. Access restrictions for the hospital by a staff physician

    d. The hospital's provision of access to its health IT items and services to selected groups of physicians to meet the community's healthcare needs

Regional Health Information Organizations

Regional health information organizations (RHIOs) are organizations formed and operated to facilitate the exchange of EHRs among hospitals, physicians, and others in the healthcare system. For an organization to be granted tax-exempt status under Code Sec. 501(c)(3), it must be organized and operated exclusively for one or more exempt purposes. Lessening the burdens of government is one of many exempt purposes under Code Sec. 501(c)(3).

COMMENT: The IRS is concerned that an RHIO might serve the commercial interests of an insurer and, therefore, operate for substantial private benefit.

As part of the *American Recovery and Reinvestment Act of 2009* (ARRA) (P.L. 111-5), Congress enacted legislation designed to promote health information technology development and information exchange. By enacting the law, Congress recognized that facilitating health information exchange and technology is important to improving the delivery of healthcare and reducing the costs of healthcare delivery and administration. The legislative history of the provisions acknowledges that certain organizations that are organized and operated to facilitate the exchange of information, and that satisfy standards established by the Department of Health and Human Services, lessen the burden of government and may qualify for exemption under Code Sec. 501(c)(3).

COMMENT: ARRA included $19 billion in subsidies were allocated to RHIOs.

In a successful tax exemption application the IRS, using a facts and circumstances standard, looks for lessening the burden of government, promoting health, or furthering educational purpose. In an unsuccessful application (IRS Letter Ruling 200942068), an organization that was not attached to a hospital or physicians group was not operated exclusively for one or more exempt purposes. The applicant organization did not provide healthcare services to patients, but to its members, which consisted of employers and health plans. The activities of the organization served a substantial nonexempt commercial purpose and conferred a substantial private benefit on the members of the organization.

Be careful to see what the exemption rules are in your state. An organization might have a harder time obtaining nonprofit status under state law because the organization is not a hospital or school. Gary Horowitz, Ernst & Young, Iselin, NJ, has advised practitioners assisting a client in implementing an RHIO to think about whether there is taxable income for subsidies to physicians, if there is unrelated business income to hospitals on fees earned to put the RHIO into place, and if there would be private business use of tax-exempt bond proceeds.

COMMENT: Steve Grodnitsky, TE/GE, said that the IRS has received a large number of applications for Code Sec. 501(c)(3) status as RHIOs. He said the IRS "is trying to wrap its arms around the legal issues involved" with these entities and determine whether they qualify for tax-exempt status. For instance, the IRS is looking at whether these organizations promote health, further educational purposes, lessen the burdens of government, or provide improper benefits that would "knock them out of 501(c)(3)," said Grodnitsky. He added that RHIOs may, in fact, lessen the burdens of government.

Grodnitsky also revealed that the IRS is receiving a number of international healthcare cases "involving hospital systems established as subordinate organizations that contract with a foreign entity to provide some sort of medical service, or educational services, or management consulting services, all to get organizations in other countries up and running." The issue is whether these organizations qualify for Code Sec. 501(c)(3) status. Many of these cases involve organizations in the Middle East and Latin America, he said.

STUDY QUESTION

6. Regional health information organizations (RHIOs) are formed and operated to:

    a. Service the commercial interests of an insurer

    b. Facilitate the exchange of EHRs among providers in the healthcare system

    c. Safeguard patient privacy and accessibility to protected health information

    d. Share patients' health information with providers worldwide

¶ 710 GROUP PURCHASING ORGANIZATIONS

Group purchasing organizations (GPOs) are easily overlooked by exempt organizations, which is unfortunate, because GPOs can help many healthcare organizations save costs and discover better ways of acquiring supplies. There has been considerable activity lately regarding GPOs, said Mike Vecchioni, Ernst & Young LLP, Detroit, at a December 2014 health sciences tax conference, "with organizations deciding to form new GPOs, with new partners, or GPOs that have been in existence are busting up or reorganizing."

A GPO is an intermediary that negotiates contracts for medical equipment or supplies on behalf of its members. For its members, a GPO can obtain better prices and services from vendors. GPOs can be structured in various taxable or tax-exempt forms. To be a tax-exempt entity, an organization whose primary purpose is providing shared services can be exempt only if it is organized and operated under Code Sec. 501(e). Providing shared services, such as group purchasing, to otherwise unrelated charitable organizations is not, in and of itself, charitable but rather is an ordinary business activity.

One of the real shortcomings of 501(e), Vecchioni said, is that its restrictions are numerous and it becomes more difficult to adhere to the section's requirements as the organization grows and is involved in more complex or technically advanced transactions.

In addition, a Code Sec. 501(e) cooperative is entitled to the benefits of Code Sec. 501(c)(3) organizations, such as the ability to receive tax-deductible contributions and use the proceeds of qualified 501(c)(3) bonds.

The Code Sec. 501(e) structure, Vecchioni said, is intended to encourage cooperative activities between and among hospitals to make the healthcare industry more cost effective.

¶ 711 HOSPITAL REPORTING, SCHEDULE H

Form 990, Schedule H, Hospitals, must be completed by an organization that operates at least one facility that is, or is required to be, licensed, registered, or similarly recognized by a state as a hospital. This includes a hospital that is operated through a disregarded entity or a joint venture taxed as a partnership. It does not include hospitals that are located outside the United States. It also does not include hospitals that are operated by entities organized as separate legal entities from the organization that are taxed as a corporation for federal income tax purposes (except for members of a group exemption included in a group return filed by the organization). If the organization is not required to file Form 990, it is not required to file Schedule H.

    COMMENT: The definition of hospital for Schedule H purposes is not tied to Code Sec. 170(b)(1)(A)(iii) or the primary purpose of the organization.

COMMENT: "For many hospitals, there is no ability to report certain meaningful community benefits on the form," according to Melinda Hatton, American Hospital Association, Washington, D.C. "For example, if a hospital gives nurse scholarships and requires the recipient to work one week in the hospital, there is no place to report this even though there is a benefit to the community."

In addition, Hatton said that there is no place on the schedule to describe financial assistance that goes beyond the federal poverty guidelines. Another example, Hatton noted, occurs when hospitals that report under multiple employer identification numbers (EINs) provide cross subsidies so that one hospital can provide more financial assistance than otherwise would be possible. This benefit may very well not be reported on the schedule.

COMMENT: "I think it will be a challenge to get meaningful comparisons [where] the reporting will differ significantly depending on how [an organization's system] is set up," Amy Dosik, formerly of Ernst & Young, Atlanta, said. The exclusion from Schedule H of community benefit provided by related entities, other than hospitals, that do not have a community benefit reporting obligation may artificially lower the percentage of community benefit reported on a system-wide basis. Dosik suggested looking at which legal entities in a healthcare system are performing charity care and community benefit in a quantitative way and shifting some of these activities to entities that file a Schedule H to ensure that the system is getting "full credit" for the charity care and community benefit it provides.

COMMENT: If an organization's approach in its community benefit report is different from that of its Schedule H, Howard Levenson, Ernst & Young, Washington, D.C., does not foresee a problem. "If Schedule H doesn't permit you to report things that you think it should permit you to do, I think it is appropriate to articulate that in your community benefit report."

COMMENT: The community benefit report is one place people look to determine whether the organization is fulfilling its duties as a tax-exempt hospital and deserves its exemption, said Kathy Pitts, Ernst & Young, Birmingham.

MODULE 4: ENTITY CONCERNS—Chapter 8: Reducing (Self-) Employment and NII Taxes in Passthrough Entities

¶ 801 WELCOME

This chapter discusses the *Federal Insurance Contribution Act* tax (FICA or employment tax), the *Self-Employment Contribution Act* tax (SECA or self-employment tax), the additional Medicare tax, and the net investment income (NII) tax in the context of passthrough entities. It also discusses a planning technique that can be used to minimize the amounts of these taxes by operating the taxpayer's trade or business as an S corporation, rather than a partnership. Finally, it briefly reviews the application of these taxes to general and limited partners and explains why an S corporation may be a better vehicle for avoiding these taxes than a limited partnership.

¶ 802 LEARNING OBJECTIVES

Upon completion of this chapter, you will be able to:

- Recognize some of the taxes that apply to the owners of passthrough entities;
- Identify circumstances when employment taxes, self-employment tax, additional Medicare tax, and net investment income tax apply in the context of trades or businesses conducted by passthrough entities; and
- Recognize how S corporations can be used to minimize the combined amount of FICA, SECA, additional Medicare tax, and NII tax paid by the owners of a trade or business.

¶ 803 INTRODUCTION

The introduction of the additional Medicare tax—as a component of the FICA and SECA taxes—and NII tax have created new tax burdens for taxpayers who operate trades or businesses through passthrough entities, such as limited liability companies (LLCs), partnerships, and S corporations. However, there are ways to reduce these taxes through careful planning. Principal among these new strategies, partnerships (including limited liability companies (LLCs) taxed as partnerships) can convert to S corporations. By limiting wages paid to S corporation shareholder-employees, the combined FICA taxes paid by the corporation and employee-shareholders may be less than the SECA taxes paid by the owners when the trade or business operated as a partnership. Moreover, provided the shareholders materially participate in the S corporation's trade or business, it will not be a passive activity with respect to them, and they will not be subject to NII tax on their distributive shares of S corporation income.

¶ 804 TAX TREATMENT OF PASSTHROUGH ENTITIES

Partnerships and S corporations are treated as passthrough entities. This means that the entities do not generally pay taxes, but income from the entities passes through to the owners, who include it on their own tax returns. LLCs that have two or more members can choose to be taxed as corporations—either S corporations or C corporations (which pay entity-level taxes)—or as partnerships. LLCs with one member can choose to be taxed as corporations or to be disregarded as separate from their owner, in which case tax items realized by the LLC are included directly on the owner's tax return.

FICA Taxes

Social Security and Medicare taxes are imposed on both employers and employees and calculated based on the wages paid by the employer to the employee. The Social Security tax funds the federal old-age, survivors, and disability insurance (OASDI) program, and the Medicare tax funds the federal hospital insurance (HI) program. Both taxes are provided for by FICA and, thus, are collectively referred to as FICA taxes. Income received by a nonemployee for services (including those of a partner in a partnership) is not subject to FICA.

Both the Social Security tax and the Medicare tax consist of two parts: the employee's portion and the employer's portion. Employers are required to withhold their employees' portion of the taxes from the employees' FICA wages and to pay a matching amount as the employer's portion. FICA taxes are imposed on both the employer and the employee at a rate of 6.2 percent and 1.45 percent, respectively, for a total of 7.65 percent. An additional .09-percent Medicare tax is imposed on employees whose wages exceed a certain level. Employers are required to withhold their employees' portion of the taxes from the employees' FICA wages and to pay a matching amount as the employer's portion. For both the employee's portion and the employer's portion, the amount of an employee's wages that is subject to the OASDI rate is limited to an amount called the *Social Security wage base.* The Social Security wage base is determined by Section 230 of the Social Security Act and is indexed annually for inflation (Code Sec. 3121(a)(1)). The wage base is $118,500 for 2015, and this is the maximum amount subject to the employer's and employee's share of OASDI tax.

Medicare taxes (hospital insurance (HI)) are imposed on both the employee and the employer at a rate of 1.45 percent of wages. In addition, an additional .09-percent Medicare tax (see below) applies to the employee portion for wages and self-employment income over $200,000 ($250,000 for a joint return, $125,000 for married filing separately), increasing the rate to 2.35 percent for wages in excess of the applicable amount (Code Sec. 3101(b)). The employer's portion of the Medicare tax is not subject to the additional .09-percent Medicare tax and remains equal to 1.45 percent of the employee's wages, no matter how high they are (Code Sec. 3111(b)).

SECA Taxes

Every taxpayer who has self-employment income for a tax year must pay a self-employment (SECA) tax in addition to any other applicable taxes. The self-employment tax is equivalent to the Social Security and Medicare taxes required to be paid by employees and employers. As with FICA, the self-employment tax includes a Social Security—or OASDI—component and a Medicare—or HI—component.

A taxpayer's self-employment income is generally equal to his or her net earnings from self-employment for the tax year. Net earnings from self-employment are a taxpayer's gross income from the operation of a trade or business, less the allowable deductions attributable to that trade or business, plus the taxpayer's distributive share of income or loss from any business conducted as a partnership in which he or she is a *general* partner, less an adjustment for self-employment tax. (Limited partners are not usually subject to SECA taxes, as discussed further below.) Gross income from a trade or business for this purpose includes gross income received or accrued in the tax year even though the income is attributable in whole or in part to services rendered or other acts performed in a prior tax year for which the individual was not subject to the tax on self-employment income.

An individual does not pay self-employment tax if his or her net earnings from self-employment are less than $400. If the individual is an employee of a religious organization, the floor is reduced to $100.

Generally, a person is self-employed if he or she carries on a trade or business as a sole proprietor or independent contractor, is a member of a partnership that carries on a trade or business, or is otherwise in business for him- or herself (including a part-time business). A trade or business does not include the performance of services by an individual as an employee, but certain employee services are treated as a trade or business and are therefore subject to self-employment tax.

Every taxpayer who has self-employment income for a tax year must pay a self-employment tax in addition to any other applicable taxes (Code Sec. 1401). The self-employment tax is in lieu of the FICA taxes required to be paid by employees and their employers.

The self-employment tax rate is generally 15.3 percent of self-employment income. This rate is derived by combining the 12.4-percent Social Security tax and the 2.9-percent Medicare tax (Code Sec. 1401(a) and (b)). The rates are equal to the sum of the employee's and employer's FICA OASDI tax rates (6.2 percent each) and the employee's and employer's FICA Medicare tax rate (1.45 percent each). As with FICA, the Social Security component of SECA is subject to the wage base limitation ($118,500 for 2015). Both FICA taxes and SECA taxes apply in full (at a 15.3-percent rate) to employment earnings up to a threshold (e.g., $118,500 in 2015) and at a reduced rate of 2.9 percent on employment earnings above that threshold.

General partners (discussed below) and sole proprietors typically pay SECA taxes on the full amount of their net trade or business income. Limited partners pay SECA taxes only on the fairly narrow category of payments from the partnership that are for services provided and that are determined without regard to the income of the partnership. The application of SECA taxes to members of most limited liability companies (LLCs) is unclear because LLC members are neither general partners nor limited partners under state law. S corporation shareholders are not subject to SECA taxes. Instead, they are subject to FICA taxes on wages paid for services like any other employee.

SECA Tax for Partners

In computing self-employment tax, several special rules apply to individuals who are partners in partnerships. These special rules include the treatment of a partner's distributive share and guaranteed payments, payments to retired partners, and payments to deceased partners.

General partner. A general partner's net earnings from self-employment include his or her distributive share of the income of the partnership and any guaranteed payment for services rendered to the partnership or for the use of capital by the partnership (whether distributed or not). The guaranteed payments are included only to the extent they are determined without regard to the income of the partnership (Reg. § 1.1402(a)-1(b)). A guaranteed payment is offset by the partner's distributive share of any loss sustained by the partnership (Rev. Rul. 56-675, 1956-2 CB 459).

The partnership must be engaged in a trade or business for a partner's distributive share of the income to be considered net earnings from self-employment income (Reg. § 1.1402(a)-1(b)). If the partnership is engaged in a trade or business, the partner's distributive share of the income of the partnership is included in net earnings from self-employment, regardless of whether the individual partner participated in the operations (Reg. § 1.1402(a)-2(g); *Bennett v. Commissioner,* Dec. 54,699(M), TC Memo. 2002-83).

¶804

Limited partner. A limited partner's distributive share of the income from a partnership is excluded from the definition of net earnings from self-employment. This exclusion does not apply to guaranteed payments to the partner to the extent the payments are remuneration for services performed for the partnership. Accordingly, a guaranteed payment to a limited partner for the performance of services to the partnership is included in net earnings from self-employment (Code Sec. 1402(a)(13)).

Under proposed regulations, an individual is a limited partner unless the individual has personal liability for the debts of the partnership by reason of being a partner, has authority to contract on behalf of the partnership, or participates in the partnership for more than 500 hours during the partnership's tax year. An individual who fails solely the 500-hour test may, nevertheless, be a limited partner if:

- The individual owns only one class of partnership interest;
- Limited partners own a substantial and continuing interest in that class of interest; and
- The individual has the same rights and obligations as those limited partners.

Similarly, an individual who fails any one of the tests but who owns multiple classes of interest may be a limited partner with respect to one or more of the interests if other limited partners own a substantial and continuing interest in that class of interest and the individual has the same rights and obligations as those limited partners. However, an individual who provides more than a *de minimis* amount of service to a partnership providing services in the field of law, accounting, health, engineering, architecture, actuarial science, or consulting can never be a limited partner in the partnership (Prop. Reg. § 1.1402(a)-2(h)).

The Tax Court has taken a different approach to defining limited partners, holding that individuals who merely invest in a partnership and do not actively participate in the partnership's business operations are limited partners not subject to self-employment tax, whereas partners who perform services for the partnership in their capacity as partners are subject to self-employment tax. Thus, when a law firm's income was derived from legal services performed by lawyers, and those lawyers invested only a nominal amount for their partnership interest in the firm, the court held that the lawyers' distributive share of the firm's income was subject to self-employment tax because the distributive shares arose from services provided by the lawyers and not from a return on an investment (***Renkemeyer, Campbell, & Weaver, LLP, v. Commissioner,*** Dec. 58,543, 136 TC 137 (2011)).

The IRS issued the proposed regulations in 1997 to facilitate the determination by individuals as to whether they are limited partners for purposes of Code Sec. 1402(a)(13), thereby reducing the uncertainty in calculating net earnings from self-employment. In response, however, the U.S. Senate passed a resolution stating that the IRS should withdraw the proposed regulations and that Congress should determine the tax law governing self-employment for limited partners (143 Cong. Rec. 13297 (1997)). The IRS has neither withdrawn nor finalized the regulations, and Congress has not acted to clarify the law. Thus, lacking guidance from both the IRS and Congress, the court, in ***Renkemeyer,*** determined its definition of a limited partner by looking at Congress' original intent at the time it created the exclusion for limited partners under Code Sec. 1402(a)(13) in 1977. An IRS official has since indicated, however, that the IRS will not challenge transactions that rely on the proposed regulations.

Additional Medicare Tax

Form W-2 wages above a certain amount are subject to the 0.9 percent additional Medicare tax imposed on the employee as part of the FICA tax. The threshold amount is $200,000 for a taxpayer filing as single, head of household, or surviving spouse; $250,000 for a joint return; and $125,000 for a married taxpayer filing a separate return. The additional Medicare tax is imposed on the employee, not the employer. Amounts below the thresholds are not subject to additional Medicare tax.

The additional Medicare tax is also imposed on self-employment income exceeding the $200,000, $250,000, or $125,000 threshold amount. Unlike the Social Security wage base, the $200,000 and $250,000/$125,000 amounts at which the 0.9 percent Medicare tax starts to apply are not adjusted annually for inflation. A similar 0.9-percent additional Medicare tax applies for FICA purposes, and if any portion of the taxpayer's self-employment income is subject to that other additional tax, then that portion of income is excluded for purposes of determining the additional tax on self-employment income.

Net Investment Income Tax

The Affordable Care Act (ACA) imposed a 3.8-percent tax on investment income for certain high-income earners. This 3.8-percent tax, referred to as the net investment income (NII) tax, is imposed on the net amount from investments of individuals and estates and trusts for tax years beginning in tax years after December 31, 2012 (Code Sec. 1411).

The net investment income (NII) tax for individuals is 3.8 percent of the lesser of:

- The taxpayer's NII for the tax year; or
- The taxpayer's modified adjusted gross income (MAGI) in excess of $200,000 ($250,000 for joint filers and surviving spouses, $125,000 for married taxpayer filing separately) (Code Sec. 1411).

These thresholds are the same as for the additional Medicare tax, except that the $250,000 limit applies to surviving spouses (qualifying widow(er)s with at least one dependent child). They, too, are not adjusted for inflation each year.

In general, net investment income (NII) includes the sum of the taxpayer's items in the following three categories (or "baskets"), over allowable deductions that are properly allocable to them:

- Most gross income from interest, dividends, annuities, royalties and rents, unless they are from a non-Category (ii) trade or business (*Category (i) income*);
- Gross income from a trade or business that is a passive activity (see below) with respect to the taxpayer, or is a commodities or financial instruments trading business (*Category (ii) income*); and
- Net gain derived from the disposition of property, other than property held in a non-Category (ii) trade or business of the taxpayer (i.e., an active trade or business of the taxpayer that is not a commodities or financial instruments trading business) (*Category (iii) income*).

The NII tax does not apply to any item taken into account in determining self-employment income for the tax year on which an individual pays Medicare taxes (Code Sec. 1411(c)(6)). However, the contrapositive of that statement is not true—income that is not subject to self-employment tax will not necessarily be subject to NII taxes. This creates planning opportunities, one of which is discussed below.

STUDY QUESTION

1. The SECA tax for self-employed taxpayers is imposed:

    a. As an equivalent to FICA taxes to fund Social Security and hospital insurance

    b. On a limited partner's distributive share of partnership income

    c. On a self-employed taxpayer's gross income

    d. On net investment income

Passive activities (material participation). As mentioned above, the distributive share of S corporation income allocated to an S corporation shareholder can escape both the additional Medicare tax and—if he or she materially participates in the S corporation's trade or business—also escapes the NII tax.

To determine whether a shareholder-employee materially participates in an S corporation's trade or business, the same tests apply that are used in determining whether that shareholder-employee materially participates in an activity under the passive activity loss rules.

An activity is generally a passive activity if it involves the conduct of any trade or business in which the taxpayer does not materially participate (Code Sec. 469(c)(1)). Material participation in an activity requires that a taxpayer be involved in the operations of the activity on a regular, continuous, and substantial basis (Code Sec. 469(h)(1)). Participation generally includes any work done by an individual who owns an interest in the activity, or the individual's spouse (Reg. § 1.469-5(f)(1); Temporary Reg. § 1.469-5T(f)(3)). However, work done by an investor in his or her capacity as such is not treated as participation unless the investor is involved in the day-to-day management or operations of the activity. Work done in the capacity of an investor includes studying and reviewing financial statements or reports on operations of the activity, preparing or compiling summaries or analyses of the finances or operations of the activity for the individual's own use, and monitoring the finances or operations of the activity in a nonmanagerial capacity (Temporary Reg. § 1.469-5T(f)(3)).

Whether a taxpayer's participation constitutes material participation is generally determined under the facts and circumstances, or by meeting one of several tests. A taxpayer who owns an interest in a limited partnership as a limited partner generally is not treated as materially participating in the limited partnership's activities, but may nevertheless be treated as materially participating if certain requirements are met. For farming, management work may be material participation if income derived from the management work is self-employment income. An estate or trust is deemed to materially participate in an activity if an executor or other fiduciary, in his or her capacity as such, materially participates in the activity. The passive activity limitations do not directly apply to S corporations and partnerships at the entity level. Any losses and credits passed through these entities to their respective shareholders or partners are subject to the passive activity limitations at the shareholder or partner level. Thus, material participation is determined at the partner or shareholder level.

In general, an individual is treated as materially participating in an activity for purposes of the passive activity rules during the tax year only if any one of the following tests is met:

- The individual participates in the activity for more than 500 hours during the year;
- The individual's participation constitutes all of the participation in the activity by all individuals for the year;
- The individual participates in the activity for more than 100 hours during the tax year and his participation in the activity is not less than the participation in the activity of any other individual for the year;
- The activity is a significant participation activity for the individual for the tax year, and his or her aggregate participation in all significant participation activities exceeds 500 hours for the year;
- The individual materially participated in the activity for any five tax years (which do not need to be consecutive) during the 10 tax years that immediately precede the current tax year;
- The activity is a personal service activity, and the individual materially participated in the activity for any three tax years (need not be consecutive) preceding the current tax year; or
- The individual does not satisfy any of the other tests but, based on all of the facts and circumstances, the individual participates in the activity on a regular, continuous, and substantial basis for such tax year (Temp. Reg. § 1.469-5T(a)).

The 500-hour test. An individual who participates in an activity for more than 500 hours during the year is treated as materially participating in the activity (Temp. Reg. § 1.469-5T(a)(1)).

The substantially all test. An individual whose participation in an activity for a tax year constitutes substantially all of the participation in the activity by all individuals for the year (including individuals who are not owners of interests in the activity) is treated as materially participating in the activity (Temp. Reg. § 1.469-5T(a)(2)).

> **EXAMPLE:** Bill Hemmingsen is employed full time as an accountant. Bill also is the sole shareholder of an S corporation that engages in construction activities that constitute a trade or business activity. Bill is the only participant in the activity for the tax year. Each Saturday throughout the tax year, Bill works for six hours in the activity. Although Bill does not participate in the activity for more than 500 hours during the tax year, he is treated as materially participating in the activity because his participation is substantially all of the participation of all individuals in the activity for the year.

The not-less-than-others test. An individual who participates in an activity for more than 100 hours during the tax year and whose participation in the activity is not less than the participation in the activity of any other individual for the year (including individuals who are not owners of interests in the activity) is treated as materially participating in the activity (Temp. Reg. § 1.469-5T(a)(3)).

> **EXAMPLE:** Bill Hastings is employed full time as an accountant. Bill also owns an interest in a partnership that is engaged in a construction activity, which is a trade or business activity conducted entirely on Saturdays. Bill and the other partners—Mark Pearson and David Staron—are the only participants in the activity for the tax year. Each Saturday throughout the tax year, Bill, Mark, and David all work for six hours in the activity. Although Bill does not participate in the activity for more than 500 hours during the tax year, Bill is treated as materially participating in the activity because he participates in the activity for more than 100 hours during the tax year, and Bill's participation in the activity is not less than the participation of any other individual in the activity for the year.

Significant-participation-activities test. An individual is treated as materially participating in an activity if the activity is a significant participation activity for that individual for the tax year, and his or her aggregate participation in all significant participation activities exceeds 500 hours for the year (Temp. Reg. § 1.469-5T(a)(4)). A significant participation activity is a trade or business activity in which the individual participates for more than 100 hours during the tax year but does not otherwise materially participate within the meaning of any other test (Temp. Reg. § 1.469-5T(c)). In determining whether an activity is a significant participation activity, the requirement that the individual not materially participate in the activity is made without applying the significant-participation-activity rule to the particular activity.

EXAMPLE: Diana Chirchi is employed full time as a paralegal. Diana also owns interests in two partnerships that run a restaurant and a shoe store, respectively. The restaurant and shoe store are trade or business activities that are treated as separate activities under the passive activity rules. During the tax year, Diana works in the restaurant for 400 hours and in the shoe store for 150 hours. Both the restaurant and the shoe store activities are significant participation activities for Diana in the tax year. Accordingly, because Diana's aggregate participation in the restaurant and shoe store activities during the tax year exceeds 500 hours, she is treated as materially participating in both activities.

EXAMPLE: Paul Monteleone participates in five trade or business activities in which he owns a partnership interest: restaurant (120 hours), shoe store (75 hours), construction (140 hours), insurance (300 hours), and van conversions (550 hours). The shoe store and van conversions are not significant participation activities for Paul because his participation in them is less than 100 hours and more than 500 hours, respectively. These hours are not counted for purposes of the significant-participation-activities test. The restaurant (120 hours), construction (140 hours), and insurance (300 hours) activities are significant participation activities. Paul is treated as materially participating in all three of these activities because the total of 560 hours (120 + 140 + 300) exceeds 500 hours. Note that Paul is considered to have materially participated in the van conversion activity because he participated in the activity for more than 500 hours.

EXAMPLE: Kevin Postanza owns interests in two partnerships engaged in, respectively, the import-export business and insurance. He participates in two businesses during the tax year as follows: import/export (300 hours) and insurance (600 hours). Because Kevin participates in the insurance activity for more than 500 hours during the tax year, the activity is not a significant participation activity (although Kevin is considered to have materially participated in the insurance activity because he participated in the activity for more than 500 hours). With respect to the import activity, Kevin does significantly participate (i.e., he participates for more than 100 hours), but he is not considered to have materially participated in the activity because he does not satisfy the more than 500-hour requirement for all significant participation activities.

The 5-of-10-preceding-years test. An individual is treated as materially participating in an activity for the current tax year if the individual materially participated in the activity for any 5 tax years (which do not need to be consecutive) during the 10 tax years that immediately precede the current tax year (Temp. Reg. § 1.469-5T(a)(5)). The purpose of this rule is to prevent a retiring taxpayer from converting active income into passive income.

EXAMPLE: In 2005, John Beauteax acquired stock in an S corporation engaged in a trade or business activity. For every tax year from 2005 through 2009, John participated in the activity for more than 500 hours. John retired from the activity at the beginning of 2010 and has not materially participated in the activity in 2010 and subsequent years under any other test. John is treated as materially participating in the activity for tax years 2010 through 2015 because he materially participated in the activity for 5 tax years during the 10 tax years that immediately precede each of those years. John is not treated as materially participating in the activity for tax years after 2015 because for those years John has not materially participated in the activity for 5 of the 10 immediately preceding tax years.

EXAMPLE: Assume the same facts, except that John does not acquire any stock in the S corporation until 2009. John is not treated as materially participating in the activity for any tax year before 2009 because he did not own an interest in the activity for any of the preceding tax years. Accordingly, John materially participates in the activity for only one tax year before 2010, and John is not treated as materially participating in the activity for 2010 or subsequent tax years.

Personal-service-activities test. An individual is treated as materially participating in an activity for the current tax year if the activity is a personal service activity, and the individual materially participated in the activity for any three tax years (need not be consecutive) preceding the current tax year (Temp. Reg. § 1.469-5T(a)(6)). An activity is considered a personal service activity if it involves the performance of personal services in the field of health, law, engineering, architecture, accounting, actuarial science, performing arts, consulting, or any other trade or business in which capital is not a material income producing factor (Temp. Reg. § 1.469-5T(d)).

EXAMPLE: In 2012, Oz acquired stock in an S corporation engaged in the performance of personal services in the field of dentistry. For every tax year from 2012 through 2014, Oz materially participates in the activity under the 500-hour test. Oz retires from the activity at the beginning of 2015 and is not treated as materially participating in the activity for 2015 and subsequent tax years under the 500-hour test. Oz is treated as materially participating in the activity for 2015 and all subsequent tax years because he materially participated in the activity for three tax years.

Facts-and-circumstances test. If a taxpayer does not satisfy any of the other tests, he can be considered to materially participate in an activity for the tax year if, based on all of the facts and circumstances, the individual participates in the activity on a regular, continuous, and substantial basis for the tax year (Temp. Reg. § 1.469-5T(a)(7)). For this test to be satisfied, however, the individual must participate in the activity for more than 100 hours during the tax year (Temp. Reg. § 1.469-5T(b)(2)). The fact that the taxpayer satisfies the requirements of any participation standard (whether referred to as material participation) under Code Sec. 1402 (relating to self-employment) or Code Sec. 2032A (relating to the valuation of farm property for purposes of the estate tax) or any other provision (other than Code Sec. 469) is not taken into account in determining whether the taxpayer materially participates in an activity for purposes of the facts-and-circumstances test.

The regulations do not address what facts and circumstances are to be taken into account for purposes of this test. However, the legislative history discusses several factors to be considered in determining material participation (S. Rep. 99-313, at 733-735 (1986)). None of these factors alone is to be considered conclusive in determining material participation. These factors are:

- *Principal business factor*—A taxpayer is more likely to materially participate in an activity that is his her principal business and less likely to materially participate in an activity that is not her principal business.

- *Regular presence factor*—A taxpayer is more likely to materially participate in an activity when the taxpayer is regularly present at the place where the principal operations of the activity are conducted. However, a taxpayer can materially participate in the operation of an activity without being present at the activity.

- *Knowledge or experience factor*—A taxpayer who has little or no knowledge or experience in an activity is less likely to materially participate in the activity.

- *Management factor*—If a taxpayer merely approves or ratifies decisions made by others, the taxpayer's participation is not substantial. The degree of a taxpayer's knowledge about or experience with an activity is significant in determining whether the participation of the taxpayer and management amounts to material participation.

STUDY QUESTION

---

2. The NII tax is calculated on baskets of income over allowable deductions from all of the following *except:*

    a. Royalties and rents

    b. Passive activity gross income

    c. Trades or businesses in which the taxpayer materially participates

    d. Net gain from disposition of nonbusiness property

Application of FICA, SECA, and NII Taxes to S Corporations

An employee of an S corporation (including a shareholder-employee) is subject to FICA taxes (including additional Medicare tax, if applicable). However, the distributive share of S corporation income allocated to S corporation shareholders is not subject to FICA or SECA taxes (including additional Medicare tax), so if an S corporation shareholder-employee receives lower wages and larger distributions, he or she can minimize the amount of FICA taxes paid. The main thing to remember is that compensation paid to a shareholder must be reasonable (see below).

The shareholder's distributive share of S corporation income and gain—reported on Schedule K-1—is not subject to additional Medicare tax. Moreover, as long as the shareholder materially participates (see below) in the S corporation's trade or business, his or her distributive share of S corporation income is not subject to NII tax, which is imposed on the net amount from investments, as the shareholder's material participation will make the income nonpassive and take it out of Category (ii) (or Category (iii) if applicable).

Reasonable compensation. The IRS is aware that S corporations may be tempted to underpay shareholder-employees for the services that they perform for the corporation (making up the shortfall in the form of dividends) to avoid self-employment and payroll taxes. The government may seek to recharacterize these dividends as compensation.

The same factors are used to determine reasonableness of compensation paid to a shareholder-employee of an S corporation as are used to determine reasonableness of compensation paid to shareholders of a C corporation. However, there is a shift in emphasis—in the case of an S corporation, the IRS tries to keep salaries up to a reasonable limit rather than down.

Reasonableness is determined on the basis of all of the facts and circumstances of the particular case (*Charles Schneider & Co., Inc. v. Commr,* 32 TCM 555, Dec. 32,013(M), TC Memo. 1973-130, aff'd, CA-8, 74-2 USTC ¶ 9563, 500 F2d 148, cert. denied, 420 US 908). No single factor is controlling (*Mayson Manufacturing Co. v. Commr,* CA-6, 49-2 USTC ¶ 9467, 178 F2d 115). However, the Ninth Circuit and the Tax Court have used five criteria to determine the reasonableness of compensation:

- The employee's role in the company;
- An external comparison of the employee's salary with similarly situated employees;
- The character and condition of the company;
- Whether the relationship of the company to the employee creates a conflict of interest with respect to the awarding of compensation and, if so, whether the level of compensation would provide a satisfactory level of return on equity for a hypothetical independent investor; and
- The internal consistency of salaries paid to all employees of the company.

Among the other factors considered from *Owensby & Kritikos, Inc. v. Commr* (50 TCM 29, Dec. 42,133(M), TC Memo. 1985-267, aff'd, CA-5, 87-2 USTC ¶ 9390, 819 F2d 1315) are:

- The employee's qualifications;
- The nature, extent, and scope of his or her work;
- The size and complexities of the business; and
- A comparison of salaries paid with the income of the business and with distributions to stockholders.

In *Mayson Manufacturing Co. v. Commr* (CA-6, 49-2 USTC ¶ 9467, 178 F2d 115) the following factors were considered:

- The prevailing general economic conditions; the prevailing rates of compensation for comparable positions in comparable concerns;
- The salary policy of the employer as to all employees; and
- In the case of small corporations with a limited number of officers, the amount of compensation paid to the particular employee in previous years.

Additional factors considered in determining reasonableness of compensation are special employee qualifications in terms of expertise or efforts, and a large salary or payment at the end of a company's tax or accounting year. Although limited experience and lack of formal credentials can be taken into account to determine the reasonableness of compensation, perceived deficiencies in formal training should not be used as a direct offset from compensation determined by the use of comparables when there is no evidence of the experience or credentials of the persons earning the salaries used for comparison and the business is not of the character requiring formal education (*Max Burton Enterprises, Inc. v. Commr,* 74 TCM 652, Dec. 52,254(M), TC Memo. 1997-421).

More specific factors that have been considered by the courts include:

- The volume and profitability of business (*New York Talking Machine Co. v. Commr,* 13 BTA 154, Dec. 4297 (1928));
- Comparison of an unrelated successor's salary (*Roux Laboratories, Inc. v. US,* DC Fla., 76-2 USTC ¶ 9751);
- The necessity of paying same amount to replace an employee and the employee's ability to get same amount of compensation elsewhere (*J.D. Van Hooser & Co. v. S.R. Glenn,* DC Ky., 43-1 USTC ¶ 9395, 50 FSupp 279.);
- Gross sales, net profits, dividends paid, and capital investment (*Universal Manufacturing Co., Inc. v. Commr,* 68 TCM 305, Dec. 50,014(M), TC Memo. 1994-367; *Faucette Co., Inc. v. Commr,* 17 TC 187, Dec. 18,459 (1951); *Long Island Drug Co., Inc. v. Commr,* 35 BTA 328, Dec. 9560 (1937), aff'd, CA-2, 40-1 USTC ¶ 9446, 111 F2d 593, cert. denied, 311 US 680);

- The cash condition of the employer (***Wenatchee Bottling Works v. T.W. Henricksen,*** DC Wash., 40-1 USTC ¶ 9270, 31 FSupp 763); and
- The value of an officer's services as a director (***Express Publishing Co. v. Commr,*** CA-5, 44-2 USTC ¶ 9397, 143 F2d 386).

The IRS has issued a fact sheet that addresses various issues with respect to wage compensation for S corporation officer/shareholders and that includes the following factors that courts have considered in determining reasonable compensation (IRS Fact Sheet FS-2008-25, Nov. 20, 2008):

- Training and experience;
- Duties and responsibilities;
- Time and effort devoted to the business;
- Dividend history;
- Payments to nonshareholder employees;
- Timing and manner of paying bonuses to key people;
- What comparable businesses pay for similar services;
- Compensation agreements; and
- The use of a formula to determine compensation.

STUDY QUESTION

---

3. The IRS will reallocate wages and or distributions paid to S corporation shareholder-employees so that the shareholder-employee's wages are:

   a. As low as possible so each shareholder's distributive share of S corporation income will be higher

   b. Below the level of compensation paid to C corporation shareholders

   c. Reasonable compensation for the services the shareholder-employee performed

   d. As high as possible because the income of the S corporation is taxed at a low corporate rate

---

Using an S Corporation to Minimize Taxes

The taxation of employment income earned by owners of passthrough entities treats business owners differently according to the legal form of their ownership and the legal form of the payment that they receive. In part, this is a holdover from earlier years when limited partners were prohibited by state law from holding managerial roles in their firms and LLCs did not exist. The differential treatment distorts choice of organizational form and provides tax planning opportunities for business owners, e.g., by some S corporation owners who receive substantial income in the form of distributions rather than as wages. As a result of these differences, some business owners pay employment taxes on nearly all their earnings (general partners and sole proprietors), other similarly situated owners pay employment taxes on only a portion of their earnings (S corporation owner-employees), and others pay little employment tax at all (limited partners and many LLC members). Thus, many owners of passthrough entities successfully avoid payroll tax on income that is equivalent to self-employment earnings and that would be subject to employment taxes if the business had a different legal structure.

The fact that the distributions from an S corporation to its shareholder-employees who materially participate in the S corporation's trade or business escape both FICA and SECA tax—including additional Medicare tax—and NII tax creates the opportunity for S corporations and their shareholders to minimize these taxes by making sure wages paid to the shareholder employees do not exceed reasonable compensation. The reduction in W-2 wages paid to shareholder-employee will increase S corporation income by a like amount. Remember, a shareholder's distributive share of S corporation income is not subject to either additional Medicare tax, or NII tax—as long as he or she materially participates in the S corporation's trade or business.

The planning technique discussed here works best with single-shareholder S corporations or with S corporations where the wages paid to the shareholder-employees are proportionate to their interests in the S corporation. Because of the single-class-of-stock requirement, all distributions and allocations made to S corporation shareholders must be proportionate to their ownership interest in the S corporation.

STUDY QUESTIONS

---

4. Under Temp. Reg. § 1.469-5T(a), if a taxpayer participates in multiple trade or business activities of an S corporation and aggregated hours from activities exceeds 500, he or she could meet the criteria for the:

    a. Personal-services-activities test

    b. Substantially all test

    c. Significant-participation-activities test

    d. Not-less-than-others test

---

5. The test for material participation in S corporation activities that requires participation of just 100 hours in one activity is the:

    a. Personal-services-activities test

    b. Substantially all test

    c. Significant-participation-activities test

    d. Not-less-than-others test

Application to Partnerships

On the other hand, the planning technique currently being used in S corporations is not available for partnerships. Typically, the distributive share of a general partner in a partnership operating a trade or business would be subject to SECA taxes, including (to the extent his or her salary exceeded the relevant threshold) additional Medicare tax. A taxpayer who owns an interest in a limited partnership as a limited partner generally is not treated as materially participating in the limited partnership's activities (Code Sec. 469(h)(2); Temp. Reg. § 1.469-5T(e); Prop. Reg. § 1.469-5(e)). A limited partner's distributive share of the income, gain, loss, deductions, or credits from an activity in which he or she owns a limited partnership interest, and any gain or loss recognized from the sale or exchange of the partnership interest, are presumed to be passive. A limited partner may nevertheless be treated as materially participating in a partnership if he or she satisfies either the 500-hour participation test, the 5-of-10-preceding-years participation test, or the personal-service-activity participation test.

Figure 1. Material Participation for Limited Partners

A limited partner is limited to three of the seven material participation tests:

(1) The individual participates in the activity for more than 500 hours during the year;

~~(2) The individual's participation constitutes all of the participation in the activity by all individuals for the year;~~

~~(3) The individual participates in the activity for more than 100 hours during the tax year and his participation in the activity is not less than the participation in the activity of any other individual for the year;~~

~~(4) The activity is a significant participation activity for the individual for the tax year, and his aggregate participation in all significant participation activities exceeds 500 hours for the year;~~

(5) The individual materially participated in the activity for any five tax years (which do not need to be consecutive) during the ten tax years that immediately precede the current tax year;

(6) The activity is a personal service activity, and the individual materially participated in the activity for any three tax years (need not be consecutive) preceding the current tax year; or

~~(7) The individual does not satisfy any of the other tests but, based on all of the facts and circumstances, the individual participates in the activity on a regular, continuous, and substantial basis for such tax year. Temp. Reg. §1.469-5T(a).~~

A partnership interest is treated as a limited partnership interest if it is limited in liability for partnership obligations under applicable state law to a determinable fixed amount (Temp. Reg. §1.469-5T(e)(3)(i)). For example, a partner is a limited partner if his or her liability is limited to the sum of capital contributions to the partnership plus any additional amount that the partner is required to contribute under the terms of the partnership agreement.

A partnership interest is also treated as a limited partnership interest if is it designated as a limited partnership interest in the partnership agreement or certificate of limited partnership. This characterization applies regardless of whether the liability of the partner is in fact limited under applicable state law. Thus, if an individual who is designated as a limited partner participates in the affairs of the partnership to a degree that his or her liability as to the partnership is no longer limited, the individual is nevertheless still considered a limited partner for purposes of the passive activity rules.

In certain circumstances, a partner who is both a general partner and a limited partner in a partnership is not treated as a limited partner if the individual satisfies any of the seven material participation tests (Temp. Reg. §1.469-5T(e)(3)(ii)). For this exception to apply, however, the individual must be a general partner in the partnership at all times during the partnership's tax year ending with or within the individual's tax year. If a general partner is also a limited partner but for only part of the partnership's tax year, the individual must be a general partner during that portion of the partnership's tax year that he or she directly or indirectly owns the limited partnership interest.

The Tax Court has ruled that the general partnership exception applies to the interests of individuals in an LLC or limited liability partnership (LLP) if the individual is allowed by state law to participate in the management of the entity (***Garnett v. Commissioner,*** Dec. 57,875, 132 TC 368). For example, a taxpayer who held a managing member interest in a California LLC that was classified as a partnership was a general partner because members of a California LLC can participate directly in management (***Newell v. Commissioner,*** Dec. 58,127(M), TC Memo 2010-23). The Federal Claims Court has also ruled that an individual's interest in an LLC is not a limited partnership interest if the individual may participate in management of the entity (***Thompson v. United States,*** FedCl, 2009-2 USTC ¶ 50,501, 87 FedCl 728, acq. in result only, 2010-15 IRB np). The current regulations literally require that the ownership interest be a business entity that is a partnership under applicable state law, and not merely taxed as a partnership for federal income purposes (Temp. Reg. § 1.469-5T(e)(3)).

Proposed regulations, which will be effective for tax years beginning on or after the date they are finalized, eliminate the reliance on an individual's limited liability as a limited partner under state law or as designated in the partnership agreement in determining whether an interest is a limited partnership interest (Prop. Reg. § 1.469-5(e)(3)(i)). Instead, whether an individual is a limited partner in an entity depends upon the individual's right to participate in the management of the entity, whether it is a partnership or LLC. Thus, an individual's interest in an entity is treated as an interest in a limited partnership if:

- The entity is classified as a partnership for federal income tax purposes under the check-the-box regulations; and
- The holder of the interest does not have any rights to manage the entity at any time during the entity's tax year under the applicable state law or under the operating agreement of the entity.

The general partnership interest exception continues to apply under the proposed regulations. Thus, an individual is not treated as holding a limited partnership interest in a limited partnership if he or she also holds a general partnership interest in the same partnership at all times during the partnership's tax year ending with or within the individual's tax year (Prop. Reg. § 1.469-5(e)(3)(ii)). Moreover, if a limited partner actively participates in the business, he or she may lose the liability protections of the limited partner status.

EXAMPLE: Marcus and Liam are equal (50-percent) members in an LLC taxed as a partnership. They are considered general partners for purposes of the material participation rules. For 2015, the partnership has $1 million in income from its trade or business, which it allocates $500,000 each to Marcus and Liam. Each partner will pay no NII tax and the following amounts in the SECA components of Social Security, Medicare, and additional Medicare taxes (aMt):

OASDI	12.4%	×	$118,500	=	$14,694
HI	2.9%	×	500,000	=	14,500
aMt	0.9%	×	300,000	=	2,700
					$31,894

Now assume that the business is run through an S corporation. Marcus and Liam are still 50-percent owners of the business as the corporation's shareholders, but the corporation also hires them as employees. Assume the corporation can establish that reasonable compensation for their services is $100,000 each, With respect to each shareholder-employee, the combined FICA tax imposed on the S corporation and the shareholder-employee would be as follows:

OASDI	12.4%	×	$100,000	=	$12,400
HI	2.9%	×	100,000	=	2,900
aMt	0.9%	×	0	=	0
					$15,300

If they run their business as an S corporation in the above example, each of Marcus and Liam will save $16,594 in SECA/FICA taxes ($31,894 – $15,300).

What if either Marcus or Liam is a 50-percent limited partner? In that case, the limited partner will not be subject to SECA taxes but will be subject to NII tax of $11,400 (3.8% × $300,000), unless he materially participates in the partnership's trade or business. However, for practical purposes, it will be difficult for the limited partner to materially participate, because he will have to meet one of the three most rigorous material participation tests—and if the limited partner participates too much, he could lose the limited liability protections afforded limited partners under state law.

Could conducting the business as an S corporation help the limited partner? Yes. An S corporation shareholder is not considered a limited partner and can qualify as materially participating in the S corporation's business under any of the seven material participation tests, which makes it easier for the shareholder to avoid NII tax. Furthermore, participating in a corporation's business will not put a shareholder's limited liability protection under state law in jeopardy.

STUDY QUESTION

---

6. Which of the following material participation tests does **not** apply to limited partners?

   a. The personal-service-activity test

   b. The significant-participation-activities test

   c. The 5-out-of-10 preceding years test

   d. The 500-hour test

MODULE 5: LEGISLATION—Chapter 9: Tax Reform and Interim Measures

¶ 901 WELCOME

This chapter explores proposals and prospects for federal tax reform. Ever since passage of the last comprehensive tax reform law—the *Tax Reform Act of 1986*—lawmakers have been adding new tax provisions, eliminating others, and tinkering with many. The result is a tax code that nearly all taxpayers, tax professionals and lawmakers agree, is in need of revision.

¶ 902 LEARNING OBJECTIVES

Upon completion of this chapter, you will be able to:

- Identify the working group and committee initiatives that lawmakers have created to examine tax reform;
- Recognize standalone tax bills that have passed the House, Senate, or both chambers;
- Identify legislative proposals to amend the *Patient Protection and Affordable Care Act* (P.L. 111-148);
- Identify tax reform proposals in President Obama's fiscal year (FY) 2016 budget proposals; and
- Recognize tax-related provisions in trade legislation.

¶ 903 INTRODUCTION

The various tax reform proposals and bills discussed in this chapter were current as of the time the chapter was prepared. Legislation can, and often does, change before final passage. Other bills that have been introduced likely will not make it to the full House and/or Senate for a vote.

Comprehensive federal tax reform is a topic much in the news in 2015. Both President Obama and the Republican-controlled Congress have made proposals and counterproposals for tax reform. There has been no shortage of tax bills introduced since the beginning of 2015, some new and some that have been previously offered over the course of the past few years. The bills represent markers for lawmakers who will use them to negotiate their inclusion, or some of the proposals therein, when tax writers begin to undertake serious tax reform negotiations. Additionally, tax extenders will need to be addressed as the *Tax Increase Prevention Act of 2014* merely extended the incentives through 2014. Democrats and Republicans generally agree that the research tax credit should be made permanent, but they split on issues such as tradeoffs from enhancing the earned income credit (EIC) and other credits aimed at families. Extension of enhanced Code Sec. 179 expensing and bonus depreciation are also discussed frequently.

> **COMMENT:** Both President Obama and Congressional Republicans have called for revenue neutral tax reform. Their definitions of *revenue neutral* often differ based on projections of economic growth and the impact of tax reform on the economy. House Republicans have approved the use of dynamic scoring for major

bills, and Senate Republicans may go along. The White House counters that dynamic scoring distorts the economic impact of tax cuts.

¶ 904 CONGRESSIONAL TAX WRITING COMMITTEES

Both tax writing committees—the Senate Finance Committee and the House Ways and Means Committee—have been engaged in tax reform proposals in 2015.

Senate Finance Committee

In July 2015, the Senate Finance Committee (SFC) unveiled reports from bipartisan working groups on tax reform. The reports, which were the culmination of six months of work, did not make concrete proposals for tax reform. However, they did draw attention to the need for tax reform and could help encourage movement of stand-along tax bills, including a package to renew the so-called tax extenders. SFC Chair Orrin Hatch (R-Utah) and ranking member Ron Wyden (D-Ore.) launched the tax reform working groups earlier this year. The working groups reviewed a number of previous tax reform proposals, including the 2012 Framework for Business Tax Reform from President Obama, a comprehensive tax code overhaul prepared by then Ways and Means Chair Dave Camp (R-Mich.) and others.

> **COMMENT:** The SFC created five working groups: individual income tax; business income tax; savings and investment; international tax; and community development and infrastructure.

Business tax reform. Thirty-one industrialized nations have lowered their corporate tax rates since 2001, the SFC noted on July 8. The U.S. corporate tax rate has remained unchanged. Various proposals to reduce the rate have stalled, primarily because of disputes over how to, or whether to, recoup the lost revenue. Considered in the context of a tax reform offsets that have failed to win support include repeal of the last-in, first-out (LIFO) method of accounting, repeal of the Code Sec. 199 domestic production activities deduction, and others.

Research tax credit. The SFC noted that the Code Sec. 41 research tax credit has been extended 16 times since it was first enacted in 1981, often on a retroactive basis after the credit had expired. "Yet it is likely that very few businesses that conduct R&D expect the credit will not be reinstated. To say that the credit is a temporary provision of the tax code is to state something that may be technically accurate, but does not actually reflect reality," the SFC said on July 8.

Energy tax incentives. A number of energy tax incentives (such as incentives for biodiesel fuel, the production tax credit, and more) are temporary. Their temporary nature provides taxpayers with little certainty, the SFC noted on July 8. As a result, taxpayers may choose to forgo the investments these provisions are meant to encourage.

Individual tax reform. Like business tax reform, individual tax reform has been hindered over disagreements about revenue raisers. According to the SFC, a one percentage point across-the-board rate reduction would cost $690 billion over 10 years. "Difficult choices would need to be made if even a modest reduction in rates were to be achieved while continuing to raise similar amounts of revenue," the SFC noted on July 8. Revenue could be generated by reducing or eliminating, for example, the home mortgage interest deduction, the child tax credit, and the Code Sec. 36B premium assistance tax credit.

> **COMMENT:** Eliminating the home mortgage deduction and the Code Sec. 36B credit would generate some $700 billion in revenues, the SFC estimated.

Education tax reform. The SFC reviewed education tax incentives and observed that the number of education credits and deductions could be ripe for streamlining and consolidation. "Complexities associated with multiple incentives make it difficult for taxpayers to take into account the value of the incentives in budgeting for college expenses, while income-related phaseouts create both computational and transactional complexity for taxpayers," the SFC noted on July 8.

Tax administration. The sequence of return filing dates complicates a taxpayer's ability to prepare an accurate return, the SFC explained. The information that a taxpayer is required to assemble with respect to all income-generating investments or activities may not be available until shortly before, after, or contemporaneous with one's filing date.

> **COMMENT:** The SFC acknowledged that reordering the due dates for filing income tax returns so that both partnerships and S corporations file before C corporations and individuals may reduce the need for routine use of extensions, but did not endorse a specific proposal.

International tax reform. The SFC reviewed options for moving from a worldwide tax system to a territorial tax system. "Every other G-7 country has adopted some form of territorial system—and all of these countries have lower corporate tax rates than the U.S. This means that no matter what jurisdiction a U.S. multinational company is competing in, it is competing at a disadvantage," the SFC noted on July 8.

Retirement savings/pension reform. The SFC identified three key goals for retirement savings/pension reforms: increasing access to tax deferred retirement savings; increasing participation and levels of savings; and discouraging individuals from borrowing from their savings before retirement while promoting lifetime income. Although the working group did not endorse any specific proposals, its members emphasized that tax reform must include retirements savings/pension reforms.

House Ways and Means Committee

House Ways and Means Committee Chairman Paul Ryan (R-Wis.) has said several times in 2015 that that he would be open to approaching an overhaul of the tax code in phases as long as it leads to comprehensive tax reform. "We're willing to do it in pieces, then move to a big across-the-board bill, which I think is cleaner and better," said Ryan in January 2015. "I'm happy to do tax reform in two phases if that's necessary, so long as the first phase doesn't preclude but actually precipitates the second phase, which is to finish the job of lowering the rates across the board."

In March 2015 Ryan said that in the ongoing process of negotiations with the Obama Administration, he was hopeful that all involved can find common ground. He acknowledged, however, that the administration does not agree with House Republicans on all things, but he believes there may be common ground on business tax reform. He said that his committee and staff members are exploring that and are "working very hard at doing their research and getting our scores and engaging with Treasury to see if we can find that common ground on reform."

In July 2015, Ryan said that said that he is looking for short-term solutions as a down payment on more comprehensive tax reform. Ryan pointed out, however, that there is no sure thing when it comes to tax reform.

STUDY QUESTION

---

1. As a starting point for comprehensive tax reform, the Obama Administration and House Ways and Means Committee may agree to initiate:

- **a.** Individual tax rate adjustments
- **b.** Business tax reform
- **c.** International tax reform pieces of an income tax overhaul
- **d.** Estate and gift tax reforms

¶ 905 TAX EXTENDERS

While lawmakers debate comprehensive tax reform, the clock is ticking on the fate of the tax extenders. The *Tax Increase Prevention Act of 2014* (TIPA) only extended the popular but temporary tax breaks for 2014.

> **COMMENT:** Among the now-expired extenders are the state and local sales tax deduction, higher education tuition deduction, transit benefits parity, research tax credit, Indian employment, and many others.

In April, House Ways and Means Chairman Ryan said that he plans to complete tax extenders by the end of the summer if negotiations fail with the Obama Administration to combine them with some kind of tax reform. "Sooner is better than later as far as I'm concerned, and we're pretty clear about what we think should be permanent," Ryan said. "I think we should have a robust debate about tax reform and that debate should take place sooner rather than later," he added. Ryan said he believed extenders can either be part of a limited tax reform package this summer, or if lawmakers are unable to come to agreement with the administration, then he would move to extenders and do those in those as early as possible in the fall.

> **COMMENT:** One provision that traditionally was part of an extenders package—the health coverage tax credit—was moved to trade legislation (discussed below) in 2015.

Stand-Alone Tax Legislation

Since the start of 2015, several stand-alone tax bills have been approved by the House or Senate, or both chambers.

Research Tax Credit

House lawmakers on May 20 approved legislation, the American Research and Competitiveness Bill of 2015 (HR 880), to simplify and make permanent the research tax credit. The House bill provides no revenue offsets, however, and President Obama has promised to veto the measure, which is estimated to add $180 billion to the federal deficit over the next 10 years. In a Statement of Administration Policy, the White House said, "The president supports enhancing, simplifying, and making permanent the credit, and offsetting the cost by closing tax loopholes. The administration wants to work with Congress to make progress on measures that strengthen the economy and help middle-class families, including pro-growth business tax reform. However, HR 880 represents the wrong approach."

The bill would make permanent the alternative simplified method for calculating the research tax credit and increase the rate to 20 percent. That is, the research credit is equal to 20 percent of qualified research expenses that exceed 50 percent of the average qualified research expenses for the three preceding tax years. The rate is reduced to 10 percent if a taxpayer has no qualified research expenses in any one of the three preceding tax years. The provision repeals the traditional 20 percent research credit calculation method. The measure also would make permanent the basic research credit and the energy research credit—both with credit rates of 20 percent—and changes the base period for the basic research credit from a fixed period to a three-year rolling average.

The bill also provides that, in the case of an eligible small business, as defined in Code Sec. 38(c)(5)(C), the research credit determined under Code Sec. 41 for tax years beginning after December 31, 2014, is a specified credit. Thus, the research credits of an eligible small business may offset both regular and alternative minimum tax (AMT) liability. The bill is generally effective for tax years beginning after December 31, 2014. The provision to make the research credit permanent applies to amounts paid or incurred after December 31, 2014.

Highway Funding

In May, Congress passed the Highway and Transportation Funding Bill of 2015 (HR 2353), a two-month extension of current funding through the highway trust fund. Lawmakers sought a longer extension, at least until the end of 2015, but were unable to reach an accord. The cost of such an extension would have required $11 billion in revenue offsets. Senate Finance Committee Chairman Hatch, who had taken responsibility for finding revenue offsets, said he had devised a 50/50 plan that includes offsets and spending cuts. Hatch added, however, that he was willing to go along with the House short-term extension. "I am committed to finding a long-term solution on highways," said Hatch. "I plan to keep working with my colleagues, particularly [Senate Environment and Public Works Committee] Chair [James] Inhofe (R-Okla.), whose committee deals with much of the highway policy, as well as those who serve on the Finance and Ways and Means Committees, on finding a way to get us there."

The short-term highway bill amends the Internal Revenue Code by extending revenue from other sources for two months: the sport fish restoration and boating trust fund (Code Sec. 9504), and the leaking underground storage tank trust fund (Code Sec. 9508(e)(2)).

> **COMMENT:** In June, SFC Chair Hatch said he had ruled out a gas tax hike to help replenish the Highway Trust Fund. Hatch also dismissed the idea of a so-called repatriation holiday, which, according to the Joint Committee on Taxation (JCT), loses nearly $120 billion over 10 years. Hatch said it was not a "serious proposal" to pay for a long-term highway bill.

Code Sec. 529 Plans

The Senate Finance Committee in April approved a bipartisan bill to improve and extend Code Sec. 529 college plans. The bill would change the way that Code Sec. 529 education savings accounts currently operate. The full House approved a similar measure (HR 529) in February.

The legislation would make some changes to current law. It would allow the purchase of a computer to be considered a qualified expense. It would also remove distribution aggregation requirements, which are considered an outdated burden on 529 plan administrators. When 529 college savings plans originated in 1996, the funds were taxed before they were deposited into the account, and then taxed a second time when they were disbursed to pay for higher education expenses. However, the law was changed in 2001 and made permanent in 2006, so that 529 savings are only taxed once—before they are put into a 529 account. Only disbursements used to pay for nonqualified expenses are taxable. Another provision provides tax and penalty relief in instances where a student may have to withdraw from school for illness or other reasons. Under current law, any refunds from the college are subject to immediate taxation and a 10 percent tax penalty. The bill eliminates this tax and penalty if the refund is redeposited in a 529 account. It also permits a family to set the refund aside to pay for the student's education should he or she return to college or to use it for another family member.

> **COMMENT:** Under the current tax code, distributions from 529 plans are generally not included in the income of the donor or the designated beneficiary, as long as the distributions do not exceed the beneficiary's qualified higher education expenses (Code Sec. 529(c)(3)(B)). A qualified tuition program (QTP) (also known as a *qualified tuition plan*) is a program under which an individual may prepay tuition credits or make cash contributions to an account on behalf of a beneficiary for payment of qualified higher education expenses. The program must be established and maintained by a state, state agency, or an eligible educational institution, i.e., virtually any accredited public, nonprofit, or private college or university. Eligible schools generally include any accredited post-secondary educational institution, so long as contributions made to the program are held in a qualified trust, that is, one that meets the requirements under Code Sections 408(a)(2) and(5).

> **COMMENT:** Over the past few years the value and use of 529 accounts has increased dramatically. From 2012 to 2013 alone, there was a net increase of 19.1 percent in 529 account assets. According to recent estimates, total investment by families in 529 plans is now more than $247 billion, with the average account size calculated at $20,474 as of the end of 2014.

STUDY QUESTION

---

2. Which of the following is *not* a feature of the American Research and Competitiveness Bill of 2015 (HR 880) regarding the research tax credit?

    a. The proposed change for the credit enables eligible small businesses to apply the credit against both their regular and alternative minimum tax liability

    b. The bill increases the credit to 20 percent of eligible expenses

    c. The bill eliminates use of the alternative simplified method for calculating the credit

    d. The president would veto the bill as the wrong approach to pro-growth business tax reform

---

Estate Tax

House lawmakers in April approved the Death Tax Repeal Bill (HR 1105) to permanently repeal the estate tax. The measure also repeals the generation-skipping transfer (GST) tax for all future transfers. The White House has said President Obama will veto the bill. "HR 1105 is fiscally irresponsible and, if enacted, would add $269 billion to the deficit over 10 years, according to the Joint Committee on Taxation. The bill would worsen the nation's long-term fiscal challenges, jeopardizing programs and investments important to the middle class and national security," the White House said in a statement of administration policy.

> **COMMENT:** Under current law, the estate and gift tax exclusion amount and the GST exemption amount is $5 million, which is indexed annually for inflation after 2011; the exclusion and exemption amounts are $5.43 million for 2015. A

decedent's estate may elect to allow the unused portion of the decedent's applicable exclusion amount to be available to his or her surviving spouse or the spouse's estate (referred to as "portability").

State and Local Tax Deduction

The House passed in April the State and Local Sales Tax Deduction Fairness Bill (HR 622), which would permanently extend the optional deduction for state and local sales taxes in lieu of deducting state and local income taxes. This option expired at the end of 2014 as part of the last extenders package. The White House said it would veto HR 622 if it came to the president's desk for signature, stating that the cost of the measure is not offset and would add to long-term deficits. "By making permanent the deduction for state and local sales taxes, HR 622 would add $42 billion to the deficit over the next 10 years," said the White House in a statement of administration policy.

> **COMMENT:** The deduction is not only potentially beneficial to taxpayers in states without an income tax. Taxpayers who make a big ticket purchase, such as a motor vehicle, before year-end could benefit by weighing the deduction for state and local general sales taxes against their deduction for state and local income taxes.

Charitable Giving

The House in February approved the Fighting Hunger Incentive Bill of 2015, which would extend and expand tax breaks for food inventory donations, land donations for conservation, and other related provisions. The bill also would make permanent certain tax-free distributions from individual retirement accounts for charitable purposes. President Obama has said he will veto the measure if it appears on his desk because it is not offset by revenue raisers.

> **COMMENT:** The special treatment for charitable gifts from IRAs allows individuals age 70½ and older to continue to be allowed to make tax-free distributions from IRAs to a qualified charitable organization. The treatment is capped at a maximum of $100,000 per taxpayer each year.

"Doc Fix Bill"

In April, President Obama signed the *Medicare Access and CHIP Reauthorization Act of 2015* (P.L. 114-10), also known as the "doc fix bill." The bill amends Title XVIII of the *Social Security Act* to repeal the Medicare sustainable growth rate (SGR) and strengthen Medicare access by improving physician payments and making other improvements, to reauthorize the Children's Health Insurance Program, and for other purposes. Before being amended by P.L. 114-10, Code Sec. 6331(h)(3) provided that a continuous IRS levy to collect an unpaid tax liability of a Medicare provider was limited to 30 percent of a qualified payment. Under the "doc fix" bill, the IRS can levy up to 100 percent of a qualified payment owed to a Medicare provider to collect an unpaid tax liability.

> **COMMENT:** The Congressional Budget Office (CBO) has estimated that the bill would raise $600 million over 10 years.

Public Safety Officers

In April, President Obama signed the *Slain Officer Family Support Act of 2015* (P.L. 114-7) extending the tax deadline for individuals making charitable donations to organizations supporting the families of slain New York Police Department (NYPD) Detectives Wenjian Liu and Rafael Ramos. Donors could apply such tax deductions to their 2014 tax return. Previously, individuals contributing to organizations that provide

¶905

financial support to the families of the slain detectives were required to make their contributions by December 31, 2014, to qualify for a tax deduction with their 2014 filing. This bill extended the date of eligibility from January 1 to April 15, 2015, allowing deductions to be treated as if they were made on December 31, 2014, for tax purposes.

In May, President Obama signed legislation, the *Don't Tax Our Fallen Public Safety Heroes Act* (P.L. 114-14), which clarifies federal law to ensure that both federal and state benefits for public safety officers fallen or injured in the line of duty are treated the same in the tax code. Under the legislation, neither would be subject to federal income tax. The bill was introduced by House Ways and Means Committee members Erik Paulsen (R-Minn.), Bill Pascrell (D-N.J.), and Rep. Dave Reichert (R-Wash.). Joining Paulsen in introducing the legislation were the bipartisan cochairs of the House Law Enforcement Caucus. Companion legislation approved by the Senate was introduced by Sens. Kelly Ayotte (R-N.H.), and Jeanne Shaheen (D-N.H.).

In June, President Obama signed the *Defending Public Safety Employees' Retirement Act* (P.L. 114-26). Generally, taxpayers who receive an early distribution from a qualified retirement plan are subject to a 10 percent penalty, unless an exemption exists. Current law provides an exemption for qualified public safety officers. The *Defending Public Safety Employees' Retirement Act* expands the exemption to include certain federal law enforcement officers, federal firefighters, customs and border protection officers, and air traffic controllers. The provision applies to distributions made after December 31, 2015.

COMMENT: Many federal public safety officers are able to retire at age 50 after 20 years of service. The act is intended to provide penalty relief to these individuals.

IRS Oversight

The House in April approved a series of bills dealing with oversight of the IRS. The package of bills includes:

- HR 1058, the Taxpayer Bill of Rights Bill of 2015, which would incorporate a taxpayer's bill of rights into the core responsibilities of the IRS commissioner. This would include rights to pay no more than the correct amount of tax, to privacy, and to challenge the IRS's decisions;

- HR 1152, would prohibit officers and employees of the IRS from using personal email accounts to conduct official business;

- HR 1026, the Taxpayer Knowledge of IRS Investigations Bill, which amends the tax code to stop the IRS from using a provision that is designed to protect taxpayer privacy, but can be used to protect government employees who improperly look at or reveal taxpayer information;

- HR 1295, would improve the process for making determinations with respect to whether organizations are exempt from taxation under Code Sec. 501(c)(4);

- HR 1314, provides for a right to an administrative appeal relating to adverse determinations of tax-exempt status of certain organizations;

- HR 709, the Prevent Targeting at the IRS Bill, which would make political targeting a terminating offense at the IRS;

- HR 1104, the Fair Treatment for All Gifts Bill, which would ensure fair and equal gift tax audit treatment for taxpayers who donate to tax-exempt organizations; and

- HR 1562, the Contracting and Tax Accountability Bill, which would prohibit federal agencies from awarding contracts or grants to persons or companies that have seriously delinquent tax debt.

STUDY QUESTION

3. The *Defending Public Safety Employees' Retirement Act:*

    a. Qualifies local public safety employees to claim the same retirement benefits as federal public safety employees

    b. Waives the 10 percent early withdrawal penalty for retirement accounts of eligible public safety employees

    c. Makes tax-free any withdrawals by eligible employees of amounts from their retirement savings

    d. Lowers the full retirement age of federal public safety employees to 55

Housekeeping Bills

In February, the Senate Finance Committee approved a package of housekeeping bills. These include:

- Modifications to Alternative Tax for Certain Small Insurance Companies;
- Modifications to the Excise Tax on Cider;
- An Exception to the Private Foundation Excess Business Holdings Rules for Certain Philanthropic Business Holdings;
- Creation of a Waste-Heat-to-Power Investment Tax Credit;
- Conversion of the Tax on Liquefied Natural Gas and Liquefied Petroleum Gas to an Energy Equivalent Basis;
- An Exclusion from Gross Income Certain Clean Coal Power Grants; and
- Creation of a Military Spouse Job Continuity Credit.

Taxpayer Bill of Rights

Senate Finance Committee members Charles E. Grassley (R-Iowa) and John Thune (R-S.D.) in June introduced the Taxpayer Bill of Rights Enhancement Bill of 2015 (Sen 1578), which they predicted would improve customer service at the IRS, create new taxpayer protections, and update and strengthen existing taxpayer protections. Provisions in the bill would:

- Significantly increase civil damages and criminal penalties for the unauthorized disclosure or inspection of tax return information and significantly increases civil damages for improper IRS collection activities;
- Impose an affirmative duty on the commissioner of the IRS to ensure that employees are familiar with, and act in accordance with, all taxpayer protections;
- Update the "10 deadly sins," established by the *IRS Restructuring and Reform Act of 1998* (P.L. 105-206)—those actions by IRS employees that require mandatory termination—to include official actions taken for political purposes;
- Permit the Treasury Department to provide status updates and, in certain instances, require status updates, regarding investigations into misconduct by IRS employees—or, in some circumstances, third parties—to taxpayers who are the subject of the misconduct;

- Strengthen a provision that permits taxpayers to bring a cause of action against the IRS for unauthorized collections actions; and

- Extend the declaratory judgment remedy currently available to Code Sec. 501(c)(3) groups to other 501(c) groups, including 501(c)(4) social welfare organizations.

Craft Brewers

Senate Finance Committee ranking member Wyden in June 12 introduced legislation, the Craft Beverage Modernization and Tax Reform Bill (Sen 1562), which would, among other provisions, reduce excise taxes for brewers. Wyden's proposal would provide a rate of $16-per-barrel on the first 6-million barrels for all brewers and beer importers compared to the current $18-per-barrel. The bill also defines small brewers as those producing less than 2 million barrels annually, with the application of an excise tax of $3.50-per-barrel for the first 60,000 barrels, jumping to $16 after that. The measure also expands the excise tax credit for small wine producers.

Additionally, the bill provides for an exemption for the aging period of beer, wine, and spirits from certain capitalization rules. The IRS has held that producers of wine must include the time that wine ages in bottles as part of the production period, which concludes when the wine vintage is officially released to the distribution chain. Those same rules apply to barrel aging of beer, wine, and distilled spirits. Wyden's bill would exclude aging periods for beer, wine, and distilled spirits from the production period for purposes of these capitalization rules.

¶ 906 PATIENT PROTECTION AND AFFORDABLE CARE ACT

A number of bills were introduced in Congress in the first half of 2015 to repeal, amend, or otherwise change the *Patient Protection and Affordable Care Act* (PPACA, known as the Affordable Care Act, ACA) (P.L. 111-148).

Medical Device Excise Tax

In June, the House Ways and Means Committee approved the Protect Medical Innovation Bill of 2015 (HR 160), which would repeal the medical device tax. The full House subsequently approved the bill. The medical device tax was intended to help pay for the Affordable Care Act and levies a 2.3 percent tax on medical device manufacturers. Under the bill, the medical device tax repeal applies to sales in calendar quarters beginning after the date of enactment. Thus, the tax would not be refundable.

COMMENT: According to the Joint Committee on Taxation (JCX-88-15), the estimated cost of the measure would be $24.4 billion over 10 years.

COMMENT: The medical device tax does not attach to many consumer medical devices, such as eye glasses, contact lenses, and hearing aids. Under IRS regulations (TD 9604) a device will be considered to be of a type generally purchased by the general public at retail for individual use if:

- It is regularly available for purchase and use by individual consumers who are not medical professionals; and

- The design of the device demonstrates that it is not primarily intended for use in a medical institution or office or by a medical professional.

Whether these two factors result in a retail exemption for a given device is based on an evaluation of all the relevant facts and circumstances. These two factors are not, however, exclusive. There may be additional facts and circumstances relevant to whether the retail exemption applies.

Hire More Heroes Bill

The Senate Finance Committee in January approved the Hire More Heroes Bill (HR 22). The legislation would permit an employer, when determining whether it must provide health care coverage to its employees under the Affordable Care Act, to exclude employees who have coverage under a health care program administered by the Department of Defense.

> **COMMENT:** The employer mandate, Code Sec. 4980H, a key provision of the PPACA, requires all businesses with more than 50 full-time or full-time equivalent employees (currently defined as employees who work more than 30 hours per week) to provide employer-sponsored insurance. Businesses face a $2,000 noncompliance penalty for each employee beyond the 30th they hire after 50, in addition to the salary and benefits they must provide to their employees.

Volunteers

The House unanimously approved the Protecting Volunteer Firefighters and Emergency Responders Bill (HR 1191), which provides that emergency services volunteers are not counted as full-time employees by the IRS under the employer mandate of the Affordable Care Act.

> **COMMENT:** Under the employer mandate provision, employers with 50 or more employees must provide health insurance or pay penalties. If volunteers were considered employees, fire companies could exceed the 50-employee threshold in several different ways: a volunteer department by itself based on size; by being part of a combined, paid-volunteer fire department; or by being part of a municipality that has 50 or more public employees in total. Initially, the IRS declined to indicate how it would classify hours of service for emergency volunteers under the Affordable Care Act, meaning that fire companies and municipalities could be forced to provide volunteers with health insurance or pay a fine.

ACA Alternative

In February, Senate Finance Chairman Hatch, along with Sen. Richard Burr (R-N.C.) and House Energy and Commerce Chairman Fred Upton (R-Mich.) unveiled the Patient Choice, Affordability, Responsibility, and Empowerment (CARE) Bill, which would cap the exclusion for employer-provided health coverage and provide a targeted tax credit to help buy health care. Under the CARE Bill, there would be no mandate for individuals to buy health care coverage and employers would not be required to provide any. In addition, the plan would not allow a patient to be denied coverage based on a preexisting condition. The plan would also ban insurance companies from imposing lifetime limits on a consumer and would adopts age-rating changes that would lower costs for younger individuals and allow them to stay on their parents' health plan up to age 26, unless a state chose otherwise.

¶ 907 OBAMA's FY 2016 TAX PROPOSALS

President Obama unveiled a number of individual and business tax reform proposals as part of his FY 2016 budget recommendations to Congress. The FY 2016 proposals also aim to reform international taxation, particularly with respect to accumulated foreign earnings, simplify the tax system for small businesses, and enhance and streamline the myriad education incentives available to middle-class individuals.

COMMENT: There are approximately 160 total proposals in the president's FY 2016 budget release, of which 27 are new, 45 are modified or combined from proposals made in 2014, and 85 are substantially the same as proposals issued for FY 2015.

International Tax Reforms

The Obama Administration budget's international tax proposals represent an attempt to build a hybrid territorial/worldwide system of international taxation. New for the FY 2016 budget is a two-part solution to allow foreign profits to be repatriated into the U.S. to provide domestic growth without foregoing revenues that otherwise should have been taxed:

- *19 percent minimum tax on foreign income.* The administration proposed a minimum cumulative tax of 19 percent on earnings of a U.S. corporation that has stock in a controlled foreign corporation (CFC) or that has foreign earnings from a foreign branch or from performing services abroad. The tax would be imposed on current foreign earnings regardless of whether they are repatriated to the United States. This would allow all foreign earnings to be repatriated without further U.S. taxes; and

- *14 percent, one-time tax on previously untaxed foreign income.* In connection with the imposition of a minimum tax, the administration would impose a one-time, 14-percent tax on earnings accumulated in CFCs that have not previously been subject to U.S. tax. A foreign tax credit would be allowed. The accumulated income could then be repatriated to the United States without further tax. The proposal would apply to earnings accumulated for tax years beginning before January 1, 2016. The tax would be payable ratably over five years.

Additional proposals designed to reform the U.S international tax system include measures that would:

- Restrict corporate inversions by limiting the ability of U.S. corporations to expatriate by broadening the definition of an inversion to a greater than 50 percent ownership of the foreign parent by the former U.S. shareholders (replacing the current 80 percent test);

- Provide tax incentives for locating business activity in the United States and remove tax deductions for shipping jobs overseas;

- Limit the shifting of income through intangible property transfers;

- Close loopholes under Subpart F of the tax code;

- Restrict the use of hybrid arrangements that create stateless income; and

- Restrict deductions for excess interest of members of financial reporting groups.

STUDY QUESTION

4. The Protect Medical Innovation Bill of 2015 (HR 160) would:

- **a.** Treat full-time and seasonal employees the same for purposes of the Affordable Care Act's employer shared responsibility requirements

- **b.** Repeal the Affordable Care Act's medical device excise tax

- **c.** Treat Medicare as minimum essential health coverage for purposes of the Affordable Care Act's individual shared responsibility requirements

- **d.** Amend the Affordable Care Act to make it retroactive to January 1, 2008

Small Business Tax Relief/Simplification

Proposed tax relief for small businesses in the president's FY 2016 budget includes:

- Expand and permanently extend Code Sec. 179 expensing to a $500,000 for 2015 and $1 million in 2016, with inflation adjustments thereafter;
- Expand use of the cash method of accounting to small businesses with less than $25 million in average annual gross receipts;
- Permanently extend the 100 percent exclusion for income from tax qualified small business stock held by individuals for more than five years;
- Increase and consolidate the deduction for startup and organizational expenditures; and
- Expand the Code Sec. 45R credit for small employers to provide health insurance to apply to up to 50 (rather than 25) full-time equivalent employees, with phaseout between 20 and 50 employees (rather than between 10 and 25).

Individuals

The tax side of the administration's proposals for individuals focuses primarily on child care, education, and two-earner couples:

- *A $3,000 maximum credit per child for care for children under age 5.* The child and dependent care credit under Code Sec. 21would be increased to a maximum of $3,000 per child for expenses incurred for the care of children under age 5 to enable gainful employment of the parent(s) or other qualified taxpayer. The regular credit for those ages 5 through 12 would also phase out at higher income levels. Flexible spending accounts for child care, however, would be eliminated.
- *A $500 "second earner" tax credit for dual-earner couples.* This new credit would be fully phased out at adjusted gross income (AGI) exceeding $210,000.
- *Consolidation of overlapping education provisions.* Provisions would be consolidated, and the $2,500 American opportunity tax credit (AOTC) would be expanded to include more students. The AOTC would be permanently available for the first five years of post-secondary education (replacing the Hope tax credit entirely); a larger portion of the AOTC would be refundable, and the credit amount would be indexed for inflation each year. The credit would also be better coordinated with Pell grants. In exchange, the administration proposed the repeal of the lifetime learning credit and student loan interest deduction to simplify the overall scheme for education benefits.

Revenue Raisers

The Obama Administration highlighted three principal reforms through which it says many of its investments in the middle class will be funded:

- *Elimination of "stepped up basis" at death; similar gift consequences.* Transfers of appreciated property generally would be treated as a sale of the property, with the donor or deceased owner of the appreciated asset realizing capital gain at the time the asset is given or bequeathed. Generally, a $100,000-per-person exclusion would exist for inherited appreciated assets, along with exceptions for surviving spouses, small businesses, charities, and residences, among others;
- *Raising the top effective capital gains and dividends rate to 28 percent.* This rate increase would include a rise in the top capital gain and qualified dividend rate from 20 percent to 24.2 percent, which rises to 28 percent when the current net investment income tax of 3.8 percent is included; and

- *Imposition of a tax on large financial institutions for highly leveraged activities.* Large financial firms would pay a 7-basis-point fee on their liabilities.

Additional revenues would be raised in the form of provisions, among others, that have also appeared in prior years, including:

- Limiting to 28 percent the value of itemized deductions and other tax preferences;
- Implementing the "Buffett Rule." This rule, which is a carryover from prior year budget proposals, would require the wealthy to pay at least a 30 percent effective tax rate; and
- Taxing carried interest profits as ordinary income applicable to income earned by hedge fund managers and others.

Business Provisions

Provisions within the Obama Administration's budget directed toward business, many of which have appeared in prior years, include, among others:

- An enhanced and permanent research tax credit and other incentives;
- Extend and modify incentives to hire veterans and other employment tax credits;
- Modify and permanently extend the renewable electricity production tax credit and the investment tax credit;
- Provide a new carbon dioxide investment and sequestration tax credit;
- Modify and permanently extend the new markets tax credit;
- Modify and permanently extend the low-income housing tax credit;
- Provide and expand America fast forward bonds; and
- Provide qualified public infrastructure bonds.

IRS Budget

President Obama's FY 2016 budget would fund the IRS at $12.9 billion, representing an increase of nearly $2 billion compared to FY 2015. The president called for significant increases in operations support, taxpayer services, and enforcement.

> **COMMENT:** The House Appropriations Committee in June approved a fiscal year (FY) 2016 appropriations bill to provide $10.1 billion to fund the IRS for FY 2016. The bill represents a cut of approximately $838 million, compared to the IRS's FY 2015 budget.

STUDY QUESTION

5. Which of the following is **not** a reform proposed by the Obama Administration to raise government revenues?

    a. Impose a tax on the highly leveraged activities of large financial institutions

    b. Eliminate the renewable electricity production tax credit

    c. Raise the effective tax rate on capital gains and dividends

    d. Eliminate the stepped-up basis used for transfers of property as gifts or upon the death of the transferor

¶ 908 TRADE LEGISLATION

In June, President Obama signed the *Bipartisan Congressional Trade Priorities and Accountability Act of 2015* (P.L. 114-26) and the *Trade Preferences Extension Act of 2015* (P.L. 114-27)). The trade bills enhance or change several tax provisions as well as extend the health coverage tax credit (HCTC).

Trade Adjustment Assistance

Trade Adjustment Assistance (TAA) is a group of programs that provide federal job-training and other assistance to workers, firms, farmers, and communities that have been adversely impacted by foreign trade, including workers who have been separated from employment because their jobs moved overseas or as a result of increased imports. The TAA was originally created by the *Trade Expansion Act of 1962* and has been subsequently reauthorized.

Generally, a petition must be filed with the U.S. Department of Labor (DOL) by or on behalf of a group of workers who have lost or may lose their jobs or experienced a reduction in wages as a result of foreign trade. After DOL investigates the facts behind the petition, it applies statutory criteria to determine whether foreign trade was an important cause of the threatened or actual job loss or wage reduction. If DOL grants the petition to certify the worker group, individual workers in the group may apply to their state workforce agency for TAA benefits and services. In 2010, DOL certified 2,718 TAA petitions, covering 280,873 workers. More than two-thirds of covered workers accessed TAA benefits, DOL reported.

Trade readjustment allowances (TRA) are available to covered workers to provide income support while they participate in full-time training. The amount of each weekly TRA payment is based on the weekly unemployment insurance (UI) benefit amount already received by the covered worker. A covered worker must have been entitled to receive UI benefits before he or she may receive TRA and must have exhausted his or her UI entitlement. There are three types of TRA: basic TRA, additional TRA, and completion TRA. Another program, the Alternative Trade Adjustment Assistance (ATAA) program, provides benefits to workers age 50 or older who do not earn more than $50,000 annually in their new employment, to accept reemployment at a lower wage.

> **COMMENT:** Training programs under TAA include classroom training, on-the-job training, customized training designed to meet the needs of a specific employer or group of employers, apprenticeship programs, post-secondary education, or remedial education, which may include GED preparation, literacy training, basic math, or English as a second language.

Health Coverage Tax Credit

The *Trade Preferences Extension Act of 2015* renews the Code Sec. 35 health coverage tax credit (HCTC), which had expired after 2013. Covered individuals (and in some cases family members) may claim the HCTC to help offset the cost of health insurance. Covered individuals generally must qualify for Trade Adjustment Assistance (TAA) or qualify as an eligible Pension Benefit Guaranty Corporation (PBGC) pension recipient. The new law makes the HCTC retroactive to January 1, 2014, and available for months beginning before January 1, 2020.

Generally, a covered individual is an individual who is:

- An eligible TAA recipient;
- An eligible alternative TAA recipient; or
- An eligible Pension Benefit Guaranty Corporation (PBGC) pension recipient.

COMMENT: An individual is an eligible PBGC pension recipient for any month if the individual is age 55 or older as of the first day of the month and receives a benefit for the month, any portion of which is paid by the PBGC.

For purposes of the HCTC, qualified health insurance eligible for the credit is:

- COBRA continuation coverage;

- State-based continuation coverage provided by the state under a state law that requires such coverage;

- Coverage offered through a qualified state high-risk pool;

- Coverage under a health insurance program offered to state employees or a comparable program;

- Coverage through an arrangement entered into by a state and a group health plan, an issuer of health insurance coverage, an administrator, or an employer;

- Coverage offered through a state arrangement with a private sector health care coverage purchasing pool;

- Coverage under a state-operated health plan that does not receive any federal financial participation;

- Coverage under a group health plan that is available through the employment of the eligible individual's spouse;

- Coverage under individual health insurance if the eligible individual was covered under individual health insurance during the entire 30-day period that ends on the date the individual became separated from the employment that qualified the individual for the TAA allowance, the benefit for an eligible alternative TAA recipient, or a pension benefit from the PBGC, whichever applies; and

- Coverage under an employee benefit plan funded by a voluntary employee beneficiary association (VEBA) established under an order of a bankruptcy court (or by agreement with an authorized representative).

Information Reporting

The *Trade Preferences Extension Act of 2015* overhauls the penalty structure for information returns and payee statements. The changes to the penalty structure are effective for information returns and payee statements required to be filed/furnished after 2015. The penalty for a single failure would increase from $100 to $250; the maximum penalty for all failures during a calendar year would increase from $1.5 million to $3 million. If the failure is corrected within 30 days of the required filing date, the penalty for a single violation would increase to $50 (up from $30); the penalty for all failures would increase to $500,000 (up from $250,000). The lower limitations for persons with gross receipts of $5 million or less would increase.

COMMENT: If the failure to properly file a correct information return is due to intentional disregard of the rules, the penalty is at least $250 for each improper return, and there is no cap on the total penalties imposed. The penalty does not apply to certain inconsequential errors, *de minimis* failures, or failures due to reasonable cause.

COMMENT: Many information reporting requirements have specific penalty provisions for failure to provide the required information.

Child Tax Credit

A U.S. citizen or resident living abroad may be eligible to elect to exclude from U.S. taxable income certain foreign earned income and foreign housing costs under Code Sec. 911. The *Trade Preferences Extension Act of 2015* limits the child tax credit for taxpayers who elect to exclude from gross income for a tax year any amount of foreign earned income or foreign housing costs. These taxpayers would not be able to claim the refundable portion of the child tax credit for the tax year.

Corporate Taxes

The *Trade Preferences Extension Act of 2015* shifts corporate estimated tax payments for corporations with at least $1 billion in assets. The amount of corporate estimated tax due in July, August, or September 2020 is increased by 8 percent and the amount of the next required installment is reduced to reflect the prior increase.

Education

Educational institutions are required to provide Form 1098-T, *Tuition Statement,* to students who attend their institution and file a copy of Form 1098-T with the IRS. Under the *Trade Preferences Extension Act of 2015,* the American opportunity tax credit (the revised HOPE credit) and the lifetime learning credit under Code Sec. 25A, as well as the tuition and fees deduction under Code Sec. 222, will not be allowed unless the taxpayer submits with his or her return a valid information return (Form 1098-T, *Tuition Statement*) or other written statement from the educational institution. For most individuals, the provision requiring them to attach Form 1098-T to their return is effective for tax years beginning after 2015.

> **COMMENT:** In March 2015, the Treasury Inspector General for Tax Administration (TIGTA) estimated that more than 3.6 million taxpayers received some $5.6 billion in potentially erroneous education credits for tax year (TY) 2012. TIGTA identified nearly 2.1 million taxpayers who received education credits without a Form 1098-T.

STUDY QUESTION

6. Which of the following is *not* a type of qualified health insurance eligible for the health coverage tax credit?

    a. Coverage under a college plan for students under age 22

    b. Coverage under a state-operated health plan that does not receive any federal financial participation

    c. Coverage through a qualified state high-risk pool

    d. COBRA continuation coverage

¶ 909 CONCLUSION

Tax reform in 2015 could come as a series of bills or as a comprehensive tax bill. At the time this course was prepared, the outcome of tax reform legislation in 2015 is unclear. However, Congress will need to act before year-end on a number of tax bills, most notably the tax extenders package. If Congress does not act on tax reform in 2015, however, consensus is that there is a solid framework of reports and proposals present to enable tax reform to move forward in 2016, either before or after the new president is elected.

¶ 10,100 Answers to Study Questions

¶ 10,101 MODULE 1—CHAPTER 1

1. a. *Incorrect.* The FTE calculation is based on a total number of hours of service not exceeding 120 hours per employee for the month.

b. *Correct.* **The FTEs are determined by adding the number of hours of service and dividing it by 120.**

c. *Incorrect.* Full-time equivalent employees are not disregarded in counting the number of full-time employees for qualifying ALE status.

d. *Incorrect.* Shareholders who do not provide services to the corporation are not considered employees.

2. a. *Incorrect.* The seasonal worker exemption from the shared responsibility rules does not apply for fewer than 50 full-time employees and FTEs exceeds a monthly average of 50.

b. *Incorrect.* The minimum number of days of employment for seasonal workers is 120.

c. *Correct.* **This total head count for the three-month period means that the seasonal worker exception does not apply for ALE status.**

d. *Incorrect.* The seasonal worker exclusion applies only in determining ALE status and no the shared responsibility payments.

3. a. *Incorrect.* The Code Sec. 4980H(a) rules apply if substantially all of the employer's eligible employees were offered coverage but not satisfied the affordability or MV requirements.

b. *Incorrect.* The two payment regimes specify that an ALEM is never liable under both the enrollment and affordability/MV regimes for the same calendar month.

c. *Correct.* **The affordability and MV requirements only apply if the ALEM does not offer such coverage to substantially all of its full-time employees.**

d. *Incorrect.* The Code Sec. 4980H(b) regime does not apply if no employee obtained subsidized coverage.

4. a. *Incorrect.* The payment calculation includes regular full-time and seasonal employees considered full-time multiplied times another factor.

b. *Correct.* **The payment is the product of full-time employees receiving a credit times 1/12 of the maximum $250 per month under Code Sec. 4980H(b).**

c. *Incorrect.* For 2015, the number of covered dependents does not control the employer's shared responsibility payments.

d. *Incorrect.* Before the payment is calculated, the number of hours that seasonal employees work is converted to full-time equivalent employees' hours.

5. a. *Incorrect.* Counting employee hours or service is integral to determining whether an ALEM must offer MEC or MV coverage that satisfies the employer shared responsibility requirements.

b. *Correct.* **Service hours performed by a bona fide volunteer are not counted as employee hours for the payment requirements.**

c. *Incorrect.* Hours of service are counted by ALEs for purposes of whether the employer averages at least 50 full-time employees.

d. *Incorrect.* This determination is a reason that employee hours of service are counted.

6. a. *Incorrect.* The IRS reporting requirements for Forms 1094-C and 1095-C will reveal whether the employer successfully provided MEC and MV coverage to eligible employees.

b. *Incorrect.* By filing a Form 1094-C to the IRS and Forms 1095-C to eligible employees, both the government and employees can determine whether the employer provided coverage required for ALEs under the ACA.

c. *Correct.* The two forms are retrospective and do not project future health care coverage for employees.

d. *Incorrect.* The reporting requirements will reveal whether the employer-sponsored coverage is affordable to employees and provides minimum value coverage.

¶ 10,102 MODULE 1—CHAPTER 2

1. a. *Incorrect.* Taxpayers can apply to have the credit paid in advance to help them afford premium payments throughout the year.

b. *Correct.* The IRS administers the credit through taxpayer and employer reporting on Form 1095, Form W-2, and Form 8965, *Health Coverage Exemptions,* and Form 8962, *Premium Tax Credit.*

c. *Incorrect.* The tax credit is refundable; if the taxpayer qualifies for a credit and the amount of the credit is larger than the year's income tax liability owed, he or she receives a refund for the difference.

d. *Incorrect.* The credit is intended to help both low- and middle-income taxpayers. Individuals eligible for Medicaid coverage are generally not eligible for a premium tax credit. Certain limited Medicaid coverage for family planning, pregnancy, emergency, or tuberculosis is not MEC and does not preclude a premium tax credit.

2. a. *Incorrect.* The exemption applies only to taxpayers who do not have MEC for fewer than three months in a tax year.

b. *Correct.* Only the first gap of fewer than three months within one tax year is eligible for the exemption.

c. *Incorrect.* If the gap extends for three months or longer within a year, the taxpayer is not exempt for any of the months and may be liable for a shared responsibility payment for the whole period (unless the taxpayer has an exemption).

d. *Incorrect.* For the current year, the short coverage gap is satisfied for December if it is the first gap in the year and the period is less than three months. For the following year, so long as the individual resumed coverage after February, January and February would be exempted as a short coverage gap because it is the first gap of the year and the gap is less than three months.

3. a. *Incorrect.* Part I is used by the taxpayer who claims a coverage exemption and files Form 8965 with his or her tax return.

b. *Incorrect.* Part II is used by the taxpayer who is filing a return although not required to do so, and Form 8965 is submitted with the return.

c. *Incorrect.* Part III is completed by a taxpayer who claims the coverage exemption on his or her tax return rather than applying for the exemption through the marketplace.

d. *Correct.* **A taxpayer with income lower than the filing threshold is exempt from the shared responsibility payment and does not need to file either a return or Form 8965.**

4. a. *Incorrect.* This payment does not exclude a payment for the spouses.

b. *Incorrect.* This amount exceeds the payment for the family members that were required to have coverage or an exemption.

c. *Correct.* **This is the maximum shared responsibility payment for the 2015 tax year. They subtract $20,600 (filing threshold) from $70,000 (household income). The result is $49,400. 2 percent of $49,400 equals $988. Eduardo and Julia's flat dollar amount is $975. The family's annual national average premium for bronze level coverage for 2015 is $9,936 ($2,484 × 4). Because $988 is greater than $975 and is less than $9,792, Eduardo and Julia's shared responsibility payment is $988 for 2015.**

d. *Incorrect.* This amount is the maximum the family would have paid if their household income were higher.

5. a. *Incorrect.* To use the alternative method, the couple must have been married during the tax year.

b. *Correct.* **The couple must file jointly to be eligible to use the alternative method.**

c. *Incorrect.* A member of the tax family must have been enrolled in a qualified health plan before the first full month of the couple's marriage in order to use the alternative method.

d. *Incorrect.* Someone in the tax family (not necessarily one of the spouses) must have received an advance credit in order to qualify for use of the alternative method.

6. a. *Incorrect.* In a case in which one of the spouses has been domestically abused (Situation 2), that taxpayer may claim the premium tax credit by filing separately.

b. *Incorrect.* When a spouse has abandoned his or her partner (Situation 2), the abandoned taxpayer may file separately and claim the credit.

c. *Correct.* **Neither spouse must receive an advance credit in order to apply one of the situations in which a spouse may file separately and qualify for the credit.**

d. *Incorrect.* A taxpayer qualifying to claim head of household status may file separately (Situation 1) to claim the premium tax credit.

¶ 10,103 MODULE 2—CHAPTER 3

1. a. *Incorrect.* The American opportunity tax credit or lifetime learning credit may be applied to tuition during the same tax year as distributions from a qualified tuition plan are applied to the *other* expenses.

b. *Incorrect.* Such a redemption is allowed under the coordination rules of Code Sec. 135.

c. *Correct.* **The qualified expenses must be reduced by education credits as well as scholarships and fellowship grants, and then the distribution applies to the balance tax-free.**

d. *Incorrect.* As long as qualified education expenses exceed the amount of the bond earnings and credit amounts, taxpayers may use both for the same year if their adjusted gross income is lower than the maximum for both benefits.

2. a. *Incorrect.* A 10 percent penalty applies to withdrawals not used for education or rolled over to another beneficiary except upon the death or disability of the beneficiary.

b. *Correct.* The contributor and beneficiary may also change the account's investment strategy once every calendar year.

c. *Incorrect.* Payments made directly to the institution are not subject to gift tax limits and may be made in addition to taking withdrawals from QTPs to pay *other* educational expenses. Expenses paid directly by the contributor to the institution cannot be used to avoid paying tax on withdrawals from QTP's.

d. *Incorrect.* Distributions from a qualified state tuition program may be taken the same year that the distributee claims either the AOTC or LLC. Expenses paid for by a distribution from a QTP cannot be used to claim either the AOTC or LLC.

3. a. *Incorrect.* The maximum contribution for a Coverdell is $2,000 per year, and the maximum allowed without gift tax to a qualified tuition plan is $14,000 per donor (and more made ratably over five years)

b. *Correct.* Taxable distributions from either type of account carry a 10 percent penalty in addition to their tax liability if the withdrawals are not used for qualified education expenses.

c. *Incorrect.* Only Coverdell ESAs specify that the account balance must be used or rolled over when the student reaches age 30.

d. *Incorrect.* Owners of Coverdell accounts may choose the investment type, but contributors to a qualified tuition plan must use the investments made by the state administering the plan.

4. a. *Incorrect.* Bond interest is excludible if the taxpayer named on the bond uses the proceeds to pay qualified educational expenses for him- or herself, the taxpayer's spouse or dependents.

b. *Incorrect.* The taxpayer must have attained the age of 24 before the issue date for bond interest to be excludible.

c. *Correct.* The exclusion of interest begins to phase out for taxpayers whose MAGI is more than $115,750 for joints returns and $77,200 for other returns, up to the complete phaseout at $145,750/$92,200.

d. *Incorrect.* A qualified bond is a Series EE bond issued after December 31, 1989 or a Series I bond.

5. a. *Correct.* The credit applies to the first $10,000 of tuition paid, for a maximum amount of $2,000.

b. *Incorrect.* The credit cannot be claimed for the amount of books and other course materials not required by the institution and not paid to the institution for purposes of enrollment.

c. *Incorrect.* In 2015 eligibility for claiming the credit begins to phase out for single taxpayers with MAGI in excess of $55,000 and for married taxpayers filing jointly with MAGI in excess of $110,000.

d. *Incorrect.* Married taxpayers must file jointly to be eligible for claiming the LLC.

6. a. *Correct.* The credit is allowed for 100 percent of the first $2,000 of qualified expenses and 25 percent of the next $2,000, for a total credit maximum for the year of $2,500.

b. *Incorrect.* The AOTC applies to expenses related to course materials.

c. *Incorrect.* Although educational institutions provide a Form 1098-T for the calendar year, a taxpayer must elect to claim an educational credit using Form 8863, *Education Credits (American Opportunity and Lifetime Learning Credits),* which is attached to the taxpayer's federal income tax return.

d. *Incorrect.* The credit is 40 percent refundable for these tax years unless the taxpayer is a child subject to the kiddie tax on his or her income.

7. a. *Incorrect.* Payment for services as part of this program is not treated as taxable income.

b. *Correct.* **Payments received for personal services are pay reported to the cadet on Form W-2.**

c. *Incorrect.* The need-based Pell grant amounts are not taxable if used for qualified education expenses.

d. *Incorrect.* Payments of veterans' education, training, or subsistence under Department of Veterans Affairs laws are tax free.

8. a. *Incorrect.* The 10 percent penalty does not apply if IRA funds are used for qualified higher education expenses of the taxpayer, or his or her spouse, child, or grandchild.

b. *Correct.* **Funds withdrawn from a traditional IRA are taxable when a taxpayer of whatever age takes a distribution.**

c. *Incorrect.* The funds may be paid for qualified expenses within 60 days of withdrawal from the IRA account.

d. *Incorrect.* A child or grandchild is not required to be the taxpayer's dependent to use the withdrawn funds for qualified higher education expenses.

9. a. *Incorrect.* The individual claiming the student loan interest deduction cannot be claimed as a dependent on another taxpayer's income tax return.

b. *Incorrect.* To claim an interest deduction, the loan must be in the name of the borrower (student) who files the income tax return.

c. *Correct.* **The individual is ineligible for the interest deduction on a student loan if he or she is married and files a separate return.**

d. *Incorrect.*.The student's age is not a factor if the loan is in his or her name.

¶ 10,104 MODULE 2—CHAPTER 4

1. a. *Correct.* **If the married taxpayer qualifies for head of household filing status, he or she is treated as unmarried and is eligible to claim the standard deduction even with a spouse who itemizes deductions. Otherwise, if one spouse itemizes, the other spouse is not allowed to take the standard deduction**

b. *Incorrect.* Both spouses filing separately are not required to take the standard deduction.

c. *Incorrect.* A nonresident alien or dual-status alien is not eligible for the standard deduction.

d. *Incorrect.* Married filing separately taxpayers are eligible for a deduction, but certain circumstances limit the choice between taking the standard deduction and itemizing.

2. a. *Incorrect.* Each spouse may contribute the same as if he or she was unmarried: $5,500 if younger than age 50, and $6,500 if older than age 50.

b. *Correct.* **The phaseout threshold for the MAGI of joint filers is less than double that for single filers who are covered by an employer retirement plan.**

c. *Incorrect.* Spouses do not have to file separate returns because they are married, and the phaseout threshold for contribution deductions is $0 for separate filers.

d. *Incorrect.* Contribution amounts are unaffected by employer plans.

3. a. *Incorrect.* The coverage is exempt from taxation because Baylea's employer plan covers medical expenses of her spouse.

b. *Incorrect.* The couple is not required to file separately for the lower threshold to apply.

c. *Correct.* **Because one spouse is age 65 and they file jointly, the lower AGI percentage for deducting medical expenses applies to both of their expense amounts.**

d. *Incorrect.* The higher threshold does not apply to the couple's combined AGI.

4. a. *Correct.* **The decedent's estate may elect to allow the unused portion to be usable by the surviving spouse or the spouse's estate.**

b. *Incorrect.* The credit is applied first to the decedent's estate and then any remaining credit may be ported to the spouse if requested.

c. *Incorrect.* The gift tax marital deduction does not apply if the spouse is not a U.S. citizen, but the gift tax exclusion of $147,000 for 2015 applies.

d. *Incorrect.* Portability is not an issue for lifetime transfers to a surviving spouse because the deduction is based on their marital status at the time of the transferor's death.

5. a. *Incorrect.* The amount of the spouses' relative efforts in acquiring the property is not a determining factor in whether it is community property or quasi-community property.

b. *Correct.* **Such property would have been community property had the spouses lived in a community property state at the time of acquisition.**

c. *Incorrect.* The locale of the sale of community property is not determinative in whether it is quasi-community property.

d. *Incorrect.* Such property remains separate property.

6. a. *Incorrect.* The penalty on distributions made before the retirement age does not apply under a QDRO.

b. *Correct.* **Restrictions such as the antialienation rules do not apply for distributions under a QDRO.**

c. *Incorrect.* The participant is not treated as receiving the amount for tax purposes except if it is made to a payee other than his or her spouse, such as their child.

d. *Incorrect.* The ex-spouse who receives the plan benefits is treated as though he or she were the participant; thus, no rollover or distribution is required.

¶ 10,105 MODULE 3—CHAPTER 5

1. a. *Correct.* A foreign estate is not a U.S. person under FATCA, although other estates are.

b. *Incorrect.* A domestic corporation or partnership is considered a U.S. person under FATCA.

c. *Incorrect.* A domestic trust is considered a U.S. person under FATCA.

d. *Incorrect.* Any domestic entity serving to hold specified foreign financial assets is a specified person.

2. a. *Incorrect.* Under FATCA requirements, unless the account is owned by a bona fide resident of the U.S. territory, it is subject to reporting on Form 8938.

b. *Incorrect.* A currency swap and similar agreements with a foreign counterparty are other specified foreign financial assets.

c. *Correct.* The stock is not reportable on Form 8938 if a bona fide resident of Guam (a U.S. possession) is the owner.

d. *Incorrect.* An interest in a foreign entity is reportable on Form 8938 even if the account is not maintained by an FFI.

3. a. *Correct.* Each spouse includes just half of the value of the jointly owned assets in his or her foreign financial assets for reporting.

b. *Incorrect.* Each of the owners not married to each other must list the entire value of the jointly owned asset in determining his or her total assets.

c. *Incorrect.* A parent electing to include a child's unearned income by filing Form 8814 lists the jointly owned asset's value on the parent's Form 8938.

d. *Incorrect.* When one spouse is not a specified person, each spouse includes the entire value of the jointly owned asset in determining the total specified foreign financial assets.

4. a. *Incorrect.* The limitations period is extended to six years even for classes of assets that the IRS excepts from the reporting requirements if the assets increase gross income by $5,000 or more.

b. *Incorrect.* The statutory period is extended to six years even when omissions of gross income of more than $5,000 are properly reported.

c. *Correct.* If the omitted income is less than $5,000, the normal three-year limitations period applies.

d. *Incorrect.* The duration of the limitations period is extended to six years even when the assets' value is less than the reporting threshold if gross income from the assets increases by at least $5,000.

5. a. *Incorrect.* The maximum fine for tax evasion is $250,000.

b. *Incorrect.* Filing a false return incurs up to a $250,000 fine, which is half as much as the fine for another individual tax violation.

c. *Correct.* Failure to file an FBAR carries a fine of up to $500,000, double the fine applied to other individual tax law violations.

d. *Incorrect.* Defrauding the government carries a fine of up to $250,000; the violation's maximum prison term is five years.

6. a. *Incorrect.* All penalties for U.S. citizens dwelling in the United States have not been eliminated, but the procedure applies to more noncompliant taxpayers.

b. *Correct.* **Starting in 2014, the procedures apply to taxpayers whose failure to disclose offshore assets was nonwillful, and the low-risk threshold is not required.**

c. *Incorrect.* The Streamlined Procedure has been expanded to include more taxpayers, not narrowed in scope.

d. *Incorrect.* The liability threshold for eligibility to use the procedure was not raised.

7. a. *Incorrect.* Preventing treaty abuse is Action 6 of the project, and an output report was issued regarding the action in September 2014.

b. *Incorrect.* Making dispute resolution mechanisms more effective is Action 14 of the project and is one of the 2015 deliverables.

c. *Incorrect.* Strengthening CFC rules is Action 3 of the project and is one of the 2015 deliverables.

d. *Correct.* **The project seeks to prevent the artificial avoidance of the permanent establishment status.**

¶ 10,106 MODULE 3—CHAPTER 6

1. a. *Incorrect.* The advance consent procedure is only required if the taxpayer previously made a change under the repair regulations and is making the same change again

b. *Correct.* **The automatic consent procedure continues to apply to a taxpayer who did not previously file Form 3115 to comply with the repair regulations**

c. *Incorrect.* The late partial disposition election may not be made for a tax year that begins after 2014.

d. *Incorrect.* The revocation of a prior-year general asset account election had to be made no later than for the 2014 tax year.

2. a. *Correct.* **The relief applies to small business taxpayers that did not file Form 3115 for the 2014 tax year to change to the required methods or that did not attach a rejection statement to their 2014 return.**

b. *Incorrect.* The last-minute relief does not apply to retroactively filed 2014 returns.

c. *Incorrect.* If the last minute relief was accepted, taxpayers were treated as applying the repair regulations on a cut-off basis without the computation of a Code Sec. 481(a) adjustment

d. *Incorrect.* The last-minute relief treated taxpayers as changing to all methods required by the repair regulations.

3. a. *Incorrect.* The cost of the new floor would not be considered an ordinary business expense if the lessor claimed a loss on the old floor's basis.

b. *Correct.* **The replacement floor is considered a restoration that must be capitalized if a loss is deducted on the old floor.**

c. *Incorrect.* A hardwood floor is a structural component and, therefore, is section 1250 property.

d. *Incorrect.* The floor is a structural component that remains part of the building unit of property although it is depreciated as a separate asset over 39 years.

4. a. *Incorrect.* The UNICAP provisions do not target the place of production to determine the capitalization versus deduction of acquisition or production costs.

b. *Incorrect.* The UNICAP rules do not have a dollar threshold.

c. *Correct.* **The UNICAP rules, which trump the provisions of the *de minimis* safe harbor, concern whether the property is acquired or produced for resale or produced for the taxpayer's own use.**

d. *Incorrect.* The UNICAP rules target acquisition or production costs, not worthless property.

5. a. *Incorrect.* The deduction election does not apply to receipts of the taxpayer in a single tax year

b. *Correct.* **Taxpayers whose average annual gross receipts do not exceed $10 million in the three preceding tax years may make an annual election to deduct limited improvements if the building's unadjusted basis is $1 million or less.**

c. *Incorrect.* The election must be made on a timely filed original return (including extensions) and can only be made on an amended return with IRS permission

d. *Incorrect.* The ceiling on deductions for limited improvements is the lesser of $10,000 or 2% of the unadjusted basis of the building

6. a. *Correct.* **When a portion of a separately depreciated asset, such as a building or an item of section 1245 property, is retired a taxpayer may make a partial disposition election to claim a loss equal to the remaining undepreciated basis of the retired component.**

b. *Incorrect.* A taxpayer makes a partial disposition election by claiming the loss on the return. It is not necessary to file an election statement.

c. *Incorrect.* When an entire asset is retired, recognition of gain or loss is mandatory.

d. *Incorrect.* Although the retirement of a portion of an asset does not result in gain or loss unless a partial disposition election is made, the sale of a portion of an asset (or an entire asset) results in the recognition of gain or loss without making the election.

¶ 10,107 MODULE 4—CHAPTER 7

1. a. *Incorrect.* Mere participation in a PSO does not prevent a provider from qualifying as a tax-exempt organization.

b. *Incorrect.* Code Sec. 501(o) provisions apply to for-profit as well as tax-exempt providers that may be organized as a PSO.

c. *Correct.* **Any provider or other person who has a financial interest in a PSO is treated as a private shareholder for the hospital providing patient care.**

d. *Incorrect.* The PSO may lose its tax-exempt status if it exhibits a pattern of violating the law's antidumping provisions.

2. a. *Correct.* **Healthcare systems use criteria such as zip codes or regional approaches to delineate their community.**

b. *Incorrect.* Separate chapters or sections of the CHNA are documented for all of a hospital facility consisting or multiple buildings to assess health needs of the different populations and their geographic areas; an implementation strategy is adopted separately for each facility.

c. *Incorrect.* The CHNA describes how input was obtained for the assessment from not only experts and medical providers but also the community served.

d. *Incorrect.* The assessment must be conducted at least once every three years.

3. a. *Correct.* The hospital may nevertheless be subject to penalties or even have its exempt status revoked, but correcting and disclosing the violation may help the hospital to indicate that the failure was not willful.

b. *Incorrect.* When a multihospital organization operates a facility that fails to satisfy the requirements, the IRS final regulations imposes an income tax on the organization.

c. *Incorrect.* The excise tax applies when the hospital does not properly conduct a CHNA and adopt an implementation strategy.

d. *Incorrect.* The revocation can occur when the hospital fails to meet the consumer protection standards of Code Sec. 501(r).

4. a. *Incorrect.* This first category of correction under Reg. § 1.501(r)-2(b) is excused as not a Code Sec. 501(r) compliance failure.

b. *Correct.* A willful failure is caused by gross negligence, reckless disregard, or willful neglect and is not excused under the regulations.

c. *Incorrect.* The revenue procedure provides that such minor omissions are not considered noncompliance with Code Sec. 501(r).

d. *Incorrect.* This second category of failure involves correction and disclosure under Reg. § 1.501(r)-2(c).

5. a. *Incorrect.* As long as the terms do not refer to cash payments from hospitals to physicians, the hospital benefits for EHR subsidies does not disqualify them from being considered Code Sec. 501(c)(3) organizations.

b. *Correct.* If the net earnings of a hospital have inured to the benefit of staff physicians outside of the EHR arrangement, the safe harbor is not applicable to the hospital.

c. *Incorrect.* Access restrictions are acceptable under the IRS directive to prevent violations of federal and state privacy laws or the physician's contractual obligations to patients.

d. *Incorrect.* As long as the access is related to meeting the healthcare needs of the community, access to various physician groups at different times is not impermissible private benefit under the IRS directive.

6. a. *Incorrect.* Although these commercial interests are a concern of the IRS in connection with RHIOs, their purpose is not provision of insurer benefits.

b. *Correct.* Although the purpose of RHIOs is facilitation of EHR information among hospitals, physicians, and other healthcare system members, the IRS is concerned that the organizations might serve insurers' interests and generate substantial private benefit.

c. *Incorrect.* Patient privacy and accessibility rights are not the focus of RHIOs.

d. *Incorrect.* Although the IRS receives a number of international healthcare cases related to sharing EHR data, whether these organizations qualify for tax-exempt status is unresolved.

¶ 10,108 MODULE 4—CHAPTER 8

1. a. *Correct.* SECA taxes are imposed on sole proprietors and general partners (a well as on guaranteed payments to limited partners in exchange for performing services for their partnership) to fund Social Security and Medicare.

b. *Incorrect.* Self-employment taxes are not imposed on the distributive share limited partners in partnerships unless the payments are for services performed by the limited partners.

c. *Incorrect.* SECA taxes apply to a self-employed person's net earnings from self-employment (gross trade or business income minus allowable deductions plus income or loss on partnership interests).

d. *Incorrect.* Not all taxpayers subject to the SECA tax are subject to the net investment income tax.

2. a. *Incorrect.* Income from royalties and rents are included in one of the baskets (Category (i)) of income on which NII tax is calculated.

b. *Incorrect.* Gross income from passive activities is included in one of the baskets of income (Category (ii)) on which the NII tax is imposed.

c. *Correct.* The tax is not imposed if the taxpayer satisfies a material participation test.

d. *Incorrect.* Net gain on the disposition of nonbusiness property is included in one of the baskets (Category (iii)) on which NII tax is imposed.

3. a. *Incorrect.* The IRS does not seek to lower the salaries of shareholder-employees for their services to their S corporation.

b. *Incorrect.* The IRS position is not to adjust the levels of compensation between C and S corporation shareholders.

c. *Correct.* The IRS seeks to keep shareholder-employee compensation reasonable and recharacterizes dividends that are disguised compensation.

d. *Incorrect.* The IRS seeks to ensure that shareholder-employees performing services for the corporation do not avoid paying self-employment and payroll taxes on the income; S corporations are not, as a general rule, taxed at the entity level on the S corporation's income.

4. a. *Incorrect.* The personal-service-activities test of an individual's material participation is applied to services activity such as law or accounting for any three tax years preceding the current tax year.

b. *Incorrect.* This test is satisfied only if the individual whose participation in the S corporation activity composes substantially all of the participation by all individuals.

c. *Correct.* This test aggregates all of the individual's significant participation activities for the tax year, which must exceed 500 hours; certain other criteria apply under this test as well.

d. *Incorrect.* This test is satisfied if an individual participates for at least 100 hours during the tax year and that level of participation is at least that of any other individual for the year.

5. a. *Incorrect.* This test considers whether an individual materially participated in an activity not focused on capital as a material income-producing factor for three tax years preceding the current year.

b. *Incorrect.* This test is not a measure of the total hours of participation but compares the individual's participation to the level of any other participant.

c. *Incorrect.* This test aggregates the hours that the individual participates in all significant participation activities for a minimum of 500 total hours.

d. *Correct.* **An individual whose participation in the S corporation exceeds 100 hours and is not less than participation by any other individual for the tax year satisfies this test.**

6. a. *Incorrect.* By satisfying the personal-service-activities test, a limited partner is treated as materially participating in a partnership.

b. *Correct.* **The significant-participation-activities test as applied to shareholder-employees of S corporations is not used as a measure for a limited partner in a limited partnership.**

c. *Incorrect.* Satisfaction of participation requirements for any 5 tax years during the 10 preceding the current year is considered material participation by a limited partner.

d. *Incorrect.* A limited partner is considered as materially participating in a limited partnership by participating in an activity of the partnership for at least 500 hours during the tax year.

¶ 10,109 MODULE 5—CHAPTER 9

1. a. *Incorrect.* Rep. Paul Ryan has indicated that the committee and the president differ in their opinions about tax rates.

b. *Correct.* **Rep. Paul Ryan stated that the committee and president can find common ground on business tax reform.**

c. *Incorrect.* Rep. Paul Ryan indicated that reforming the international taxation system would not be helpful to efforts at comprehensive tax reform.

d. *Incorrect.* Estate and gift taxes are not the focus of the committee's efforts at overhauling the tax code, although the president has proposed reinstating the 2009 estate and gift tax rates in his FY 2016 budget proposals.

2. a. *Incorrect.* Eligible small businesses could offset both their regular tax and AMT liabilities under the bill.

b. *Incorrect.* The bill repeals the traditional 20 percent credit method for calculating the credit and increases the rate to a variable 20 percent.

c. *Correct.* **The legislation would make the alternative simplified method permanent.**

d. *Incorrect.* President Obama promised a veto of the bill, stating its approach to business tax reform has the wrong emphasis.

3. a. *Incorrect.* The act is not targeted at local public safety employees but rather federal officials.

b. *Correct.* **The act provides penalty relief to eligible federal public safety employees who take distributions from certain retirement plans.**

c. *Incorrect.* Eligible federal public safety employees would still be subject to federal income tax on retirement account withdrawals at any age.

d. *Incorrect.* The act does not set a full retirement age but focuses on the benefits available to federal public safety employees and their associated income tax liability.

4. a. *Incorrect.* The Affordable Care Act currently makes a distinction between full-time and seasonal employees for purposes of the employer shared responsibility requirements.

b. *Correct.* **The proposal would repeal the Affordable Care Act's medical device excise tax.**

c. *Incorrect.* The Affordable Care Act treats Medicare as minimum essential health coverage for purposes of the individual shared responsibility requirement.

d. *Incorrect.* The Affordable Care Act is effective as of its date of enactment, March 26, 2010, although some provisions carry delayed effective dates.

5. a. *Incorrect.* Large firms would pay a fee of 7 basis points on their tax liabilities.

b. *Correct.* **The credits for producing renewable electricity and for investments would be permanently extended, not cut, under the president's proposals.**

c. *Incorrect.* The top effective capital gains and dividends tax rate would be raised to 28 percent, on top of which the net investment income tax of 3.8 percent would be added.

d. *Incorrect.* Property transferred at death or by gift would be treated as a sale of the property, subjecting the transferor to capital gains tax.

6. a. *Correct.* **The credit targets PBGC pension recipients and individuals either adversely affected by foreign trade or individuals whose wages were reduced as a result of foreign trade, not individuals covered under a college plan for students under age 22.**

b. *Incorrect.* Coverage for individuals covered under such a state-operated health plan is eligible for the credit.

c. *Incorrect.* Coverage offered through a qualified state high-risk pool enables covered individuals to claim the credit.

d. *Incorrect.* Consolidated Omnibus Budget Reconciliation Act (COBRA) continuation coverage enables covered individuals to claim the credit.

Index

References are to paragraph (¶) numbers.

¶ 10,200 CPE Quizzer Instructions

This CPE Quizzer is divided into five Modules. To obtain CPE Credit, go to **CCH-Group.com/PrintCPE** to complete your Quizzers online for immediate results and no Express Grading Fee. There is a grading fee for each Quizzer submission.

Processing Fee:	Recommended CPE:
$56.00 for Module 1	4 hours for Module 1
$70.00 for Module 2	5 hours for Module 2
$56.00 for Module 3	4 hours for Module 3
$56.00 for Module 4	4 hours for Module 4
$28.00 for Module 5	2 hours for Module 5
$266.00 for all Modules	19 hours for all Modules
IRS Program Number:	**Federal Tax Law Hours:**
4VRWB-T-01420-15-S for Module 1	4 hours for Module 1
4VRWB-T-01421-15-S for Module 2	5 hours for Module 2
4VRWB-T-01419-15-S for Module 3	4 hours for Module 3
4VRWB-T-01422-15-S for Module 4	4 hours for Module 4
4VRWB-T-01423-15-S for Module 5	2 hours for Module 5
	19 hours for all Modules

Instructions for purchasing your CPE Tests and accessing them after purchase are provided on the **CCHGroup.com/PrintCPE** website.

To mail or fax your Quizzer, send your completed Answer Sheet for each Quizzer Module to **CCH Continuing Education Department, 4025 W. Peterson Ave., Chicago, IL 60646**, or fax it to (773) 866-3084. Each Quizzer Answer Sheet will be graded and a CPE Certificate of Completion awarded for achieving a grade of 70 percent or greater. The Quizzer Answer Sheets are located at the back of this book.

Express Grading: Processing time for your mailed or faxed Answer Sheet is generally 8-12 business days. To use our Express Grading Service, at an additional $19 per Module, please check the "Express Grading" box on your Answer Sheet and provide your CCH account or credit card number **and your fax number**. CCH will fax your results and a Certificate of Completion (upon achieving a passing grade) to you by 5:00 p.m. the business day following our receipt of your Answer Sheet. **If you mail your Answer Sheet for Express Grading, please write "ATTN: CPE OVERNIGHT" on the envelope.** NOTE: CCH will not Federal Express Quizzer results under any circumstances.

Recommended CPE credit is based on a 50-minute hour. Participants earning credits for states that require self-study to be based on a 100-minute hour will receive 1/2 the CPE credits for successful completion of this course. Because CPE requirements vary from state to state and among different licensing agencies, please contact your CPE governing body for information on your CPE requirements and the applicability of a particular course for your requirements

---

Date of Completion: If you mail or fax your Quizzer to CCH, the date of completion on your Certificate will be the date that you put on your Answer Sheet. However, you must submit your Answer Sheet to CCH for grading within two weeks of completing it.

Expiration Date: December 31, 2016

Evaluation: To help us provide you with the best possible products, please take a moment to fill out the course Evaluation located after your Quizzer. A copy is also provided at the back of this course if you choose to mail or fax your Quizzer Answer Sheets.

One **complimentary copy** of this course is provided with certain copies of CCH publications. Additional copies of this course may be downloaded from **CCH-Group.com/PrintCPE** or ordered by calling 1-800-248-3248 (ask for product 10024491-0003).

¶ 10,301 Quizzer Questions: Module 1

1. The pay or play rules of the Affordable Care Act specify that applicable large employers (ALEs) must:

   a. Pay their employees to obtain health insurance through a marketplace

   b. Pay employees to cover shared responsibility payments under the individual mandate

   c. Offer minimum essential health insurance coverage to employees or make shared responsibility payments to the government

   d. Offer premium assistance to all employees for their nondiscriminatory health coverage

2. For ACA purposes, a company's status as an ALE is determined by:

   a. Whether the employer offers all employees a form of health insurance coverage

   b. The number of full-time employees that are employed during the employer's peak quarter

   c. Summing the number of full-time and full-time equivalent employees for the year and dividing by 12 for a dividend of at least 50

   d. The reasonable expectation that a long-standing employer will employ an average of at least 50 full-time employees during a benchmark month

3. Shared responsibility rules count employees in determining an ALE for any of the following *except:*

   a. Farm workers employed full-time for seven months during the calendar year

   b. Real estate agents working for all but two weeks of the year

   c. Store stockpeople employed 32 hours per week

   d. Workers who are not offered family or sabbatical leave during the year

4. The payment regime for the employer shared responsibility payments for 2015 is triggered if:

   a. The employer is an applicable large employer member (ALEM) and one of its employees qualifies for subsidized coverage through a marketplace when the coverage is unaffordable

   b. The employer offers self-only minimum essential coverage (MEC) to eligible employees

   c. The employer does not immediately offer coverage to new full-time employees

   d. The employer reaches a count of 99 full-time employees during the year

5. The limited nonassessment period for an otherwise-eligible employee of an ALEM is:

   a. One month

   b. Two months

   c. Three months

   d. Six months

6. Under transition relief for 2015 for the Code Sec. 4980H(a) payment regime, employers must make shared responsibility payments if they fail to offer coverage to all but _____ of their full-time employees.

    a. 30 percent

    b. 25 percent

    c. 10 percent

    d. 5 percent

7. The shared responsibility payment rules under the Code Sec. 4980H(b) regime:

    a. Apply to employers who fail to offer minimum essential coverage to eligible employees

    b. Require payment for coverage that does not meet affordability or minimum value standards

    c. Require double the penalty applied for employers liable for payments under the Code Sec. 4980H(a) regime

    d. Apply to employees who were offered but did not enroll in minimum essential coverage by their employer

8. Using the monthly measurement method of determining full-time employees for the employer shared responsibility payment on Form 1094-C, ALEMs report their monthly full-time total:

    a. Minus employees in a limited nonassessment period

    b. Plus the number of seasonal employees working for four or more months

    c. Plus amounts of nonhourly employees who worked more than 30 hours a week in any month

    d. Minus weeks-worked equivalency for which nonhourly employees were credited with at least one hour of service

9. A standard measurement period used as a lookback period by ALEMs for determining for ongoing employees' full-time status:

    a. Cannot be less than 1 month and not more than 3 consecutive months

    b. Cannot be less than 2 months and not more than 6 consecutive months

    c. Cannot be less than 3 months and not more than 12 consecutive months

    d. Cannot be less than 4 months and not more than 18 consecutive months

10. The Authoritative Transmittal Form 1094-C must be:

    a. Provided quarterly to each eligible employee describing whether he or she qualified for MEC during each month of the quarter

    b. Provided annually to each employee to report insurance eligibility of his or her dependents as covered individuals

    c. Provided annually to the IRS by each ALEM reporting aggregate employer-level data for all full-time employees

    d. Provided annually to each full-time employee so he or she may determine whether to claim a premium assistance credit

11. The cap on the individual shared responsibility payment for 2015 is _____ per family in a tax household.

    a. $47.50

    b. $95.00

    c. $975.00

    d. $500.00

12. Coverage under which program does ***not*** constitute minimum essential coverage (MEC)?

    a. Students' self-funded health coverage through universities

    b. CHIP coverage

    c. Accident and disability policies

    d. Medicare Part A coverage and Medicare Advantage plans

13. The affordability exemption from having MEC is available if either an employer-sponsored plan or marketplace plans costs more than _____ of the taxpayer's household income.

    a. 1 percent

    b. 2 percent

    c. 5 percent

    d. 8 percent

14. To calculate household income to complete Form 8965, *Health Coverage Exemptions,* a taxpayer:

    a. Combines his or her modified adjusted gross income plus the MAGI of each dependent in the tax household who files a return

    b. Subtracts tax credit amounts from his or her adjusted gross income

    c. Combines his or her gross income with that of dependents in the tax household who will file returns

    d. Subtracts tax owed on Form 1040, 1040A, or Form 1040EZ from his or her gross income

15. A taxpayer cannot qualify for the premium tax credit while he or she is eligible for MEC from an employer ***unless***:

    a. The taxpayer chooses a plan offering more extensive coverage from a different insurer

    b. The coverage is unaffordable or does not provide minimum value

    c. The taxpayer works part-time

    d. The taxpayer is married, living with a spouse, and files separately

16. Part 2 of Form 8962, *Premium Tax Credit,* compares the taxpayer's calculated amount for the credit to:

    a. His or her gross income

    b. The taxpayers whose income is too high for receiving the credit

    c. The cost of the second lowest cost silver plan

    d. His or her tax family's MAGI

17. The taxpayer's modified adjusted gross income (MAGI) is the AGI plus all of the following inclusions *except:*

    a. Supplemental Security Income

    b. Nontaxable Social Security benefits

    c. Tax-exempt interest

    d. Excluded foreign income

18. Which of the following circumstances does *not* trigger the need to repay an excess advance premium tax credit?

    a. The married taxpayer is filing separately for the tax year

    b. The taxpayer's income for the tax year significantly exceeded the income the taxpayer estimated when enrolling in coverage and the taxpayer did not tell the marketplace

    c. One of the taxpayer's dependents died during the tax year, and the taxpayer did not tell the marketplace

    d. For whatever reason, the advance amount is more than the credit amount

19. If taxpayers are divorced, legally separated, married filing separate returns, or share a health care policy with another tax family, they must use Form 8962, Part 4, to:

    a. Calculate their MAGI as a percentage of the federal poverty line

    b. Make a shared policy allocation

    c. Separately account for each month's credit

    d. Perform an alternative credit calculation for the year of marriage

20. The alternative credit calculation applied for the year of marriage of the taxpayer:

    a. Subtracts the credit received by the lower-income spouse from the higher-income spouse

    b. Divides the alternative size families for both spouses and divides household income 50/50

    c. Eliminates the excess advance premium credit

    d. Establishes revised monthly advance premiums for the following tax year

¶ 10,302 Quizzer Questions: Module 2

21. In 2015 if a married couple elects gift-splitting to fund their child's qualified tuition program and elects to have the contribution treated as if made ratably over five years, the total they can invest in the current tax year without incurring gift tax is:

    a. $6,500

    b. $13,000

    c. $28,000

    d. $140,000

22. The maximum contribution allowed per beneficiary per year to a Coverdell educational savings account is:

    a. $2,000

    b. $5,500

    c. $14,000

    d. $28,000

23. Which of the following types of tax incentive offerings can be used to pay for elementary and high school expenses?

    a. Lifetime learning credit

    b. Coverdell ESA

    c. Educational U.S. savings bonds

    d. Qualified tuition programs

24. Educational U.S. savings bonds:

    a. May be redeemed to make tax-free contributions to a qualified tuition plan or Coverdell ESA

    b. May be redeemed without coordination of expenses used for claiming the educational tax credits

    c. Must be purchased in the name of the student who will use the proceeds for educational expenses

    d. Have a 20-year maturity period

25. The American opportunity tax credit (AOTC) is:

    a. Available for an unlimited number of years for postsecondary and graduate educational costs

    b. Available only for students enrolled in a degree, certificate or other credential program

    c. Payable up to a maximum of $5,000 per year

    d. Available only for costs of the oldest dependent attending college in a single tax year

26. The lifetime learning credit (LLC) is:

    a. Available for an unlimited number of years for postsecondary and graduate educational costs

    b. Available only for students enrolled in a degree, certificate or other credential program

    c. Payable up to a maximum of $5,000 per year

    d. Available only for costs of the oldest dependent attending college in a single tax year

27. A penalty tax of _____ applies to taxable distributions from a Coverdell ESA.

    a. 2 percent

    b. 5 percent

    c. 10 percent

    d. 25 percent

28. Distributions from a Coverdell ESA are subject to the penalty tax if:

    a. The distribution returns excess contributions and earnings, and a timely corrective distribution is made

    b. The beneficiary withdraws the funds after becoming disabled according to Code Sec. 72(m)(7)

    c. The beneficiary withdraws the balance of the account after completing his or her undergraduate degree

    d. The distribution is made to the beneficiary's estate after his or her death

29. When a student's loan has not yet entered repayment status, payments he or she makes are known as:

    a. Voluntary payments

    b. Preterm installments

    c. Deferred payments

    d. Prepaid writedowns

30. The student loan interest deduction is:

    a. Not available for loans to pay room and board and transportation costs

    b. Claimed as an adjustment to income and does not require the student to itemize deductions

    c. Not applicable to loan origination fees

    d. Not available for loan interest if the borrower uses a credit card to pay qualified education expenses

31. Under a qualified state tuition program, room and board expenses for higher education:

    a. Are not eligible if students live off-campus

    b. Are payable up to the school's posted room and board fees or $2,500 per year

    c. Are payable only if students are carrying a full-time course load

    d. Are not payable in a tax year when students or parents claim any of the tax credits for other educational expenses

32. Distributions from a Coverdell ESA:

    a. Are included in the taxpayer's gross income if the student does not attend school full-time

    b. Are excluded from gross income only if made in the name of the original beneficiary

    c. Are deemed as paid from both contributions and earnings

    d. Must exhaust the account by the time the student reaches age 25

33. The American opportunity or lifetime learning credit:

    a. May be claimed in the same year the beneficiary takes a tax-free distribution from a Coverdell ESA

    b. Is a one-time deduction for qualified tuition and related expenses during the student's first year of postsecondary education

    c. Can apply to the same expenses the beneficiary pays with a tax-free distribution from a Coverdell ESA

    d. Is available to individuals for whom a personal exemption deduction is claimed by another taxpayer

34. Which of the following does **not** reduce the amount of qualified tuition considered for the AOTC or LLC?

    a. Tax-free scholarships and fellowships under Code Sec. 117

    b. Amounts deducted by an individual as educational business expenses under Code Sec. 162

    c. Expenses paid by gift or inheritance under Code Sec. 102

    d. Educational assistance excludable from the gross income of the student or taxpayer claiming the credit

35. For purposes of the gift tax exclusion, educational expenses that are paid directly to an educational institution:

    a. Apply only to postsecondary tuition, room and board, and books

    b. May not exceed the amount of tuition for the current school term

    c. Are excludible only if the AOTC or LLC is not claimed for the year

    d. Apply to tuition-only expenses for primary, secondary, or postsecondary education

36. Which of the following is **not** required for a married taxpayer filing a separate federal tax return to claim personal exemptions for his or her spouse?

    a. The spouse cannot be claimed as a dependent by another taxpayer

    b. The taxpayer declines to take a personal exemption in order to claim one for his or her spouse

    c. The spouse is not filing his or her own federal return

    d. The spouse had no gross income for the tax year

37. An unmarried same-sex taxpayer may claim a dependency exemption for his or her partner's child if:

    a. The taxpayer and partner file jointly

    b. The taxpayer and partner are each claiming a dependency exemption for the child on their separate returns

    c. The taxpayer adopts the partner's child

    d. The child lives with the couple for the entire tax year

38. Geoffrey Hamilton, a 43-year-old taxpayer who has no retirement plan at work, is married to Raj Khan, who is age 41 and unemployed. They may together contribute a total of _____ to traditional IRAs for 2015.

    a. $5,500

    b. $11,000

    c. $12,000

    d. $15,000

39. Ira Shindel, a 52-year-old taxpayer who earns $55,000 in 2015, is married to Bernie Stark, a 49-year-old who earns $72,000 in 2015, but neither is covered by an employer retirement plan. They may together contribute a total of _____ to their Roth IRAs.

    a. $5,500

    b. $11,000

    c. $12,000

    d. $13,000

40. Lisa Patta participates in her employer's retirement plan, but her spouse Natalia Wocyck, has no plan at work. Their modified adjusted gross income (MAGI) for their joint return must total less than _____ in 2015 to avoid the threshold for phasing out deductions for their traditional IRA contributions.

    a. $61,000

    b. $71,000

    c. $98,000

    d. $118,000

41. Which of the following is *not* an option for an unmarried individual who inherits his or her partner's qualified retirement plan account?

    a. Using the account balance to purchase an annuity

    b. Leaving the funds in the account

    c. Making a trustee-to trustee transfer into an IRA set up in the deceased partner's name for the benefit of the beneficiary

    d. Closing the account by taking a lump-sum distribution

42. Phaseouts of tax deductions often favor unmarried partners compared to married couples because:

    a. They may each claim their children as dependents, lowering their adjusted gross incomes

    b. Each partner may claim deductions not allowed to joint filers with lower exemptions

    c. Unmarried taxpayers each have higher adjusted gross income thresholds for figuring itemized deductions

    d. Phaseout limitations for married couples are lower than twice the amount for single taxpayers

43. Under related-party antiabuse rules:

    a. Unmarried same-sex couples are subject to the same loss limitations as married couples

    b. Stock constructively owned by a spouse's estate is considered owned by the surviving spouse

    c. Stock owned by a partner's child is not considered owned by a related party if the taxpayer has legally adopted the spouse's child

    d. The mother of a spouse is not considered a family member for stock ownership purposes

44. Gifts to a noncitizen spouse are eligible for a gift tax annual exclusion of up to _____ in 2015.

    a. $14,000

    b. $28,000

    c. $147,000

    d. $2,117,800

45. When same-sex couples divorce, alimony payments:

    a. Include child support amounts

    b. Are taxable to the recipient

    c. Do not include cash payments to a third party on behalf of the payee ex-spouse

    d. Include payments for maintenance for a home owned by the payor ex-spouse but used by the payee ex-spouse

¶ 10,303 Quizzer Questions: Module 3

46. FATCA currently requires all of the following specified persons with foreign assets exceeding the threshold to file Form 8938 *except:*

    a. Specified domestic closely held corporations and partnerships

    b. Domestic entities indirectly holding specified foreign assets

    c. Nonresident aliens electing to be resident aliens to file joint returns

    d. Any individual who is a resident alien for any part of the year

47. If a foreign financial institution (FFI) fails to meet FATCA requirements, a U.S. withholding agent must withhold _____ on any withholdable payment to the FFI.

    a. 10 percent

    b. 20 percent

    c. 30 percent

    d. 40 percent

48. Under FATCA requirements, _____ is a reportable specified foreign financial asset.

    a. A financial accounts in a domestic branch of a foreign bank

    b. A security issued by a person other than a U.S. person

    c. All assets in a financial account subject to the mark-to-market rules

    d. An account at a foreign branch of a U.S. financial institution

49. Specified persons who are joint filers living abroad are subject to FATCA requirements when their specified foreign assets exceed _____ on the last day of the year or _____ anytime during the year.

    a. $50,000; $75,000

    b. $100,000; $150,000

    c. $200,000; $300,000

    d. $400,000; $600,000

50. To report the value of a specified foreign financial asset for Form 8938, the taxpayer:

    a. Lists its total worth in the currency type used for the account without converting it to US dollars

    b. Identifies the value in the foreign currency, then converts it to US dollars using the averages of the monthly or quarterly exchange rates used for paying estimated tax

    c. Identifies the value in the foreign currency, then converts it to US dollars using the Treasury Department's year-end spot rate

    d. Identifies the beginning value of the asset for that tax year, then converts it to US dollars using the Treasury Department's year-end spot rate for the immediately preceding year

51. An accuracy-related penalty of _____ applies under FATCA to tax underpayments involving undisclosed foreign financial assets.

   a. 10 percent

   b. 20 percent

   c. 30 percent

   d. 40 percent

52. For purposes of the FBAR rules, a U.S. person can have a financial interest in a foreign account unless he or she:

   a. Is a deemed owner of the financial interest's account

   b. Is a constructive owner acting on behalf of the U.S. person who owns the foreign account

   c. Is a discretionary beneficiary in a discretionary trust

   d. Is the owner of record or holder of legal title of the foreign financial account

53. Which officers or employees are subject to FBAR requirements?

   a. Ones with signature or other authority of a bank-owned account

   b. Ones having a financial interest in an account of the institution

   c. Ones registered with and examined by the Commodity Futures Trading Commission

   d. Ones of an entity with a class of security listed on any U.S. national securities exchange

54. An exception to FBAR reporting applies to:

   a. Employee welfare plan accounts of government entities

   b. Annuity policies with cash value

   c. Mutual fund accounts issuing shares to the general public

   d. Accounts with brokers or deals for futures or options

55. The 2014 Offshore Voluntary Disclosure Program imposes an accuracy-related penalty for offshore taxpayers' noncompliance of:

   a. 10 percent

   b. 20 percent

   c. 30 percent

   d. 40 percent

56. The eligibility limitations for automatic changes in accounting method prohibit a taxpayer from filing the same method change:

   a. Twice within a three-year period

   b. Twice within a five-year period

   c. Three times within a five-year period

   d. Four times within a seven-year period

57. For purposes of the relief permitted for filing accounting method changes, a small business taxpayer must have total assets of less than _____ as of the first day of the tax year or average annual gross receipts of _____ or less for the prior three tax years.

    a. $1 million; $1 million

    b. $5 million; $10 million

    c. $10 million; $10 million

    d. $25 million; $50 million

58. If a unit of Section 1245 property is acquired and installed in a building:

    a. The lessor may deduct the cost of the property but a lessee may not

    b. The property must be capitalized and depreciated

    c. Neither the lessor nor the lessee may capitalize the acquisition costs

    d. The basis of the property is treated as zero dollars

59. If an original structural component of a building is retired, a lessor may claim a loss by:

    a. Making a partial disposition election

    b. Continuing to depreciate the retired component through its remaining useful life

    c. Capitalizing the replacement component

    d. Treating the retired component as a separate unit of property

60. If a taxpayer with an applicable financial statement uses the *de minimis* safe harbor election, materials, supplies, and units of property may be expensed if their total cost, or itemized cost, does **not** exceed:

    a. $500

    b. $1,000

    c. $5,000

    d. $10,000

61. If a taxpayer does not have an applicable financial statement and uses *de minimis* safe harbor election, materials, supplies, and units of property may be expensed if their total cost, or itemized cost, does not exceed:

    a. $500

    b. $1,000

    c. $5,000

    d. $10,000

62. When property that was expensed under the *de minimis* rule is sold or otherwise disposed of, the gain:

    a. Must offset capital losses

    b. Is treated as ordinary income

    c. Is treated as gain from a capital asset under Code Sec. 1221

    d. Is treated as gain from property used in a trade or business under Code Sec. 1231

63. Under the MACRS disposition regulations, a taxpayer may make a partial disposition election of a loss on a retired structural component equal to:

    a. Its current fair value

    b. 25 percent of its purchase price

    c. The remaining basis that has not been depreciated

    d. 50 percent of the replacement component's purchase price

64. Electing to place a building in a general asset account in the year the building is placed in service is advisable if the taxpayer:

    a. Intends to demolish the structure in the future

    b. Plans to make a partial disposition election on retiring a structural component of the building

    c. Wants to dispose of the asset in the same tax year

    d. Wants to shift income or deductions among taxpayers using the account

65. If a building asset is held in a general asset account and demolished in a later tax year, a taxpayer may:

    a. Deduct the costs of demolition as ordinary losses

    b. Continue to depreciate the building until its basis is fully recovered

    c. Amortize the costs of demolition throughout the building's useful life

    d. Elect a retroactive partial disposition during the year of demolition

¶ 10,304 Quizzer Questions: Module 4

66. All of the following are methods a hospital typically uses to establish that it is a tax-exempt organization under the community benefit standard *except:*

   a. Governance by a board composed of civic leaders

   b. Medical staff admissions open to all qualified physicians

   c. Operation not for the benefit of owners

   d. Operation of a full-time emergency room open to everyone

67. Hospitals that participate in the Medicare program must accept all persons who require emergency medical care under the *Consolidated Omnibus Reconciliation Act of 1985's:*

   a. Financial assistance policy provision

   b. Antidumping provision

   c. Mandatory treatment provision

   d. Patient protection provision

68. Failure to meet the community health needs assessment (CHNA) requirements subjects a hospital organization to an excise tax of:

   a. $10,000

   b. $25,000

   c. $50,000

   d. $100,000

69. In conjunction with the CHNA requirements, the PPACA requires tax-exempt hospital organizations to:

   a. Adopt an implementation strategy for each facility to meet community needs identified in the CHNA

   b. Revise its fee structures to provide discounted care to underserved community members

   c. Provide post-discharge care to all community members without regard to their ability to pay

   d. Hold organization-sponsored community review sessions of its CHNA results

70. Final IRS regulations on PPACA requirements for the financial assistance policies (FAPs) of tax-exempt hospitals require:

   a. Development and provision of plain language summaries in the five most common languages of the patient population

   b. Include general notifications about the FAP on services' invoices and conspicuously in the hospital

   c. Discontinuation of extraordinary collection actions such as third-party collections and wage garnishments

   d. Targeting policies to middle-income patients as well as disadvantaged populations

71. Under Code Sec. 501(r), disclosure of violations of PPACA requirements by tax-exempt hospitals must include all of the following *except:*

    a. A description of the violation, including the failure's cause, location, date, number of occurrences, number of persons affected, and dollars associated with the failure

    b. A description of the hospital's departments and/or medical staff members responsible for the violation and number of occurrences tied to those departments or staff

    c. A description of the correction and how individuals affected were restored to their position

    d. A description of the practices or procedures established or revised if needed to prevent subsequent occurrences of the violation

72. The IRS challenged the tax-exempt status of the joint venture in the *St David's Health Care System, Inc.,* case and the circuit court decided the case on the basis of:

    a. The hospital's ability to operate for charitable purpose

    b. The organizational test for the joint venture

    c. The ratio of capital and profits of the partnership as an impermissible benefit to the for-profit healthcare partner

    d. Necessary total control of the governing board

73. The IRS issue with regional health information organizations (RHIOs) is:

    a. Which physicians should be considered disqualified persons

    b. Serving an insurer's interests resulting in substantial private benefit

    c. Hospitals denying certain staff physicians access to selected EHR software features

    d. Unequal increases in costs to patient populations due to implementations of RHIOs

74. Provisions of the *American Recovery and Reinvestment Act of 2009* promote health information technology development and exchange features incorporated in RHIOs because:

    a. Electronic health records better protect patient privacy

    b. Electronic health record subsidies support systems that grant all healthcare partners open access to patient information

    c. Facilitating health information exchange through RHIOs lessens the burden of government

    d. They prevent generation of unrelated business income for hospitals and physicians

75. A shortcoming of group purchasing organizations (GPOs) for tax-exempt hospitals and other exempt organizations is:

    a. Nonprofit healthcare organizations typically lack the size and scope to qualify for many economies of scale

    b. Restrictions of Code Sec. 501(e) make it difficult for exempt providers to share services in GPOs

    c. GPOs operating as Code Sec. 501(e) cooperatives are not entitled to the benefits of status of Code Sec. 501(c)(3) organizations

    d. GPOs usually exclude charitable members that are not part of large hospital networks

76. FICA taxes apply to:

    a. S corporations

    b. General and limited partnerships

    c. Employers

    d. Sole proprietors with no employees

77. SECA taxes apply to:

    a. S corporations

    b. Partnerships

    c. Employers

    d. General partners

78. Partners who perform services for their partnerships:

    a. Are not subject to SECA taxes if they are general partners

    b. Are limited partners subject to FICA taxes

    c. Are subject to SECA taxes on guaranteed payments

    d. Are general partners subject to FICA taxes

79. The additional Medicare tax rate for an employee or self-employed taxpayer earning more than the threshold for his or her filing status is:

    a. 0.9 percent

    b. 1.45 percent

    c. 3.8 percent

    d. 7.65 percent

80. The net investment income tax rate is:

    a. 0.9 percent

    b. 1.45 percent

    c. 3.8 percent

    d. 7.65 percent

81. Which of the following is *not* an issue for the IRS and courts regarding reasonable compensation of shareholder-employees?

    a. Payment of dividends in circumstances that suggest they are really compensation for services

    b. Avoidance of self-employment taxes

    c. The employee's general level of outside employment attainment

    d. Avoidance of payroll taxes

82. All of the following are bases for material participation of an S corporation shareholder-employee that enables avoidance of NII taxes *except:*

    a. Continuous participation by the shareholder-employee in corporate activities

    b. Contributions made by the shareholder-employee to the corporation in exchange for stock

    c. Participation of the shareholder-employee on a regular basis

    d. Substantial participation in the conduct of the trade or business by the shareholder-employee

83. The not-less-than-others test treats a taxpayer as materially participating in a trade or business activity if he or she participates at least as much as other individuals and for more than:

    a. 50 hours

    b. 100 hours

    c. 200 hours

    d. 500 hours

84. The personal-service-activities test of material participation requires an individual to have participated in the trade or activity for:

    a. Any 3 previous tax years

    b. Any 5 of the last 10 tax years

    c. 100 hours during 2 of the last 3 tax years

    d. 500 hours during any of the last 5 tax years

85. An individual's interest is *not* treated as an interest in a limited partnership if the interest is:

    a. Less than the partner's capital contributions to the partnership

    b. More than the partner's capital contributions to the partnership plus an additional amount per the partnership agreement

    c. A nonvoting interest

    d. Never allowed a distributive share of income of the partnership

¶ 10,305 Quizzer Questions: Module 5

86. All of the following are focuses of Senate Finance Committee tax reform working groups *except:*

    a. International tax

    b. Business income tax

    c. U.S. tariff policy

    d. Individual income tax

87. Under the "doc fix" bill, the IRS can levy up to ____ percent of a qualified payment owed to a Medicare provider to collect an unpaid tax liability.

    a. 10

    b. 25

    c. 75

    d. 100

88. The proposed Fighting Hunger Incentive Bill of 2015 would:

    a. Offer special tax treatment for charitable gifts from IRAs by individuals age 70½ and older

    b. Repeal the medical device excise tax

    c. Repeal tax breaks for land donations for conservation purposes

    d. Repeal the lifetime learning credit

89. The *Defending Public Safety Employees' Retirement Act :*

    a. Expands the exemption to the 10 percent early distributions from a government plan for qualified public safety employers to include federal law enforcement officers, federal firefighters, customs and border protection officers, and air traffic controllers

    b. Changes the early retirement age for certain federal public safety officers

    c. Links the maximum monthly distributions from retirement accounts of federal public safety officers to their years of service prior to early retirement

    d. Exempts spouses of federal law enforcement officers from the early distribution penalty on their retirement accounts

90. President Obama's fiscal year (FY) 2016 tax proposals do *not* include:

    a. A gas tax increase

    b. Enhancement of the Code Sec 45R small employer health insurance tax

    c. A $500 "second earner" tax credit for dual-earner couples

    d. A $3,000 maximum credit per child for care for children younger than age 5

91. President Obama's proposal for Code Sec. 179 expensing is to:

    a. Eliminate it for mid-size businesses

    b. Expand and permanently extend it

    c. Fold it into bonus depreciation after 2017

    d. Limit the availability of Code Sec. 179 to start-up companies

92. Social program proposals by President Obama for FY 2016 do *not* include:

   a. Extending and modifying incentives to hire veterans

   b. Closing "loopholes" for the child tax credit

   c. Eliminating the American opportunity tax credit (AOTC)

   d. Restricting eligibility to claim the refundable portion of the child tax credit

93. Groups of workers who have been separated from employment with lost jobs or reduced wages because their jobs have moved overseas may apply for benefits and services under the:

   a. Trans-Pacific Partnership pact

   b. North American Free Trade Agreement

   c. Trade Adjustment Assistance programs

   d. Unemployment Insurance Supplemental program

94. Which tax credit was extended by the trade legislation enacted in June 2015?

   a. Health coverage tax credit (HCTC)

   b. Earned income credit (EIC)

   c. Premium assistance tax credit

   d. Research tax credit

95. The *Trade Preferences Extension Act of 2015* shifts corporate estimated tax payments in 2020 for corporations with at least $_____ in assets.

   a. $500,000

   b. $1 million

   c. $1 billion

   d. $5 billion

¶ 10,400 Answer Sheets

¶ 10,401 Top Federal Tax Issues for 2016 CPE Course: MODULE 1

(10014583-0004)

Go to **CCHGroup.com/PrintCPE** to complete your Quizzer online for instant results and no Express Grading Fee.

A $56.00 processing fee will be charged for each user submitting Module 1 for grading. If you prefer to mail or fax your Quizzer, remove both pages of the Answer Sheet from this book and return them with your completed Evaluation Form to: CCH Continuing Education Department, 4025 W. Peterson Ave., Chicago, IL 60646-6085 or fax your Answer Sheet to CCH at 773-866-3084. You must also select a method of payment below.

NAME _____

COMPANY NAME _____

STREET _____

CITY, STATE, & ZIP CODE _____

BUSINESS PHONE NUMBER _____

E-MAIL ADDRESS _____

DATE OF COMPLETION _____

PTIN ID (for Enrolled Agents or RTRPs only) _____

METHOD OF PAYMENT:

☐ Check Enclosed   ☐ Visa   ☐ Master Card   ☐ AmEx

☐ Discover   ☐ CCH Account* _____

Card No. _____   Exp. Date _____

Signature _____

EXPRESS GRADING: Please fax my Course results to me by 5:00 p.m. the business day following your receipt of this Answer Sheet. By checking this box I authorize CCH to charge $19.00 for this service.

☐ Express Grading $19.00   Fax No. _____

* Must provide CCH account number for this payment option

 Wolters Kluwer

Module 1: Answer Sheet

(10014583-0004)

Please answer the questions by indicating the appropriate letter next to the corresponding number.

1. _____	6. _____	11. _____	16. _____
2. _____	7. _____	12. _____	17. _____
3. _____	8. _____	13. _____	18. _____
4. _____	9. _____	14. _____	19. _____
5. _____	10. _____	15. _____	20. _____

Please complete the Evaluation Form (located after the Module 5 Answer Sheet) and return it with this Quizzer Answer Sheet to CCH at the address on the previous page. Thank you.

¶ 10,402 Top Federal Tax Issues for 2016 CPE Course: MODULE 2

(10014584-0004)

Go to **CCHGroup.com/PrintCPE** to complete your Quizzer online for instant results and no Express Grading Fee.

A $70.00 processing fee will be charged for each user submitting Module 2 for grading. If you prefer to mail or fax your Quizzer, remove both pages of the Answer Sheet from this book and return them with your completed Evaluation Form to: CCH Continuing Education Department, 4025 W. Peterson Ave., Chicago, IL 60646-6085 or fax your Answer Sheet to CCH at 773-866-3084. You must also select a method of payment below.

NAME _____

COMPANY NAME _____

STREET _____

CITY, STATE, & ZIP CODE _____

BUSINESS PHONE NUMBER _____

E-MAIL ADDRESS _____

DATE OF COMPLETION _____

PTIN ID (for Enrolled Agents or RTRPs only) _____

METHOD OF PAYMENT:

☐ Check Enclosed ☐ Visa ☐ Master Card ☐ AmEx

☐ Discover ☐ CCH Account* _____

Card No. _____ Exp. Date _____

Signature _____

EXPRESS GRADING: Please fax my Course results to me by 5:00 p.m. the business day following your receipt of this Answer Sheet. By checking this box I authorize CCH to charge $19.00 for this service.

☐ Express Grading $19.00 Fax No. _____

* Must provide CCH account number for this payment option

 Wolters Kluwer

Module 2: Answer Sheet

(10014584-0004)

Please answer the questions by indicating the appropriate letter next to the corresponding number.

21. _____	26. _____	31. _____	36. _____	41. _____
22. _____	27. _____	32. _____	37. _____	42. _____
23. _____	28. _____	33. _____	38. _____	43. _____
24. _____	29. _____	34. _____	39. _____	44. _____
25. _____	30. _____	35. _____	40. _____	45. _____

Please complete the Evaluation Form (located after the Module 5 Answer Sheet) and return it with this Quizzer Answer Sheet to CCH at the address on the previous page. Thank you.

¶ 10,403 Top Federal Tax Issues for 2016 CPE Course: MODULE 3

(10014585-0004)

Go to **CCHGroup.com/PrintCPE** to complete your Quizzer online for instant results and no Express Grading Fee.

A $56.00 processing fee will be charged for each user submitting Module 3 for grading. If you prefer to mail or fax your Quizzer, remove both pages of the Answer Sheet from this book and return them with your completed Evaluation Form to: CCH Continuing Education Department, 4025 W. Peterson Ave., Chicago, IL 60646-6085 or fax your Answer Sheet to CCH at 773-866-3084. You must also select a method of payment below.

NAME _____

COMPANY NAME _____

STREET _____

CITY, STATE, & ZIP CODE _____

BUSINESS PHONE NUMBER _____

E-MAIL ADDRESS _____

DATE OF COMPLETION _____

PTIN ID (for Enrolled Agents or RTRPs only) _____

METHOD OF PAYMENT:

☐ Check Enclosed   ☐ Visa   ☐ Master Card   ☐ AmEx

☐ Discover   ☐ CCH Account* _____

Card No. _____   Exp. Date _____

Signature _____

EXPRESS GRADING: Please fax my Course results to me by 5:00 p.m. the business day following your receipt of this Answer Sheet. By checking this box I authorize CCH to charge $19.00 for this service.

☐ Express Grading $19.00   Fax No. _____

* Must provide CCH account number for this payment option

 Wolters Kluwer

Module 3: Answer Sheet

(10014585-0004)

Please answer the questions by indicating the appropriate letter next to the corresponding number.

46. _____	51. _____	56. _____	61. _____
47. _____	52. _____	57. _____	62. _____
48. _____	53. _____	58. _____	63. _____
49. _____	54. _____	59. _____	64. _____
50. _____	55. _____	60. _____	65. _____

Please complete the Evaluation Form (located after the Module 5 Answer Sheet) and return it with this Quizzer Answer Sheet to CCH at the address on the previous page. Thank you.

¶ 10,404 Top Federal Tax Issues for 2016 CPE Course: MODULE 4

(10014586-0004)

Go to **CCHGroup.com/PrintCPE** to complete your Quizzer online for instant results and no Express Grading Fee.

A $56.00 processing fee will be charged for each user submitting Module 4 for grading. If you prefer to mail or fax your Quizzer, remove both pages of the Answer Sheet from this book and return them with your completed Evaluation Form to: CCH Continuing Education Department, 4025 W. Peterson Ave., Chicago, IL 60646-6085 or fax your Answer Sheet to CCH at 773-866-3084. You must also select a method of payment below.

NAME _____

COMPANY NAME _____

STREET _____

CITY, STATE, & ZIP CODE _____

BUSINESS PHONE NUMBER _____

E-MAIL ADDRESS _____

DATE OF COMPLETION _____

PTIN ID (for Enrolled Agents or RTRPs only) _____

METHOD OF PAYMENT:

☐ Check Enclosed	☐ Visa	☐ Master Card	☐ AmEx
☐ Discover	☐ CCH Account* _____		

Card No. _____   Exp. Date _____

Signature _____

EXPRESS GRADING: Please fax my Course results to me by 5:00 p.m. the business day following your receipt of this Answer Sheet. By checking this box I authorize CCH to charge $19.00 for this service.

☐ Express Grading $19.00   Fax No. _____

* Must provide CCH account number for this payment option

 Wolters Kluwer

Module 4: Answer Sheet

(10014586-0004)

Please answer the questions by indicating the appropriate letter next to the corresponding number.

66. _____	71. _____	76. _____	81. _____
67. _____	72. _____	77. _____	82. _____
68. _____	73. _____	78. _____	83. _____
69. _____	74. _____	79. _____	84. _____
70. _____	75. _____	80. _____	85. _____

Please complete the Evaluation Form (located after the Module 5 Answer Sheet) and return it with this Quizzer Answer Sheet to CCH at the address on the previous page. Thank you.

¶ 10,405 Top Federal Tax Issues for 2016 CPE Course: MODULE 5

(10035677-0002)

Go to **CCHGroup.com/PrintCPE** to complete your Quizzer online for instant results and no Express Grading Fee.

A $28.00 processing fee will be charged for each user submitting Module 5 for grading. If you prefer to mail or fax your Quizzer, remove both pages of the Answer Sheet from this book and return them with your completed Evaluation Form to: CCH Continuing Education Department, 4025 W. Peterson Ave., Chicago, IL 60646-6085 or fax your Answer Sheet to CCH at 773-866-3084. You must also select a method of payment below.

NAME _____

COMPANY NAME _____

STREET _____

CITY, STATE, & ZIP CODE _____

BUSINESS PHONE NUMBER _____

E-MAIL ADDRESS _____

DATE OF COMPLETION _____

PTIN ID (for Enrolled Agents or RTRPs only) _____

METHOD OF PAYMENT:

☐ Check Enclosed	☐ Visa	☐ Master Card	☐ AmEx
☐ Discover	☐ CCH Account* _____		

Card No. _____   Exp. Date _____

Signature _____

EXPRESS GRADING: Please fax my Course results to me by 5:00 p.m. the business day following your receipt of this Answer Sheet. By checking this box I authorize CCH to charge $19.00 for this service.

☐ Express Grading $19.00   Fax No. _____

* Must provide CCH account number for this payment option

 Wolters Kluwer

Module 5: Answer Sheet

(10035677-0002)

Please answer the questions by indicating the appropriate letter next to the corresponding number.

86. _____	89. _____	92. _____	95. _____
87. _____	90. _____	93. _____	
88. _____	91. _____	94. _____	

Please complete the Evaluation Form (located after the Module 5 Answer Sheet) and return it with this Quizzer Answer Sheet to CCH at the address on the previous page. Thank you.

¶ 10,500 Top Federal Tax Issues for 2016 CPE Course: Evaluation Form

(10024491-0003)

Please take a few moments to fill out and mail or fax this evaluation to CCH so that we can better provide you with the type of self-study programs you want and need. Thank you.

About This Program

1. Please circle the number that best reflects the extent of your agreement with the following statements:

		Strongly Agree				Strongly Disagree
a.	The Course objectives were met.	5	4	3	2	1
b.	This Course was comprehensive and organized.	5	4	3	2	1
c.	The content was current and technically accurate.	5	4	3	2	1
d.	This Course was timely and relevant.	5	4	3	2	1
e.	The prerequisite requirements were appropriate.	5	4	3	2	1
f.	This Course was a valuable learning experience.	5	4	3	2	1
g.	The Course completion time was appropriate.	5	4	3	2	1

2. This Course was most valuable to me because of:

_____ Continuing Education credit   _____ Convenience of format

_____ Relevance to my practice/employment   _____ Timeliness of subject matter

_____ Price   _____ Reputation of author

_____ Other (please specify) _____

3. How long did it take to complete this Course? (Please include the total time spent reading or studying reference materials and completing CPE Quizzer).

Module 1_____   Module 2_____   Module 3_____   Module 4 _____   Module 5 _____

4. What do you consider to be the strong points of this Course?

5. What improvements can we make to this Course?

General Interests

(10024491-0003)

1. Preferred method of self-study instruction:

_____ Text _____ Audio _____ Computer-based/Multimedia _____ Video

2. What specific topics would you like CCH to develop as self-study CPE programs?

_____

_____

_____

3. Please list other topics of interest to you _____

_____

_____

About You

1. Your profession:

_____ CPA _____ Enrolled Agent

_____ Attorney _____ Tax Preparer

_____ Financial Planner _____ Other (please specify)

_____

2. Your employment:

_____ Self-employed _____ Public Accounting Firm

_____ Service Industry _____ Non-Service Industry

_____ Banking/Finance _____ Government

_____ Education _____ Other _____

3. Size of firm/corporation:

_____ 1 _____ 2-5 _____ 6-10 _____ 11-20 _____ 21-50 _____ 51+

4. Your Name _____

Firm/Company Name _____

Address _____

City, State, Zip Code _____

E-mail Address _____

THANK YOU FOR TAKING THE TIME TO COMPLETE THIS SURVEY!